ANIMATENESS
Under The WildLife Protection Laws

RAGHITHA

BLUEROSE PUBLISHERS
India | U.K.

Copyright © Raghitha 2024

All rights reserved by author. No part of this publication may be reproduced, stored in a retrieval system or transmitted in any form or by any means, electronic, mechanical, photocopying, recording or otherwise, without the prior permission of the author. Although every precaution has been taken to verify the accuracy of the information contained herein, the publisher assumes no responsibility for any errors or omissions. No liability is assumed for damages that may result from the use of information contained within.

BlueRose Publishers takes no responsibility for any damages, losses, or liabilities that may arise from the use or misuse of the information, products, or services provided in this publication.

For permissions requests or inquiries regarding this publication, please contact:

BLUEROSE PUBLISHERS
www.BlueRoseONE.com
info@bluerosepublishers.com
+91 8882 898 898
+4407342408967

ISBN: 978-93-6452-157-4

Cover design: Raghitha
Typesetting: Sagar

First Edition: July 2024

Contents

Introduction..1
The Wildlife (Protection) Act, 1972 4
Legislative Interventions for the Protection
of Animals: Important Laws.......................................221
Important Wildlife Conservations 236
Conclusion 272

Author's Information

Born in the year 1986 in Thrissur district, Kerala. Parents are V. Ramachandran and Bhama Ramachandran. Married to Srisha. Living in Chennai. School education is done from various schools in Thrissur district, Kerala. Law completed from Govt. Law College, Thrissur (2006-2011), Kerala. The First Book "What to Speak" is about the fundamental right to speech and expression guaranteed by the Constitution of India under Article 19 (1) (a).

Detailed Contents

1. **Introduction**

2. **Wild Life (Protection) Act, 1972**

    - History Behind Wildlife Legislation in India
    - Importance of Wildlife (Protection) Act, 1972
    - Limitations of Wildlife (Protection) Act, 1972
    - Need for the Amendment of Wildlife (Protection) Act, 1972
    - Various Amendments under Wildlife (Protection) Act, 1972
        o Wildlife (Protection) Amendment Act, 1982
        o Wildlife (Protection) Amendment Act, 1986
        o Wildlife (Protection) Amendment Act, 1991
        o Wildlife (Protection) Amendment Act, 1993
        o Wildlife (Protection) Amendment Act, 2002
            ▪ Critical Appraisal of Wildlife (Protection) Amendment Act, 2002
        o Wildlife (Protection) Amendment Act, 2006
        o Wildlife (Protection) Amendment Bill, 2013
        o Wildlife (Protection) Amendment Bill, 2021
        o Wildlife(Protection) Amendment Act, 2022
    ▪ Objectives of the Act, 2022
    ▪ Proposed Amendments
    ▪ The Concerns Associated with Act, 2022
    ▪ The Wildlife (Protection) Amendment Act, 1972 (last updated 1/4/2023)

        o **Chapter I**
        Preliminary

        o **Chapter II**
        Authorities to be appointed or constitutes under the Act

- Chapter III
  Hunting of Wild Animals

- Chapter IIIA
  Protection of Specified Plants

- Chapter IV
  - Protected Areas
  - Sanctuaries
  - National Parks
  - Closed Area

- Chapter IVA
  Central Zoo Authority and Recognition of Zoos

- Chapter IVB
  National Tiger Conservation Authority

- Chapter IVC
  Wildlife Crime Control Bureau

- Chapter V
  Trade or Commerce in Wild Animals, Animal Articles and Trophies

- Chapter VA
  Prohibition of Trade or Commerce in Trophies, Animal Articles etc., Derived from Certain Animals

- Chapter VB
  Regulation of International Trade in Endangered Species of Wild Fauna and Flora as per Convention on International Trade in Endangered Species of Wild Fauna and Flora

- Chapter VI
  Prevention and Detection of Offences

- **Chapter VIA**
  Forfeiture of Property Derived from Illegal Hunting and Trade

- **Chapter VII**
  Miscellaneous
  - Changes in Wildlife (Protection) Amendment Act, 2022
  - Challenges and Criticisms of Wildlife (Protection) Amendment Act, 2022

3. **Legislative Interventions for the Protection of Animals: Important Laws**

   - Prevention of Cruelty to Animals Act, 1960
     - Cow Slaughter and Cattle Preservation Act, 1964
     - The Karnataka Prevention of Cow Slaughter and Cattle Preservation Act, 1964
     - Jallikattu Amendment Act, 2017
     - Main features of legislations enacted by the States/Union Territories on Cow Slaughter
     - The Rajasthan Camel (Prohibition of Slaughter and Regulation of Temporary Migration or Export) Act, 2015

   - The Wild Life (Protection) Act, 1972
   - Cosmetic Rules, 2020
   - Constitutional Protection for Animal Rights
   - Indian Penal Code (IPC), 1860 replaced by Bharatiya Nyaya Sanhitha (BNS) Bill 2023, Provisions for Animal Protection

4. **Important Wildlife Conservations**

   - Environmental Conservations
   - Animal Conservations
   - Marine Conservation
   - Human Conservation

- Environmental Conservations
- Environment Pollution
    - Water Pollution
    - Air pollution
    - Land or Soil Pollution
    - Noise or Sound Pollution
    - Food Pollution
    - Radio-Active Pollution
- Animal Conservation
    - Project Snow Leopard, 2009
    - Project Tiger, 1973
    - Project Elephant, 1992
    - Project Rhino Vision, 2020 (launched in 2005)
    - Project Hangul, 1970
    - Crocodile Conservation Project, 1975
    - The Manipur Brow-Antlered Deer Project, 1981
    - Project Himalayan Musk Deer, 1981
    - Lesser Cats Project, 1976
    - The Gir Lion Sanctuary Project 1972, re launched in 2020
    - Sea Turtle Project, 1999
    - Ganges Dolphin Project, 2021
    - Protected Areas
    - Wildlife Corridors
- Marine Conservation
- Human Conservation
    - Conservation of Plants Project
    - Animals that Helps People and the Eco system
    - Birds
    - Dogs
        - Legislation and Public Health Laws Related to Rabis Control
    - Bees
    - Pangolin
    - Goat
    - Horse
    - Sharks
    - Giraffe

- o Whales
- o Rats
- Animals as legal persons.
- PETA
- CITES
- MIKE Programme

5. **Conclusion.**
   - **Table of cases.**
   - **Sources of Information.**

Introduction

India has an immense variety of natural resources. The country is rich in plant and animal heritage, which sustains millions of people. The environment is the surrounding in which we are living, it consists of both biotic and abiotic elements. The environment includes water, air and land constituting the nature and their inter relations among themselves and with human beings and other living and non- living things. For the very existence of human being, for a healthy and safe living, hygienic, natural and quality environment is the basic essential. A clean environment is required for the peaceful and healthy survival of humans. Human activities negatively affect the environment. It includes pollution, global warming, extinction of species, etc. India is the country, is very rich in flora and fauna. It is the land consisting of 10% of the world's species. According to the International Union for Conservation of Nature, India constitutes 7-8% all species, including plants and animals. These are approximately, 91,000 animal species which include insects, fish, birds, mammals, reptiles, and amphibians and molluscs.

Ever since human evolved, we have changed the land cover of the earth constantly. Forests are the natural habitat of large scale wildlife growth of trees, shrubs, and different variety of plants which gradually becoming smaller in size in every year. Forest plays a vital role in the balance of ecological system. They preserve the soil to retain water and allow them to flow slowly. Trees are responsible for purity of air by releasing oxygen while they are in the process of photosynthesis. Forest is the nation's wealth, the teak wood, timber, sandal woods, medicinal drugs, fruits, flowers, food, fabric, raw materials, etc. are the gifts from the forests. There are references about forest in the Vedas and ancient literatures. Trees are worshipped as Gods. Forest serve as natural habitats for large populations of wildlife as well as the growth of trees, shrubs, and a wide variety of plants. As a result, it is our responsibility to protect forest conservation. Trees and plants in the forest are an integral part of the eco system. It sustains life on the planet, provides clean air and shelter. Forest helps conserve bio diversity. A forest is a big region of land dominated by trees, aquatic biomes, multiple species of animals and a million micro organisms. 31% earth's land surface is covered by forests. Deforestation is the permanent destruction or loss of forests for the expansion of land for agriculture, livestock etc., conservation of forest and wildlife is necessary to keep the population of different animal and bird species.

Wildlife plays an important role in balancing the environment and provides stability to different natural process of nature and these plants are rare, threatened, or endangered. Naturally-occuring rare plants will be given the highest consideration. The wildlife helps to preserve the animal and plant species from becoming extinct. The wildlife provides shelter to the wild animals. Wildlife means undomesticated animal species and uncultivated plants living in their natural habitat such as forest, grassland, ocean, river, desert, mountains and other natural eco systems are included, all living organisms that live in their natural environment, neither human nor domesticated , especially mammals, birds, fish, insects and plants in forests. There is rapid decline of wild animals in India. Many species of birds and animals are extinct in our country like the pink-headed duck, Asiatic cheetah, and some species are endangered like Bengal tiger, Asiatic lion, Indian rhinoceros etc. India is blessed with rich and diverse wildlife housing numerous species that contribute to the country's ecological balance. Recognizing the critical importance of preserving this natural heritage, the Indian Judiciary has played an important role in shaping and enforcing laws pertaining to wildlife conservation. It was the major concern and which necessitates the need to bring the legislation for the protection of wildlife. The Wildlife (Protection) Act 1972, was enacted for the protection of plants, birds and wild animals, in order to ensure environmental and ecological security. The Act prohibits hunting, poaching, trade of endangered species. This Act aim to safeguard the nation's ecological and environmental stability by addressing the preservation of India's wildlife heritage. Two Primary Laws govern conservation of wildlife and its habitat. The Wildlife (Protection) Act of 1972, and The Indian Forest Act of 1927 (IFA). Other Laws such as The Forest Conservation Act of 1980 (FCA), The Environment Protection Act of 1986 (EPA) have also a positively impacted wildlife conservation. World Wildlife Day (WWD) is celebrated every year on 3rd March, to recognize the unique role and contributions of wildlife to people and the planet. The Supreme Court of India in T.N. Godavarman Thirumulpad V Union of India (2012) referred to a quote, Isha –Upanishads (as early as 1500-600 B.C.) taught us the following truth:-"The universe along with its creatures belongs to the Lord. No creature is superior to any other. Human beings should not be above nature. Let no one species encroach over the rights and privileges of other species". The quote was referred for a reason. It was emphasize the quintessential importance of preserving and conserving the environment and its components. Nature is the creator and the destroyer.

WPA, 1972 has been one of the most successful environmental legislations in world history. The WPA, was enacted in 1972 by the Prime Minister Mrs. Indira Gandhi. Recently, it under went its most significant Amendments. India is rich in plant and animal heritage. The concern for the protection of wildlife can be traced, back to the 3rd century when king Ashoka issued a decree at the end of his reign stating that "twenty years after his coronation, he released that the animals are not meant to be killed and should be conserved and protected prohibiting the forest fires". The Flora and Fauna should be protected and conserved as the animals and plants are of great economic importance to the humans in providing various products and by products in maintaining the balance of the nature. International Union for Conservation of Nature, Red list is a critical indicator of the health of the world's biodiversity. In this list, 'threatened' embraces the categories of Critically Endangered, Endangered and Vulnerable. Previously in India, this list contained 132 species of plants and animals in 2018 as of the 2023-1 update from the IUCN Red list, over 950 species of animals land over 600 species of plants are listed as Critically Endangered, Endangered, or Vulnerable. India's Wildlife Protection Act 1972, is a comprehensive piece of legislation that regulates Sanctuaries, National Parks, and Zoos among other protected locations. Its primary aim is to curb the illegal trade in the wildlife and the derivative parts.

The Wildlife (Protection) Act, 1972

The Wildlife Protection Act, 1972 is a crucial legislation enacted in India on 9th September 1972. Indian Parliament enacted the wildlife (Protection) Act in 1972, which provides for the safeguard and protection of the wildlife (flora and fauna) in the country. This is important legislation and forms an integral part of the environment and ecology. This Act provides for the protection of wild plants and wild animals. According to the Indian Wildlife Protection Act, the hunting and harming of the wild animals are strictly prohibited. The Act lays down restrictions on hunting many animal species. It safeguards the diverse wildlife found within the country's borders. It serves as a frame work for poaching, conserving, and managing wildlife. It aims to preserve natural habitats and ensure the well-being of wildlife species. It also promotes measures to combat illegal activities. The Wildlife Protection Act is vital in preserving India's wildlife heritage. It maintains ecological balance and fosters sustainable co existence between humans and wildlife. The Act includes various schedules that classify different species based on their level of protection and conservation status. It also establishes protected areas, permits the declaration of wildlife sanctuaries, national parks, and regulates activities related to wildlife.

History behind Wildlife Legislation in India

The initial legislation was introduced during the British Indian Government's rule in 1887, known as the Wild Birds Protection Act 1887. This law aimed to prohibit the possession and sale of specific wild birds killed or captured during their breeding season. A subsequent legal measure, The Wild Birds and Animals Protection Act, was passed in 1912. This Act was modified by introducing the Wild Birds and Animals Protection (Amendment) Act 1935. During the British Raj, wildlife preservation was not a prominent concern. It was not until 1960 that the issue of wildlife conservation and preventing certain species from becoming extinct gained significant attention.

Importance of wildlife Protection Act, 1972

The Wildlife Act of 1972 protects the country's natural animals, birds, and plants to promote ecological and environmental security. This statute established hunting limitations for a variety of animal species. Wildlife is a part of 'forest' and this was a State List until the Parliament passed this law in 1972. Now it is in Concurrent List.

- India is a treasure-trove of varied flora and fauna. Many species were seeing in rapid decline in numbers.

- A drastic decrease in the flora and fauna can cause ecological imbalance, which affects many aspects of climate and ecosystem.

- The most recent Act passed during the British era in this regard was the Wild Birds and Animals Protection, 1935. This needed to be upgraded as the punishments awarded to poachers and traders of wildlife products were disproportionate to huge financial benefits that accrue to them.

- There were five national parks in India prior to the enactment of this Act.

- The Wildlife Protection Act 1972, preserves the country's wild animals, birds and plants in order to ensure ecological and environmental security.

- This Act has laid down restriction on hunting various kinds of animal species.

- It also includes provisions related to harvesting and various other ancillary matters connected thereto.

- It has six schedules, including a list of endangered species, a list of wild creatures posing a threat to human life, a list of animals designated as vermin, and a list of defined goods, plants, and possessions, among others, that span India.

- The schedules which includes the list of endangered species list of wild animals that are threatening to humans lives, list of animals declared as vermin and list of specified trade, plants, possession etc. which extend all over the India.

- The Act provides for the formation of wildlife Advisory Boards, Wildlife Wardens, specifies their powers and duties.

- The six schedules and 66 sections of the Act give varying degrees of protection. Schedule I and part II provide absolute protection, offences under these are prescribed the highest penalties.

- The Species listed in schedule III and schedule IV are also protected, but penalties are much lower.

- Animals under schedule V eg; common crows, fruit bats, rats and mice are legally considered vermin and may be hunted freely.

- The specified endemic plants in schedule VI are prohibited from cultivation and planting.

- The Act prohibits hunting of wild animals and specified in the act schedules unless the hunting is carried out under a valid licence.

- It provides for the punishment of offences under the Act. This includes imprisonment, fines and confiscation of property.

- The Act prohibits hunting of endangered species.

- The Act provides for licences for the sale, transfer and possession of some wildlife species.

- Protection and management of wildlife habitat.

- The Establishment of protected area.

- Management of Zoo's. The provisions paved the way for the formation of the Central Zoo Authority. Central body is responsible for oversight Zoos in India, it established in 1992.

- Permits the declaration of wildlife sanctuaries and national parks.

- Regulates activities related to wildlife.

Limitations of the Wildlife Act 1972

- The Act prohibited the hunting of endangered species.

- This Act provides for the protection of the country's wild animals, birds and plant species, in order to ensure environmental and ecological security.

- The Act lays down restrictions on hunting many animal species.

- The Act prohibits any form of commercial sale of wild animal, its parts or trophies, the amendment sought exemption to carry out trade and transport of live elephants for religious use after permission from Central and State Governments.

- Elephants can only be owned when inherited.

- Schedules remain ambiguous.

- Scheduled animals are prohibited from being traded as per the Act's provisions.

- The Act provides for licenses for the sale, transfer, and possession of some wildlife species.

- Enforcement has been weak because of Illegal activities such as hunting and trade in wildlife and its products.

Need for the Amendment of Wildlife Protection Act 1972

- India has been blacklisted by CITES once before, and if a second blacklisting were to happen then India will no longer be able to trade in important plant specimens. This would affect the lively hood of a large section of Indian society that relies heavily on this trade.

- The rationalisation needed to be done because there were many discrepancies in the schedules and they were also ambiguous.

- Some species were listed under English names, others under scientific names, and under families while others under orders.

- Such categorisation was very confusing for wildlife and forest officials on the ground to implement.

Various Amendments under Wildlife (protection) Act, 1972

Over the years several Amendments were made to the Act. The Wildlife Act last Amended in 2022. The Wildlife (protection) Act, 2022 has come into force since 1st April 2023.

❖ Wild Life (Protection) Amendment Act, 1982

A few species classified as vermin (Schedule V), may be hunted without restrictions. Wildlife Wardens and their staff administer the act. An amendment to the Act in 1982, introduced a provision permitting the capture and transportation of wild animals for the scientific management of the animal population.

❖ Wild Life (Protection) Amendment Act, 1986

No. 29 of 1986 (23rd May, 1986.) An act to provide for the protection of wild animals, birds and plants and for matters connected therewith or ancillary or incidental thereto with a view to ensuring the ecological and environmental security of the country. Accordingly, by 1986 Amendment Act it was provided that no one trade in wild animals specified in Schedules I and II of the Act. Further the then existing licenses for internal trade of animals and animal articles were revoked. Further total ban was imposed on trade in Indian ivory.

❖ Wild Life (Protection) Amendment Act, 1991

- The Act restricts and prohibits hunting of animals.
- Protection of certain plants from excessive exploitation.
- Setting up and managing national parks and sanctuaries.
- Setting up an managing zoological gardens.

- Creation of a zoo authority for controlling zoos and captive breeding.

- Control trade in wildlife, wildlife products and trophies (preserved components of hunted animals).

- Encouraging and assisting the formation of wildlife societies.

National Forest Policy (1988):

It aims at increasing the forest cover of the country both in plains and hills so that the optimum of 33% forest cover is achieved. Other aims are,

- Maintenance of environmental stability through preservation and restoration of ecological balance.

- Check of soil erosion and denudation of catchment areas.

- Checking on spread of sand dunes.

- Increase in forest tree cover through massive afforestation and social forestry programmes.

- Steps to create massive people's movement for afforestation, management and protection of forests. Already about 14.25 million hectares of degraded forests are being restored, managed and protected by 63,000 Joint Forest Management Committees.

❖ **Wild Life (Protection) Amendment Act, 1993**

This document defines key terms related to trade in animal trophies and articles derived from certain scheduled animals. It prohibits dealing in such trophies, articles and animal parts after a specified date, with some exemptions. It requires anyone currently carrying out such business to declare their stockpile and allows them to retain some items for personal use it granted a certificate of ownership. Unauthorised possession, sale, or transport of scheduled animal items is also prohibited.

Chapter VA

Prohibition of Trade or Commerce in Trophies, Animal Articles, etc. derived from Certain Animals.

49A. Definitions- In this Chapter,-

a. "scheduled animal" means an animal specified for the time being in Schedule I or Part II of Schedule II;

b. " scheduled animal article " means an article made from any scheduled animal and includes an article or object in which the whole or any part of such animal (has been used but does not include tail-feather of peacock, an article or trophy made therefrom and snake venom or its derivative;)

c. "specified date" means-

I. In relation to a scheduled animal on the commencement of the Wildlife (Protection) Amendment Act, 1986, the date of expiry of two months from such commencement.

II. in relation to any animal added or transferred to Schedule I or Part II of Schedule II at any time after such commencement, the date of expiry of two months such addition or transfer;

III. in relation to ivory imported into India or an article made from such ivory, the date of expiry of six months from the commencement of the Wildlife (Protection) Amendment Act 1991.

49B. Prohibition of dealing in trophies, animal articles etc. derived from scheduled

animals- (1) Subject to the other provisions of this section, on and after the specified date, no person shall

a) Commence or carry on the business as-

i. a manufacturer of, or dealer, in scheduled animal articles; or

[(ia). a dealer in ivory imported into India or article made therefrom or a manufacturer of such article: or]

ii. a taxidermist with respect to any schedule animals or any parts of such animals; or

iii. a dealer in trophy or uncured trophy derived from any scheduled animal; or

iv. a dealer in any captive animal being scheduled animal; or

v. a dealer in meat derived from any scheduled animal; or

b) Cook or serve meat derived from any scheduled animal in any eating-house

Explanation – For the purpose of this sub-section, "eating-house" has the same meaning as in the Explanation below sub-section (1) of section 44.

2) Subject to the other provisions of this section no licence granted or renewed under section 44 before the specified date shall entitle the holder thereof or any other person to commence or carry on the business referred to in Cl (a) of sub-section (1) of this section on the occupation referred into Cl (b) that sub-section after such date.

3) Notwithstanding anything contained in sub-section (1) or sub-section (2), where the Central Government is satisfied that it is necessary or expedient to do so in the public interest, it may, by general or special order published in the official Gazette, exempt, for purposes of export, any corporation owned or controlled by the Central Government (including a Government company within the meaning of section 617 of the Companies Act, 1956 (1 of 1956), or any society registered under the Societies Registration Act, 1860 (21 of 1860), or any other law for the time being in force, wholly or substantially financed by the Central Government, from the provisions of sub sections (1) and (2).

4) Notwithstanding anything contained in sub-section(1) or sub-section (2), but subject to any rules which may be made in this behalf, a person holding a licence under section 44 to carry on the business as a taxidermist may put under a process of taxidermist may put under a process of taxidermy any scheduled animal or any part thereof,

a) For or on behalf of the Government or any corporation or society exempted under sub-section (3), or

b) With the previous authorisation in writing of the Chief Wildlife Warden, for and on behalf of any person for educational or scientific purposes.

49C. Declaration by dealer –

1) Every person carrying on the business or occupation referred to in sub section (1) of section 49 B shall within thirty days from the specified date, declare to the Chief Wildlife Warden or the authorised officer,

a) his stock, if any, as at the end of the specified date of-

i. scheduled animal articles;

ii. scheduled animals and part thereof;

iii. trophies and uncured trophies derived from scheduled animals;

iv. captive animals, being scheduled animals;

v. ivory imported into India or article made therefrom

b) the place of the places at which the stocks mentioned in the declaration are kept; and

c) the description of such items, if any, of the stocks mentioned in the declaration which he desires, to retain with himself for his bonafide personal use.

2) On receipt of a declaration under sub-section (1) the Chief Wildlife Warden or the authorised officer may take all or any of the measures specified in section 41 and for this purpose, the provisions of section 41 shall, so far as may be, apply

3) Where, in a declaration made under sub-section (1), the person making the declaration express his desire to retain with himself any of the items of the stocks specified in the declaration for his bonafide personal use, the Chief Wildlife Warden, with the prior approval of the Director, may, if he is satisfied that the person is in lawful possession of such items, issue certificates of ownership in favour of such person with respect to all, or as the case may be, such of the items as in the opinion of the Chief Wildlife Warden are required for the bonafide personal use of such person and affix upon such items identification marks in such manner as may be prescribed.

Provided that no such item shall be kept in any commercial premises.

4) No person shall obliterate or counterfeit any identification mark referred to in sub-section (3),

5) An appeal shall lie against any refusal to grant certificate of ownership under sub-section (3) and the provisions of sub-sections(2),(3)and (4) of section 46 shall, so far as may be, apply in relation to appeals under this sub-section.

6) Where a person who has been issued a certificate of ownership under sub section (3) in respect any item,

a) transfers such item to any person, whether by way of gift, sale of otherwise, or

b) transfer or transports from the State in which he resides to another State any such item he shall, within thirty days of such transfer or transport, report the transfer or transport to the Chief Wildlife Warden or the authorised officer within whose jurisdiction the transfer or transport is effected.

7) No person, other than a person who has been issued a certificate of ownership under sub-section (3) shall, on and after the specified date, keep under his control, sell or offer for sale or transfer to (any person any scheduled animal or scheduled animal article or ivory imported into India or any article made therefrom).

❖ **The Wild Life(Protection) Amendment Act, 2002**

To accomodate security of wild animals, fowls and plants and for issues associated therewith or auxiliary or accidental thereto. To guarantee the natural and ecological security of the nation. Justification of the Wild Life Protection Amendment Act,2002 with further focus on Section 32 of Wild

Life Protection Act,1972. This amendment introduced the concept of community reserves and conservation reserves as protected areas. The 2002 Amendment Act which came into force in January, 2003 have made punishment and penalty for offences under the Act more stringent.

Notable Developments in the Wildlife protection Amendment Act, 2002

Schedule I or part II of Schedule-II is inclusive of offenses concerning wild creatures (or their parts and items)

Others concerning hunting or attempting to change the limits of a sanctuary or park the punishment and penalty are upgraded, the base detainment endorsed is three years which can go as far as seven years, with a base fine Rs.10,000/-

For a resulting offense of this nature, the term of detainment will not be nevertheless three years yet may arrive at seven years with a base fine of Rs.25,000/-

Likewise a substitution segment (51-A) has been embedded inside the Act, guaranteeing conditions appropriate while allowing bail: 'When a person accused of the commission of any offence concerning schedule I or Part II of Schedule II or offences concerning hunting inside the boundaries of park or wildlife sanctuary or altering the boundaries of such parks and sanctuaries, is arrested under the provisions of the Act, then not withstanding anything contained within the Code of Criminal Procedure, 1973, no such one that had been previously convicted of an offence under this Act shall be released on bail unless –(3) (11)

- The Public Prosecutor has been given a chance of contradicting the discharge on bail;(3)

- Where the Public Prosecutor restricts the application, the court is fulfilled that there are sensible justification for accepting that he's vindicated of such offenses which he's probably not going to submit any offense while on bail.

In order to reinforce the intelligence gathering in wildlife crime, the prevailing provision for rewarding the informers has been increased from 20% of the fine and composition money respectively to 50% in each case. In addition to this, a reward up to Rs.10,000/- is additionally proposed to tend to the informants will provide assistance in detection of crime and apprehension the offender.

At present, people having proprietorship declaration (certificate) in regard of schedule I and Part II of Schedule II animals, can sell or present such articles. This has been altered so as to check unlawful exchange, and accordingly no one would now be able to obtain schedule I or Part II of Schedule II animals, articles or trophies aside from by method of legacy (with the exception of live elephants).

Severe measures have likewise been proposed to relinquish the properties of in-your-face lawbreakers who have just been indicated inside the past for appalling natural life for violations. These arrangements are practically similar to the arrangements of 'Narcotic Drugs and Psychotropic Substances Act,1985'. Arrangements have likewise been made enabling authorities to oust infringements from Protected Areas.

Offenses that are unrelated to hunting of endangered species: Offenses related with exchange and trade in trophies, animal articles and so forth got from specific animals (exemption: chapter VA section 38J) pulls in a term of detainment as long as three years as well as a fine up to Rs. 25,000/-

Critical Appraisal of Wildlife (Protection) amendment Act,2002

- The amendment Act of 2002 provided for confiscation of property derived from illegal hunting and trade by a confiscation tribunal. But investigation officer, confiscation officer and confiscation tribunal has not been appointed or created.

- There is a conflict between legislative intent of Wildlife Protection Amendment Act, 2002 and Forest Right Act, 2006, as the resource poor farmers and tribal generally come in conflict with wildlife animals as well as forest guard.

- Forest guard are not given proper training, about problem specific to forest like species diversity, study of animal behaviour, landscape planning to cope with porosity and fragmentation, understanding of zone of influence, and knowledge of animal classification.

- Forest guards are not given weapons. In case of conflict with poachers, they retreat.

Section 32 of the Wild Life (Protection) Act, 1972

Section 32 Ban on use of injurious substances (12)

No person shall use, in a sanctuary, chemicals, explosives or any other substances which may cause injury to, or endanger, any wildlife in such sanctuary.

- T. N. Godavarman Thirumulpad V Union of India (2006), The Supreme Court held the Central Empowered Committee, suggestions for the elimination of all fishing tanks and bunds used for pisciculture within Kolleru wild life sanctuary.

- Maa Dasabhuja Furniture Unit V State of Orissa and Others (2006), The Orissa High Court, dismissed a petition for allowance of license to a saw mill which was located within 10 kilometers of Chandaka Damapara Wildlife Sanctuary.

- Mohd. Hazi Rafeeq V State of Uttaranchal (2006), The Uttarakhand High Court, dismissed a petition that is contented that if an aerial distance of 10 km from the boundary of a forest is taken as a prohibited distance for a license of a saw mill close to the boundary of Rajaji National Park.

- Centre for Environmental Law, WWF India V Union of India (1995) and Goa Foundation V Union of India(2004), The Supreme Court has decided that any non-forest activity falling within sanctuaries, National Parks, and 10 kilometers of their boundaries now needs allowance prior consultation withstanding committee which is a part of National Board for Wildlife.

- Satyapal Verma V State of Jharkhand (2004), The Jharkhand High Court held that the Chief Wildlife Warden's decision under Section 29 banning movement of mineral filled trucks through Belta Wild Life Sanctuary.

- In Gujarat Navodaya Mandal V State (1988), whether Chief Wildlife Warden has any jurisdiction to pass the order under WPA,1972

   &

- State of Rajasthan V Salman khan and Others (2012) Rajasthan High Court, held that

   o A damage that is caused to the wild life qualifies as a loss to ecology.

   o By the Act of using fire arms for executing wildlife, the accused is liable for the offence of mischief as defined in sections 425 and 429 IPC.

   o Section 141 IPC covers it and it falls under the ambit of the same, mischief, criminal trespass or other offence, and can very well be taken into consideration for the offence, and can very well be taken into consideration for the offence of mischief that is when committed in relation to a wild animal also.

   o Accordingly, 'other offence' as mentioned in section 141 covers in the ambit of the same, an offence under Wildlife Protection Act.

❖ **The Wild Life (Protection) Amendment Act,2006**

The Wildlife (Protection) Act, 1972 has been amended in 2006, and a separate chapter (Chapter IVB) has been provided, which interalia, provides for constituting the National Tiger Conservation Authority (NTCA), its powers and functions, reporting requirements, constitution of State level Steering Committees,....

39 of 2006 further amended The Wildlife (Protection) Act, 1972. Its purpose is to strengthen the conservation of Tigers and other endangered species by combating crimes against them through the special Crime Control Bureau. It enacted by Parliament in the Fifty-seventh Year of Republic of India as follows:-

1. This Act may be called the Wild Life (Protection) Amendment Act, 2006.

(2) It shall come into force on such date as the Central Government may, by notification in the Official Gazette, appoint.

2. –After Chapter IVA of the Wild Life (Protection) Act, 1972 (53 of 1972) (hereinafter referred to as the principal Act), the following Chapters shall be inserted, namely;-

[CHAPTER IVB

National Tiger Conservation Authority

38K. In this Chapter,-

a) "National Tiger Conservation Authority" means the Tiger Conservation Authority constituted under section 38L;

b) "Steering Committee" means the Committee constituted under section 38U;

c) "Tiger Conservation Foundation" means the foundation established under section 38X;

d) "Tiger Reserve State" means a state having tiger reserve;

e) "Tiger Reserve" means the area notified as such under section 38V.

38L. (1) The Central Government shall constitute a body to be known as the National Tiger Conservation Authority (hereinafter in this Chapter referred to as the Tiger Conservation Authority), to exercise the powers conferred on, and to perform the functions assigned to it under this Act.

2) The Tiger conservation Authority shall consist of the following members, namely;-

a) the Minister in charge of the Ministry of Environment and Forests- Chairperson;

b) the Minister of State in the Ministry of Environment and Forests- Vice Chairperson;

c) three members of Parliament of whom two shall be elected by the House of the People and one by the Council of States;

d) Eight experts or professionals having prescribed qualifications and experience in conservation of wild life and welfare of people living in tiger reserve out of which at least two shall be from the field of tribal development;

e) Secretary, Ministry of Environment and Forests;

f) Director General of Forests and Special Secretary, Ministry of Environment and Forests;

g) Director, Wild Life Preservation, Ministry of Environment and Forests;

h) six Chief Wild Life Wardens from the Tiger Reserve States in rotation for three years;

i) an officer not below the rank of Joint Secretary and Legislative Counsel from the Ministry of Law and justice;

j) Secretary, Ministry of Tribal Affairs;

k) Secretary, Ministry of Social Justice and Empowerment;

l) Chairperson, National Commission for the Scheduled Tribes;

m) Chairperson, National Commission for the Scheduled Castes;

n) Secretary, Ministry of Panchayati Raj;

o) Inspector General of Forests or an officer of the equivalent rank having at least ten years experience in a tiger reserve or wildlife management, who shall be the Member-Secretary, to be notified by Central Government, in the Official Gazette.

3) It is hereby declared that the office of member of the Tiger Conservation Authority shall not disqualify its holder for being chosen as, or for being, a member of either House of Parliament.

38M.- 1) A member nominated under clause (d) of sub-section (2) of section 38L shall hold office for such period not exceeding three years:

Provided that a member may, by writing under his hand addressed to the Central Government, resign from his office.

2) The Central government shall remove a member referred to in clause (d) of sub-section (2) of section 38L, from office if he-

   a) is, or at any time has been, adjudicated as insolvent;

   b) has been convicted of an offence which, in the opinion of the Central Government, involves moral turpitude;

   c) is of unsound mind and stands so declared by a competent court;

   d) refuses to act or becomes incapable of acting;

   e) is, without obtaining leave of absence from the Tiger Conservation Authority, absent from three consecutive meetings of the said Authority; or

   f) has, in the opinion of the Central Government, so abused his position as to render his continuation in office detrimental to the public interest:

Provided that no member shall be removed under this sub-section unless he has been given a reasonable opportunity of being heard in the matter.

3) Any vacancy in the office of a member shall be filled by fresh appointment and such member shall continue for the remainder of the term of the member in whose place he is appointed.

4) The salaries and allowances and other conditions of appointment of the members of the Tiger Conservation Authority shall be such as may be prescribed.

5) No act or proceeding of the Tiger Conservation Authority shall be questioned or shall be invalid on the ground merely of the existence of any vacancy or defect in the constitution of the Tiger Conservation Authority.

38N. - (1) The Tiger Conservation Authority may, with the previous sanction of the Central Government, appoint such other officers and employees as it considers necessary for the efficient discharge of its functions under this Act:

Provided that the officers and employees holding office under the Directorate of Project Tiger and dealing with Project Tiger immediately before the date of constitution of the Tiger Conservation Authority shall continue to hold office in the said Authority by the same tenure and upon the same terms and conditions of service or until the expiry of the period of six months from that date if such employee opts not to be employee of that Authority.

(2) The terms and conditions of service of the officers and other employees of the Tiger Conservation Authority shall be such as may be prescribed.

38O. (1) The Tiger Conservation Authority shall have the following powers and perform the following functions, namely:-

a) to approve the Tiger Conservation Plan prepared by the State Government under sub-section (3) of section 38V of this Act;

b) evaluate and assess various aspects of sustainable ecology and disallow any ecologically unsustainable land use such as, mining, industry and other projects within the tiger reserves;

c) lay down normative standards for tourism activities and guidelines for Project Tiger from time to time for Tiger Conservation in the buffer and core area of tiger reserves and ensure their due compliance;

d) provide for management focus and measures for addressing conflicts of men and wild animals and to emphasise on co-existence in forest areas outside the National Parks, sanctuaries or tiger reserve, in the working plan code;

e) provide information on protection measures including future conservation plan, estimation of population of tiger and its natural prey species, status of habitats, disease surveillance, morality survey, patrolling, reports on untoward happenings and such other management aspects as it may deem fit including future plan conservation;

f) approve, co-ordinate research and monitoring on tiger, co-predators, prey, habitat, related ecological and socio-economic parameters and their evaluation;

g) ensure that the tiger reserves and areas linking one protected area or tiger reserve with another protected area or tiger reserve are not diverted for ecologically unsustainable uses, except in public interest and with the approval of the National Board for Wild Life and on the advice of Tiger Conservation Authority;

h) facilitate and support the tiger reserve management in the State for biodiversity conservation initiatives through eco-development and people's participation as per approved management plans and to support similar initiatives in adjoining areas consistent with the Central and State laws;

i) ensure critical support including scientific, information technology and legal support for better implementation of the tiger conservation plan;

j) facilitate on going capacity building programme for skill development of officers and staff of tiger reserves; and

k) perform such other functions as may be necessary to carry out the purposes of this Act with regard to conservation of tigers and their habitat.

2) The Tiger conservation authority may, in the exercise of its powers and performance of its functions under this Chapter, issue directions in writing to any person, officer or authority for the protection of tiger or tiger reserves and such person, officer or authority shall be bound to comply with the directions:

Provided that no such direction shall interfere with or affect the rights of local people particularly the Scheduled Tribes.

38P. (1) The Tiger Conservation Authority shall meet at such time and at such place as the Chairperson may think fit.

(2) The Chairperson or in his absence the Vice-Chairperson shall preside over the meetings of the Tiger Conservation Authority.

(3) The Tiger Conservation Authority shall regulate its own procedure.

(4) All orders and decisions of the Tiger Conservation Authority shall be authenticated by the Member-Secretary or any other officer of the said authority duly authorised by the Member-Secretary in this behalf.

38Q. - (1) the Central Government may, after due appropriation made by Parliament by law in this behalf, make to the Tiger Conservation Authority grants and loans of such sums of money as that Government may consider necessary.

(2) There shall be constituted a fund to be called the Tiger Conservation Authority Fund and there shall be credited thereto-

    i. any grants and loans made to the Tiger Conservation Authority by the Central Government;

    ii. all fees and charges received by the Tiger conservation authority under this Act; and

    iii. all sums received by the Authority from such other sources as may be decided upon by the Central Government.

(3) The fund referred to in sub-section (2) shall be applied for meeting salary, allowances and other remuneration of the members, officers and other employees of the Tiger Conservation Authority and the expenses of the Tiger Conservation Authority incurred in the discharge of its functions under this Chapter.

38R. -(1) The Tiger Conservation Authority shall maintain proper accounts and other relevant record and prepare an annual statement of accounts in such form as may be prescribed by the Central Government in consultation with the Comptroller and Auditor –General of India.

(2) The accounts of the Tiger Conservation Authority shall be audited by the Comptroller and Auditor –General of India at such intervals as may be specified by him and any expenditure incurred in connection with such audit shall be payable by the Tiger Conservation Authority to the Comptroller and Auditor-General of India.

(3) The comptroller and Auditor-General of India and any other person appointed by him in connection with the audit of the accounts of the Tiger Conservation Authority shall have the same rights and privileges and authority in connection with such audit as the Comptroller and Auditor-General generally has in connection with the audit of the Government accounts and, in particular, shall have the right to demand the production of books, accounts, connected vouchers and other documents and papers and to inspect the office of the Tiger Conservation Authority.

(4) The Accounts of the Tiger Conservation Authority as certified by the Comptroller and Auditor-General of India or any other person appointed by him in this behalf together with the audit report there on, shall be forwarded annually to the Central Government by the Tiger Conservation Authority.

38S. - The Tiger Conservation Authority shall prepare in such form and at such time, for each financial year, as may be prescribed, its annual report, giving a full account of its activities during the previous financial year and forward a copy there of the Central Government.

38T. - The Central Government shall cause the annual report together with a memorandum of action taken on the recommendations contained there in, in so far as they relate to the Central Government, and the reasons for the non-acceptance, if any, of any of such recommendations, and the audit report to be laid, as soon as may be after the reports are received, before each House of Parliament.

38U.- (1) The State Government may constitute a Steering Committee for ensuring co-ordination, monitoring, protection and conservation of tiger, co-predators and prey animals within the tiger range States.

(2) The Steering Committee shall consists of-

(a) the Chief Minister – Chairperson;

(b) the Minister in-charge of Wild Life – Vice-Chairperson;

(c) such number of official members not exceeding five including at least Two Field Directors of Tiger Reserve or Director of National Park and one from the State Government's Departments dealing with tribal affairs;

(d) three experts or professionals having qualifications and experience in conservation of wild life of which at least one shall be from the field of tribal development;

(e) two members from the State's Tribal Advisory Council;

(f) one representative each from State Government's Departments dealing with Panchayathi Raj and Social Justice and Empowerment;

(g) Chief Wild Life warden of the State shall be the Member-Secretary, to be notified by the State Government, in the Official Gazette.

38V. - (1) The State government shall, on the recommendation of the Tiger Conservation Authority, notify an area as a Tiger Reserve.

(2) The provisions of sub-section (2) of section 18, sub-sections (2), (3) and (4) of section 27, section 30, 32 and clauses (b) and (c) of section 33 of this Act shall, as far as may be, apply in relation to a Tiger Reserve as they apply in relation to a sanctuary.

(3) The State Government shall prepare a Tiger Conservation Plan including staff development and deployment plan for the proper management of each area referred to in sub-section (1), so as to ensure-

(a) protection of Tiger Reserve and providing site specific habitat inputs for a viable population of tigers co-predators and prey animals without distorting the natural prey-predator ecological cycle in the habitat;

(b) ecologically compatible land uses in the Tiger Reserves and areas linking one protected area or Tiger reserve with another for addressing the livelihood concerns of local people, so as to provide dispersal habitats and corridor for spill over population of wild animals from the designated core areas of Tiger Reserves or from tiger breeding habitats within other protected areas;

(c) the forestry operations of regular forest divisions and those adjoining Tiger Reserves are not incompatiable with the needs of Tiger Conservation.

(4) Subject to the provisions contained in this Act, the State Government shall while preparing a Tiger Conservation Plan, ensure the agricultural, livelihood, developmental and other interests of the people living in tiger bearing forests or a Tiger Reserve.

Explanation- For the purposes of this Section, the expression "tiger reserve" includes-

(i) core or critical tiger habitat areas of National Parks and Sanctuaries, where it has been established, on the basis of scientific and objective criteria, that such areas are required to be kept as inviolate for the purposes of tiger conservation, without affecting the rights of the Scheduled Tribes or such other forest dwellers, and notified as such by the State

Government in consultation with an Expert Committee constituted for the purpose;

(ii) buffer or peripheral area consisting of the area peripheral to critical tiger habitat or core area, identified and established in accordance with the provisions contained in Explanation (i) above, where a lesser degree of habitat protection is required to ensure the integrity of the critical tiger habitat with adequate dispersal for tiger species, and which aim at promoting co-existence between wildlife and human activity with due recognition of the livelihood, developmental, social and cultural rights of the local people, wherein the limits of such areas are determined on the basis of scientific and objective criteria in consultation with the concerned Gram Sabha and an Expert Committee constituted for the purpose.

(5) Save as for voluntary relocation on mutually agreed terms and conditions, provided that such terms and conditions satisfy requirements laid down in this sub-section, no Scheduled Tribes or other forest dwellers shall be resettled or have their rights adversely affected for the purpose of creating in violate areas for tiger conservation unless-

(i) the process of recognition and determination of rights and acquisition of land or forest rights of the Scheduled Tribes and such other forest dwelling persons is complete;

(ii) the concerned agencies of the State Government, in exercise of their powers under this Act, establishes with the consent of the Scheduled Tribes and such other forest dwellers in the area, and in consultation with an ecological and social scientist familiar with the area, that the activities of the Scheduled Tribes and other forest dwellers or the impact of their presence upon wild animals is sufficient to cause irreversible damage and shall threaten the existence of tigers and their habitat;

(iii) the State Government, after obtaining the consent of the Scheduled Tribes and other forest dwellers inhabiting the area, and in consultation with an independent ecological and social scientist familiar with the area, has come to a conclusion that other reasonable options of co-existence, are not available;

(iv) resettlement or alternative package has been prepared providing for livelihood for the affected individuals and communities and fulfils the requirements given in the National Relief and Rehabilitation Policy;

(v) the informed consent of the Gram Sabha concerned, and of the persons affected, to the resettlement programme has been obtained; and

(vi) the facilities and land allocation at the resettlement location are provided under the said programme, otherwise their existing rights shall not be interfered with.

38W. - (1) No alteration in the boundaries of a tiger reserve shall be made except on a recommendation of the Tiger Conservation Authority and the approval of the National Board for Wild Life.

(2) No State Government shall de-notify a tiger reserve, except in public interest with the approval of the Tiger Conservation Authority and the National Board for Wild Life.

38X. - (1) The State Government shall establish a Tiger Conservation Foundation for tiger reserves within the State in order to facilitate and support their management for conservation of tiger and biodiversity and, to take initiatives in eco-development by involvement of people in such development process.

(2) The Tiger Conservation Foundation shall, inter alia have the following objectives:-

(a) to facilitate ecological, economic, social and cultural development in the tiger reserves;

(b) to promote eco-tourism with the involvement of local stakeholder communities and provide support to safeguard the natural environment in the tiger reserves;

(c) to facilitate the creation of, and or maintenance of, such assets as may be necessary for fulfilling the above said objectives;

(d) to solicit technical, financial, social, legal and other support required for the activities of the Foundation for the achieving the above said objectives;

(e) to augment and mobilise financial resources including recycling of entry and such other fees received in a tiger reserve, to foster stake-holder development and eco-tourism;

(f) to support research, environmental education and training in the above related fields.

CHAPTER IVC

Tiger And Other Endangered Species Crime Control Bureau

38Y. - The Central Government may, for the purposes of this Act, by order published in the Official Gazette, constitute a Tiger and other Endangered Species Crime Control Bureau known as the Wildlife Crime Control Bureau consisting of-

a) the Director of Wildlife Preservation- Director ex-officio;

b) the Inspector General of Police- Additional Director;

c) the Deputy Inspector-General of Police- Joint Director;

d) the Deputy Inspector-General of Forest- Joint Director;

e) the Additional Commissioner (Customs and Central Excise)- Joint Director and;

f) such other officers as may be appointed from amongst the officers covered under sections 3 and 4 of this Act.

38Z. - (1) Subject to the provisions of this Act, the Wildlife Crime Control Bureau shall take measures with respect to-

i. collect and collate intelligence related to organized wildlife crime activities and to disseminate the same to State and other enforcement agencies for the immediate action so as to apprehend the criminals and to establish a centralised wildlife crime data bank;

ii. co-ordination of actions by various officers, State Governments and other authorities in connection with the enforcement of the provisions of this Act, either directly or through regional and border units set up by the Bureau;

iii. implementation of obligations under the various International Conventions and protocols that are in force at present or which may be ratified or acceded to by India in future;

iv. assistance to concerned authorities in foreign countries and concerned International Organisations to facilitate co-ordination and universal action for Wildlife Crime Control;

v. develop infrastructure and capacity building for scientific and professional investigation into wildlife crimes and assist State Governments to ensure success in prosecutions related to wildlife crimes;

vi. advice the Government of India on issues relating to wildlife crimes having national and international ramifications, and suggest changes required in relevant policy and laws from time to time.

(2) The Wildlife Crime Control Bureau shall exercise-

i. such powers as may be delegated to it under sub-section (1) of section 5; sub-section (1) and (8) of section 50 and section 55 of this Act; and

ii. such other powers as may be prescribed.

(3) In section 51 of the principal Act, after subsection (1B), the following sub-sections shall be inserted, namely:-

"(IC) Any person, who commits an offence in relation to the core area of a tiger reserve or where the offence relate to hunting in the tiger reserve or altering the boundaries of the tiger reserve, such offence shall be punishable on first conviction with imprisonment for a term which shall not be less than three years but may extend to seven years, and also with fine which shall not less than fifty thousand rupees but may extend to two lakh rupees; and in the event of a second or subsequent conviction with imprisonment for a term of not less than seven years and also with fine which shall not be less than five lakh rupees but may extend to fifty lakh rupees.

(ID) Whoever, abets any offence punishable under sub-section

(IC) shall, if the act abetted is committed in consequence of the abetment, be punishable with the punishment provided for that offence."

(4). In section 55 of the principal Act, after clause (aa), the following clauses shall be inserted, namely:-

"(ab) Member-Secretary, Tiger Conservation Authority; or

(ac) Director of the concerned tiger reserve: or".

(5). In section 59 of the principal Act, after the word, figures and letter "Chapter IV A", the word, figures and letter "ChapterIV B" shall be inserted;

(6). In section 60 of the principal Act, in sub-section (3), after the word, figures and letter "Chapter IV A", the word, figures and letter "Chapter IV B" shall be inserted;

(7). In section 63 of the principal Act, in subsection (1), after clause (g), the following clauses shall be inserted, namely:-

"(gi) qualification and experience of experts or professionals under clause (d) of subsection 38-1;

(gii) the salaries and allowances and other conditions of appointment of the members under sub-section (4) of section 38M;

(giii) the terms and conditions of service of the officers and other employees of the Tiger Conservation Authority under sub-section (2) of section 38N;

(giv) the form in which the annual statement of accounts of Tiger Conservation Authority shall be prepared under sub-section (1) of section 38R;

(gv) the form in which and the time at which the annual report of Tiger Conservation Authority shall be prepared under section 38S;

(gvi) other powers of the Wildlife Crime Control Bureau under clause (ii) of sub-section (2) of section 38Z".

❖ **The Wild Life (Protection) Amendment Bill, 2013**

- The Wild Life (Protection) Amendment Bill, 2013 was introduced in the Rajya Sabha on August 5, 2013. The Bill has been referred to the Standing Committee on Environment and Forests. The Bill seeks to amend the Wildlife (Protection) Act, 1972. This Act provides for the protection and conservation of wild animals, birds and plants. It also covers the management of their habitats and regulation and control of trade or commerce linked to wildlife.

- According to the Government, India is a party to the Convention on International Trade in Endangered Species of Wild Fauna and Flora (CITES) and amendments to the Act are necessary for India to fulfil its obligations under the CITES. The key amendments made by the Bill are:

- The manufacture, sale, transport or use of animal traps except for educational and scientific purposes (with permission) is prohibited.

- Under the Act, destruction, exploitation or removal of any wildlife including forest produce from a sanctuary is not permitted, except with a permit. The amendment allows certain activities such as grazing or movement of livestock, bonafide use of drinking and household water by local communities and hunting under a permit.

- Provisions to regulate international trade in endangered species of wild fauna and flora as per the CITES have been inserted. A schedule listing out flora and fauna for purposes of regulation of international trade under CITES has been added.

- The Tiger and Other Endangered Species Crime Control Bureau has been changed to Wild life Crime Control Bureau.

- The term of punishment and fines for commission of offences under the Act have been increased.

- The Bill protects the hunting rights of Scheduled Tribes in the Andaman and Nicobar Islands.

❖ **The Wild Life (Protection) Amendment Bill, 2021**

The Wildlife (Protection) Amendment Bill, 2021 was introduced in Lok Sabha by the Minister of Environment, Forest and Climate Change on December 17, 2021. The Bill amends the Wildlife (Protection) Act, 1972. The Act regulates the protection of wild animals, birds and plants. The Bill seeks to increase the species protected under the law, and implement the Convention on International Trade in Endangered Species of Wild Fauna and Flora (CITES). Key features of the Bill include:

- CITES: CITES is an international agreement between Governments to ensure that international trade in specimens of wild animals and plants does not threaten the survival of the species. Under CITES, plant and animal specimens are classified into three categories (Appendices) based on the threat to their extinction. The Convention requires countries to regulate the trade of all listed specimens through permits. It also seeks to regulate the possession of live animal specimens. The Bill seeks to implement these provisions of CITES.

- Rationalising schedules: Currently, the Act has six schedules for specially protected plants (one), specially protected animals (four), and vermin species (one). Vermin refers to small animals that carry disease and destroy food. The Bill reduces the total number of schedules to four by:

(i) Reducing the number of schedules for specially protected animals to two(one for greater protection level)

(ii) Removes the Schedule for vermin species

(iii) Inserts a new schedule for specimens listed in the Appendices under CITES (scheduled specimens).

- Obligations under CITES: The Bill provides for the Central Government to designate a:

    o Management Authority, which grants export or import permits for trade of specimens,

    o Scientific Authority, which gives advice on aspects related to impact on the survival of the specimens being traded. Every person engaging in trade of a scheduled specimen must report the details of the transaction to the Management Authority. As per CITES, the Management Authority may use an identification mark for a specimen. The Bill prohibits any person from modifying or removing the identification mark of the specimen. Additionally, every person possessing live specimens of scheduled animals must obtain a registration certificate from the Management Authority.

- Invasive alien species: The bills empowers the Central Government to regulate or prohibit the import, trade, possession or proliferation of invasive alien species. Invasive alien species refers to plant or animal species which are not native to India and whose introduction may adversely impact wild life or its habitat. The Central Government may authorise an officer to seize and dispose the invasive species.

- Control of Sanctuaries: The Act entrust the Chief Wild Life Warden to control, manage and maintain all sanctuaries in a state. The Chief Wild Life Warden is appointed by the state Government. The Bill specifies that actions of the Chief Warden must be in accordance with the management plans for the sanctuary. These plans will be prepared as per guidelines of the Central Government, and as approved by the Chief Warden. For sanctuaries falling under special areas, the management plan must be prepared after due consultation with the concerned Gram Sabha. Special areas include a Scheduled Area or areas where the Scheduled Tribes and Other Traditional Forest Dwellers (Recognition of Forest Rights) act, 2006 is applicable. Scheduled Areas are economically backward areas with a predominantly tribal population, notified under the Fifth Schedule to the Constitution.

- Conservation Reserves: Under the Act, State Governments may declare areas adjacent to national parks and sanctuaries as a conservation reserve, for protecting flora and fauna, and their habitat. The Bill empowers the Central Government to also notify a conservation reserve.

- Surrender of Captive Animals: The Bill provides for any person to voluntarily surrender any captive animals or animal products to the Chief Wild life Warden. No compensation will be paid to the person for surrendering such items. The surrendered items become property of the State Government.

- Penalties: The Act prescribes imprisonment terms and fines for violating the provisions of the Act. The Bill increases these fines.

Type of Violation	1972 Act	2021 Bill
General violation	Up to Rs.25,000	Up to Rs. 1,00,000
Specially protected animals	At least Rs.10,000	At least Rs. 25,000

❖ **Wild Life (Protection) Amendment Act, 2022**

The Rajya Sabha passed the Wild Life (Protection) Amendment Bill, 2022 which seeks to give effect to India's obligations under the Convention on International Trade on Endangered Species of Wild Fauna and Flora (CITES). The Wildlife (Protection) Act 1972, was amended in 2022 and serves as a key legislative framework for the conservation of wildlife.

Objectives of the Act, 2022

- Protection of Endangered Species: The Bill seeks to enhance punishment for illegal Wildlife trade.

- Better Management of Protected Areas: It provides for certain permitted activities like grazing or movement of livestock and Bonafide use of drinking and household water by local communities.

- Protection of Forest Lands: It is so critical because it equally inculcates in itself the protection of rights of the people who have been residing there since ages.

Proposed Amendments

- o This amendment proposed a new schedule for species listed in the Appendices under CITES.
- o Section 6 has been amended to constitute Standing Committee to exercise such powers and duties as may be delegated to it by the State Board for Wildlife.
- o Section 43 of the Act amended which permitted the use of elephants for 'religious or any other purposes'.
- o To enable the Central Government to appoint a Management Authority Section 49E has been inserted.
- o To enable the Central Government to appoint a Scientific Authority to provide guidance on matters relating to the impact on the survival of the specimens on being traded.
- o The Bill also empowers Central Government to regulate and stop the import, trade or possession of invasive plant or animal alien species.
- o The Bill also enhances the penalties prescribed for violation of provisions of the Act.
- o For 'general violations' maximum fine is increased from 25,000 to 1 Lakh.
- o In case of Specially protected animals, the minimum fine of Rs.10,000 has been enhanced to Rs.25,000.

The Concerns Associated with the Act

- Phrase "any other purpose" is vague and has potential of encouraging commercial trade of elephants.
- Some important issues regarding Human-Wildlife conflict, Eco-sensitive zone rule, etc., has not been addressed.
- According to the report provided by the Parliamentary Standing Committee, species listed in all three schedules of the Bill are incomplete.
- The scientists, botanists, biologists are short in number and needed greater inclusion of them to accelerate the process of listing all existing species of wildlife.

THE WILD LIFE (PROTECTION) ACT, 1972

(Last updated 1-4-2023)

ARRANGEMENT OF SECTIONS

CHAPTER I

PRELIMINARY SECTIONS

1. Short title, extent and commencement.
2. Definitions.

CHAPTER II

AUTHORITIES TO BE APPOINTED OR CONSTITUTES UNDER THE ACT

3. Appointment of Director and other officers.
4. Appointment of Life Warden and other officers.
5. Power to delegate.
5A. Constitution of the National Board for Wild Life.
5B. Standing Committee of the National Board.
5C. Functions of the National Board.
6. Constitution of State Board for Wild Life.
6A. Standing Committee of Board.
7. Procedure to be followed by the Board.
8. Duties of State Board for Wild Life.

CHAPTER III

HUNTING OF WILD ANIMALS

9. Prohibition of hunting.
10. [Omitted.]
11. Hunting of wild animals to be permitted in certain cases.
12. Grant of permit for special purposes.
13. [Omitted.]

14. [Omitted.]
15. [Omitted.]
16. [Omitted.]
17. [Omitted.]

CHAPTER IIIA
PROTECTION OF SPECIFIED PLANTS

17A. Prohibition of picking, uprooting, etc. of specified plant.
17B. Grants of permit for special purposes.
17C. Cultivation of specified plants without licence prohibited.
17D. Dealing in specified plants without licence prohibited.
17E. Declaration of stock.
17F. Possession, etc., of plants by licensee.
17G. Purchase, etc., of specified plants.
17H. Plants to be Government property.

CHAPTER IV
PROTECTED AREAS

Sanctuaries

18. Declaration of sanctuary.
18A. Protection to sanctuaries.
18B. Appointment of Collectors.
19. Collector to determine rights.
20. Bar of accrual of rights.
21. Proclamation by Collector.
22. Inquiry by Collector.
23. Powers of Collector.
24. Acquisition of rights.
25. Acquisition proceedings.

25A. Time-limit for completion of acquisition proceedings.
26. Delegation of Collector's powers.
26A. Declaration of area as sanctuary.
27. Restriction on entry in sanctuary.
28. Grant of permit.
29. Destruction, etc., in a sanctuary prohibited without a permit.
30. Causing fire prohibited.
31. Prohibition of entry into sanctuary with weapon.
32. Ban on use of injurious substances.
33. Control of sanctuaries.
33A. Immunisation of live-stock.
33B. Advisory Committee.
34. Registration of certain persons in possession of arms.

National Parks

35. Declaration of National Parks.
36. [Omitted.]
36A. Declaration and management of a conservation reserve.
36B. Conservation reserve management Committee.
36C. Declaration and management of community reserve.
36D. Community reserve management committee.

Closed Area

37. [Omitted.]

Sanctuaries or National Parks declared by Central Government

38. Power of Central Government to declare areas as sanctuaries or National Parks or Conservation Reserves.

CHAPTER IVA

CENTRAL ZOO AUTHORITY AND RECOGNITION OF ZOOS

38A. Constitution of Central Zoo Authority.

38B. Term of office and conditions of service of Chairperson and members, etc.

38C. Functions of the Authority.

38D. Procedure to be regulated by the Authority.

38E. Grants and loans to Authority and Constitution of Fund.

38F. Annual Report.

38G. Annual report and audit report to be laid before Parliament.

38H. Recognition of zoos.

38I. Acquisition of animals by a zoo.

38J. Prohibition of teasing, etc., in a zoo.

CHAPTER IVB

NATIONAL TIGER CONSERVATION AUTHORITY

38K. Definitions.

38L. Constitution of National Tiger Conservation Authority.

38M. Term of office and conditions of service of members.

38N. Officers and employees of Tiger Conservation Authority.

38O. Powers and functions of Tiger Conservation Authority.

38P. Procedure to be regulated by Tiger Conservation Authority.

38Q. Grants and loans to Tiger Conservation Authority and Constitution of Fund.

38R. Accounts and audit of Tiger Conservation Authority.

38S. Annual report of Tiger Conservation Authority.

38T. Annual report and audit report to be laid before Parliament.

38U. Constitution of Steering Committee.

38V. Tiger Conservation Plan.

38W. Alteration and de-notification of tiger reserves.

38X. Establishment of Tiger Conservation Foundation.

38XA. Provisions of Chapter to be in addition to provisions relating to sanctuaries and National Park.

CHAPTER IVC

WILD LIFE CRIME CONTROL BUREAU

38Y. Constitution of Wild Life Crime Control Bureau.

38Z. Powers and functions of the Wildlife Crime Control Bureau.

CHAPTER V

TRADE OR COMMERCE IN WILD ANIMALS, ANIMAL ARTICLES AND TROPHIES

39. Wild animals, etc., to be Government property.

40. Declarations.

40A. Immunity in certain cases.

41. Inquiry and preparation of inventories.

42. Certificate of ownership.

42A. Surrender of captive animals, animal article etc.

43. Regulation of transfer of animal, etc.

44. Dealings in trophy and animal articles without licence prohibited.

45. Suspension or cancellation of licences.

46. Purchase.

47. Maintenance of records.

48. Purchase of animals, etc., by licensee.

48A. Restriction on transportation of wild life.

49. Purchase of captive animal, etc., by a person other than a licensee.

CHAPTER VA

PROHIBITION OF TRADE OR COMMERCE IN TROPHIES, ANIMAL ARTICLES, ETC., DERIVED FROM CERTAIN ANIMALS

49A. Definitions.

49B. Prohibition of dealings in trophies, animal articles, etc., derived from scheduled animals.

49C. Declaration by dealers.

CHAPTER VB

REGULATION OF INTERNATIONAL TRADE IN ENDANGERED SPECIES OF WILD FAUNA AND FLORA AS PER CONVENTION ON INTERNATIONAL TRADE IN ENDANGERED SPECIES OF WILD FAUNA AND FLORA

49D. Definitions.

49E. Designation of Management Authority.

49F. Designation of Scientific Authority.

49G. Directions of Central Government.

49H. International trade in scheduled specimen and restriction in respect thereof.

49I. Conditions for scheduled specimens.

49J. Conditions for import of scheduled specimens.

49K. Conditions for re-export of scheduled specimens.

49L. Conditions for intro-function from sea of scheduled specimens.

49M. Possession transfer and breeding of living scheduled animal species.

49N. Application for Licence by breeders of Appendix I species.

49O. Licence of breeders of Appendix I species.

49P. Prohibition on alteration, etc.

49Q. Species and scheduled specimens to be Government property.

49R. Application of provisions of Act in respect of species listed in Schedule I or II and Schedule IV.

CHAPTER VI

PREVENTION AND DETECTION OF OFFENCES

50. Power of entry, search, arrest and detention.

51. Penalties.

51A. Certain conditions to apply while granting bail.

52. Attempts and abetment.
53. Punishments for wrongful seizure.
54. Power to compound offences.
55. Cognizance of offences.
56. Operation of other laws not barred.
57. Presumption to be made in certain cases.
58. Offences by Companies.

CHAPTER VI A

FORFEITURE OF PROPERTY DERIVED FROM ILLEGAL HUNTING AND TRADE

58A. Application.
58B. Definitions.
58C. Prohibition of holding illegally acquired property.
58D. Competent authority.
58E. Identifying illegally acquired property.
58F. Zeizure or freezing of illegally acquired property.
58G. Management of properties seized or forfeited under this Chapter.
58H. Notice of forfeiture of property.
58 I. Forfeiture of property in certain cases.
58J. Burden of proof.
58K. Fine in lieu of forfeiture.
58L. Procedure in relation to certain trust properties.
58M. Certain transfer to be null and void.
58N. Constitution of Appellate Tribunal.
58 O. Appeals.
58P. Notice or order not to be invalid for error in description.
58Q. Bar of Jurisdiction.
58R. Competent Authority and Appellate Tribunal to have powers of civil court.

58S. Information to competent authority.

58T. Certain officers to assist Administrator, competent authority and Appellate Tribunal.

58U. Power to take possession.

58V. Rectification of mistakes.

58W. Findings under other laws not conclusive for proceedings under this Chapter.

58X. Service of notices and orders.

58Y. Punishment for acquiring property in relating to which proceedings have been taken under this chapter.

CHAPTER VII
MISCELLANEOUS

59. Officers to be public servants.

60. Protection of action taken in good faith.

60A. Reward to persons.

60B. Reward by State Government.

61. Power to alter entries in Schedules.

62. Declaration of certain wild animals to be vermin.

62A. Regulation or prohibition of import, etc., of invasive alien species.

62B. Power to issue directions.

63. Power of Central Government to make rules.

64. Power of State Government to make rules.

65. Rights of Scheduled Tribes to be protected.

66. Repeal and savings.

SCHEDULE I

SCHEDULE II

SCHEDULE III

SCHEDULE IV

THE WILD LIFE (PROTECTION) ACT, 1972

ACT NO.53 OF 1972

[9th September, 1972.]

[An Act to provide for the [conservation, protection and management of wild life] and for matters connected therewith or ancillary or incidental thereto with a view to ensuring the ecological and environmental security of the country.]

CHAPTER I

Preliminary

1.Short title, extent and commencement- (1) This Act may be called the Wild Life (Protection) Act, 1972.

(2) It extends to the whole of India *** .]

(3) It shall come into force in a State or Union Territory to which it extends*** on such date as the Central Government may, by notification, appoint, and different dates may be appointed for different provisions of this Act or for different States or Union Territories.

2.Definitions.- In this Act, unless the context otherwise requires,-

[(1) "animal" includes amphibians, birds, mammals and reptiles and their young, and also includes, in the cases of birds and reptiles, their eggs;]

(2) "animal article" means an article made from any captive animal or wild animal, other than vermin, and includes an article or object in which the whole or any part of such animal [has been used, and ivory imported into India and an article made therefrom];

* * * *

[(4) "Board" means a State Board for Wild Life constituted under sub-section (1) of section 6;]

* * * *

(5) "captive animal" means any animal, specified in [schedule I or Schedule II] which is captured or kept or bred in captivity;

* * * *

(7) "Chief Wild Life Warden" means the person appointed as such under clause (a) of sub-section (1) of section 4;

[(7A) "circus" means an establishment, whether stationary or mobile, where animals are kept or used wholly or mainly for the purpose of performing tricks or manoeuvres;]

* * * *

[(9) "Collector" means the chief officer in charge of the revenue administration of a district or any other officer not below the rank of a Deputy Collector as may be appointed by the State Government under section 18B in this behalf;]

(10) "commencement of this Act", in relation to-

    a. a State, means commencement of this Act in that State,

    b. any provision of this Act, means the commencement of that provision In the concerned State;

[(11) "dealer" in relation to any captive animal, animal article, trophy, meat or specified plant, means a person, who carries on the business of buying or selling any such animal or article, and includes a person who undertakes business in any single transaction;]

(12) "Director" means the person appointed as Director of Wild Life Preservation under clause (a) of sub-section (1) of section 3;

[(12A) "Forest officer" means the Forest officer appointed under clause (2) of section 2 of the Indian Forest Act, 1927 (16 of 1927) or under any other Act for the time being in force in a State;

(12B) "forest produce" shall have the same meaning as in sub-clause (b) of clause (4) of section 2 of the Indian Forest Act, 1927 (16 of 1927);]

* * * *

(14) "Government property" means any property referred to in section 39 [or section 17H];

(15) "habitat" includes land, water or vegetation which is the natural home of any wild animal [or specified plant];

(16) "hunting", with its grammatical variations and cognate expressions, includes,-

    [(a) killing or poisoning of any wild animal or captive animal and every attempt to do so;

    (b) capturing, coursing, snaring, trapping, driving or baiting any wild or captive animal and every attempt to do so;]

(c) injuring or destroying or taking any part of the body of any such animal or, in the case of wild birds or reptiles, damaging the eggs of such birds or reptiles, or disturbing the eggs or nests of such birds or reptiles;

[(16A) "invasive alien species" means a species of animal or plant which is not native to India and whose introduction or spread may threaten or adversely impact wild life or its habitat;]

(17) "land" includes canals, creeks, and other water channels, reservoirs, rivers, streams and lakes, whether artificial or natural, [marshes and wetlands and also includes boulders and rocks];

(18) "licence" means a licence granted under this act;

[(18A) "livestock" means farm animals and includes buffaloes, bulls, bullocks, camels, cows, donkeys, goats, sheep, horses, mules, yaks, pigs, ducks, geese, poultry and their young but does not include any animal specified in [Schedules I, II and IV;]

[(19) "manufacturer" means a person who manufactures articles from any animal or plant specified in [Schedules I,II and III], as the case may be;

(20) "meat" includes blood, bones, sinew, eggs, shell or carapace, fat and flesh with or without skin, whether raw or cooked, of any wild animal or captive animal, other than a vermin;

(20A) "National Board" means the National Board for Wild Life constituted under section 5A;]

(21) "National Park" means an area declared, whether under section 35 or section 38, or deemed, under sub-section (3) of section 66, to be declared, as a National Park;

(22) "notification" means a notification published in the Official Gazette;

(23) "permit" means a permit granted under this Act or any rule made thereunder;

[(24) "person" shall include any firm or company or any authority or association or body of individuals whether incorporated or not;]

[(24A) "protected area" means a National Park, a sanctuary, a conservation reserve or a community reserve notified under sections 18, 35, 36A and 36C of the Act;]

(25) "prescribed" means prescribed by rules made under this act;

[(25A) "recognised zoo" means a zoo recognised under section 38H;

[(25B) "reserve forest" means the forest declared to be reserved by the State Government under section 20 of the Indian Forest act, 1927 (16 of 1927), or declared as such under any other State Act;

(26) "sanctuary" means an area declared as a sanctuary by notification under the provisions of Chapter IV of this Act and shall also include a deemed sanctuary under sub-section (4) of section 66;]

[(26A) "schedule" means a Schedule appended to this Act;]

[(27) "specified plant" means any plant specified in [Schedule III];

* * * *

(29) "State Government", in relation to a Union territory, means the Administrator of that Union Territory appointed by the President under Article 239 of the Constitution;

[(30) "taxidermy", with its grammatical variations and cognate expressions, means the curing, preparation or preservation or mounting of trophies;]

[(30A) "territorial waters" shall have the same meaning as in section 3 of the Territorial Waters, Continental Shelf, Exclusive Economic Zone and other Maritime Zones Act, 1976 (80 of 1976);]

(31) "trophy" means the whole or any part of any captive animal or wild animal, other than vermin, which has been kept or preserved by any means, whether artificial or natural, and includes-

(a) rugs, skins and specimens of such animal mounted in whole or in part through a process of taxidermy, and

[(b) antler, bone, carapace, shell, horn, rhinoceros horn, hair, feather, nail, tooth, tusk, musk, eggs, nests and honeycomb;]

(32) "uncured trophy" means the whole or any part of any captive animal or wild animal, other than vermin, which has not undergone a process of taxidermy, and includes a [freshly killed wild animal, ambergris, musk and other animal products];

(33) "vehicle" means any conveyance used for movement on land, water or air and includes buffalo, bull, bullock, camel, donkey, elephant horse and mule;

[(34) "vermin" means any wild animal notified under section 62;]

(35) "weapon" includes ammunition, bows and arrows, explosives, firearms, hooks knives, nets poison, snares and traps and any instrument or apparatus capable of anaesthetizing, decoying, destroying, injuring or killing an animal;

[(36) "wild animal" means any animal specified in [Schedule I or Schedule II] and found wild in nature;]

[(37) "wild life" includes any animal, aquatic or land vegetation which forms part of any habitat;]

(38) "Wild Life Warden" means the person appointed as such under clause (b) of sub-section (1) of section 4;

[(39) "zoo" means an establishment, whether stationary or mobile, where captive animals are kept for exhibiting to the public or ex-situ conservation and includes a circus and off-exhibit facilities such as rescue centres and conservation breeding centres, but does not include an establishment of a licensed dealer in captive animals.]

CHAPTER II

Authorities to be Appointed or Constituted Under the Act

3.Appointment of Director and other officers.- (1) The Central Government may, for the purposes of this Act, appoint,-

(a) A Director of Wild Life Preservation;

(b) such other officers and employees as may be necessary.

(2) In the performance of his duties and exercise of his powers by or under this Act, the Director shall be subject to such general or special directions, as the Central Government may, from time to time, give.

(3) The officers and other employees appointed under this section shall be required to assist the Director.]

4.Appointment of Life Warden and other officers- (1) The State Government May, for the purpose of this Act, appoint,-

(a) a Chief Wild Life Warden;

(b) Wild Life Wardens;* * *

(b) Honorary Wild Life Wardens;]

(c) such other officers and employees as may be necessary.

(2) In the performance of his duties and exercise of his powers by or under this Act, the Chief Wild Life Warden shall be subject to such general or special directions, as the State Government may from time to time, give.

(3) [The Wild Life Warden, the Honorary Wild Life Warden] and other officers and employees appointed under this section shall be subordinate to the Chief Wild Life Warden.

5. Power to delegate.- (1) The Director may, with the previous approval of the Central Government, by order in writing, delegate all or any of his powers and duties under this Act to any officer subordinate to him subject to such conditions, if any, as may be specified in the order.

(2) The Chief Wild Life Warden may, with the previous approval of the State Government, by order in writing, delegate all or any of his powers and duties under this Act, except those under clause (a) of sub-section (1) of section 11, to any officer subordinate to him subject to such conditions, if any, as may be specified in the order.

(3) Subject to any general or special direction given or condition imposed by the Director or the Chief Wild Life Warden, any person, authorised by the Director or the Chief Wild Life Warden to exercise any powers, may exercise those powers in the same manner and to the same effect as they had been conferred on that person directly by this Act and not by way of delegation.

[5A. Constitution of the National Board for Wild Life.- (1) The Central Government shall, within three months from the date of commencement of the Wild Life (Protection) Amendment Act, 2002 (16 of 2003), constitute the National Board for Wild Life consisting of the following members, namely:-

(a) the Prime Minister as Chairperson;

(b) the Minister in-charge of Forests and Wild Life as Vice-Chairperson;

(c) three members of Parliament of whom two shall be from the House of the People and one from the Council of States;

[(d) Member, NITI Aayog in-charge of Environment, Forest and Climate Change;]

(e) five persons to represent non- governmental organizations to be nominated by the Central Government;

(f) ten persons to be nominated by the Central government from amongst eminent conservationists, ecologists and environmentalists;

(g) the Secretary to the Government of India in-charge of the Ministry of Department of the Central Government dealing with Forests and Wild Life;

(h) the Chief of the Army Staff;

(i) the Secretary to the Government of India in-charge of the Ministry of Defence;

(j) the Secretary to the Government of India in-charge of the Ministry of Information and Broadcasting;

(k) the Secretary to the Government of India in-charge of the Department of Expenditure, Ministry of Finance;

(l) the Secretary to the Government of India, Ministry of Tribal Welfare;

(m) the Director-General of Forests in the Ministry or Department of the Central Government dealing with Forests and Wild Life;

(n) the Director-General of Tourism, Government of India;

(o) the Director-General, Indian Council for Forestry Research and Education, Dehradun;

(p) the Director, Wild Life Institute of India, Dehradun;

(q) the Director, Zoological Survey of India;

(r) the Director, Botanical survey of India;

(s) the Director, Indian Veterinary Research Institute;

(t) the Member-Secretary, Central Zoo Authority;

(u) the Director, National Institute of Oceanography;

(v) One representative each from ten States and Union Territories by rotation, to be nominated by the Central Government;

(w) The Director of Wild Life Preservation who shall be the Member-Secretary of the National Board.

(2) The term of office of the members other than those who are members ex officio, the manner of filling vacancies referred to in clauses (e), (f) and (v) of sub-section (1), and the procedure to be followed in the discharge of their functions by the members of the National Board shall be such, as may be prescribed.

(3) The members (except members ex officio) shall be entitled to receive such allowances in respect of expenses incurred in the performance of their duties as may be prescribed.

(4) Notwithstanding anything contained in any other law for the time being in force, the office of a member of National Board shall not be deemed to be an office of profit.

5B. Standing Committee of the National Board- (1) The National Board may, in its discretion, constitute a Standing Committee for the purpose of exercising such powers and performing such duties as may be delegated to the Committee by the National Board.

(2) The Standing Committee shall consist of the Vice-Chairperson, the Member-Secretary, and not more than ten members to be nominated by the Vice-Chairperson from amongst the members of the National Board.

(3) The National Board may constitute committees, sub-committees or study groups, as may be necessary, from time to time in proper discharge of the functions assigned to it.

5C.- Functions of the National Board –(1) It shall be the duty of the National Board to promote the Conservation and development of wild life and forests by such measures as it thinks fit.

(2) Without prejudice to the generality of the foregoing provision, the measures referred to therein may provide for-

(a) framing policies and advising the Central Government and the State Governments on the ways and means of promoting wildlife conservation and effectively controlling poaching and illegal trade of wildlife and its products;

(b) making recommendations on the setting up of and management of national parks, sanctuaries and other protected areas and on matters relating to restriction of activities in those areas;

(c) carrying out or causing to be carried but impact assessment of various projects and activities on wild life or its habitat;

(d) reviewing from time to time, the progress in the field of wild life conservation in the country and suggesting measures for improvement thereto, and

(e) preparing and publishing a status report at least once in two years on wild life in the country.]

[6.Constitution of State Board for Wild Life.-(1) The State Government shall, within a period of six months from the date of commencement of the Wild life (Protection) Amendment Act, 2002 (16 of 2003) constitute a State Board for Wild Life consisting of following members, namely:-

(a) the Chief Minister of the State and in case of the Union Territory, either Chief Minister or Administrator, as the case may be- Chairperson;

(b) the Minister in-charge of Forests and Wild Life- Vice –Chairperson;

(c) three members of the State Legislature or in the case of a Union Territory with Legislature, two members of the Legislative Assembly of that Union Territory ;

(d) three persons to represent non-governmental organizations dealing with wild life to be nominated by the State Government;

(e) ten persons to be nominated by the State Government from amongst eminent conservationists,

ecologists and environmentalists including at least two representatives of the Scheduled Tribes;

(f) the secretary to the State Government or the Government of the Union Territory, as the case may be, in-charge of Forests and Wild Life;

(g) the Officer in-charge of the State Forest Department ;

(h) the Secretary to the State Government, Department of Tribal Welfare;

(i) the Managing Director, State Tourism Development Corporation;

(j) an officer of the State Police Department not below the rank of Inspector-General;

(k) a representative of the Armed Forces not below the rank of a Brigadier to be nominated by the central Government;

(l) the Director, Department of Animal Husbandry of the State;

(m) the Director, Department of Fisheries of the State;

(n) an officer to be nominated by the Director, Wild Life Preservation;

(o) a representative of the Wild Life Institute of India, Dehradun;

(p) a representative of the Botanical Survey of India;

(q) a representative of the Zoological Survey of India;

(r) the Chief Wild Life warden, who shall be the Member-Secretary.

(2) The term of office of the members other than those who are members ex officio and manner of filling vacancies referred to in clauses (d) and (e) of sub-section (1) and procedure to be followed shall be such, as may be prescribed.

(3) The member (except members ex officio) shall be entitled to receive such allowances in respect of expenses incurred in the performance of their duties as may be prescribed.]

6A. Standing Committee of Board- (1) The Board may constitute a Standing Committee for the purpose of exercising such powers and performing such duties as may be delegated to it by the Board.

(2) The Standing Committee shall consist of the Vice-Chairperson, the Member-Secretary, and not more than ten members, to be nominated Vice-chairperson, from amongst the members of the Board.

(3) The Board or its Standing Committee referred to in sub-section (1) may, constitute committees, sub-committees or study groups, as may be necessary, from time-to-time, for proper discharge of the functions assigned to it.]

7. Procedure to be followed by the Board- (1) The Board shall meet at least twice a year at such place as the State Government may direct.

(2) The Board shall regulate its own procedure (including the quorum)

(3) No act or proceeding of the Board shall be invalid merely by reason of the existence of any vacancy therein or any defect in the constitution thereof or any irregularity in the procedure of the Board not affecting the merits of the case.

8. Duties of [State Board for Wild Life]- It shall be the duty of [State Board for Wild Life] to advise the State Government ,-

    (a) in the selection and management of areas to be declared as protected areas;]

    (b) in formulation of the policy for protection and conservation of the wild life and specified plants;]

    (c) in any matter relating to the amendment of any Schedule;* * *

    (c) in relation to the measures to be taken for harmonising the needs of the tribals and other dwellers of the forest with protection and conservation of wild life; and]

    (d) in any other matter connected with the protection of wild life, which may be referred to it by the State Government.

CHAPTER III

Hunting of Wild Animals

[9.Prohibition of hunting- No person shall hunt any wild animal specified in [Schedules I and II] except as provided under section 11 and section 12.]

[10.Maintenance of records of wild animals killed or captured.]- Omitted by the Wild Life (Protection) Amendment Act, 1991 (44 of 1991), s 10 (w.e.f. 2-10-1991).

11.Hunting of wild animals to be permitted in certain cases-(1) Notwithstanding anything contained in any other law for the time being in force and subject to the provisions of Chapter IV,-

(a) the Chief Wild Life Warden may, if he is satisfied that any wild animal specified in schedule I has become dangerous to human life or is so disabled or diseased as to be beyond recovery, by Order in writing and stating the reasons therefor, permit any person to hunt such animal or cause such animal or cause such animal to be hunted;

[Provided that no wild animal shall be ordered to be killed unless the Chief Wild Life warden is satisfied that such animal cannot be captured, transquilised or translocated:

Provided further that no such captured animal shall be kept in captivity unless the Chief Wild Life Warden is satisfied that such animal cannot be rehabilitated in the wild and the reasons for the same are recorded in writing.

Explanation- For the purposes of clause (a), the process of capture or translocation, as the case may be, of such animal shall be made in such manner as to cause minimum trauma to the said animal]

(b) the Chief Wild Life Warden or the authorised officer may, if he is satisfied that any wild animal specified in Schedule II,***, has become dangerous to human life or to property (including standing crops on any land) or is so disabled or diseased as to be beyond recovery, by order in writing and stating the reasons therefor, permit any person to hunt [such animal or group of animals in a specified area or cause such animal or group of animals in that specified area to be hunted].

(2) The killing or wounding in good faith of any wild animal in defence of oneself or of any other person shall not be an offence:

Provided that nothing in this sub-section shall exonerate any person who, when such defence becomes necessary, was committing any act in contravention of any provision of this Act or any rule or order made thereunder.

(3) Any wild animal killed or wounded in defence of any person shall be Government property.

12. Grant of permit for special purposes- Notwithstanding anything contained elsewhere in this Act, it shall be lawful for the Chief Wild Life Warden, to grant *** a permit, by an order in writing stating the reasons therefor, to any person, on payment of such fee as may be prescribed, which shall entitle the holder of such permit to hunt subject to such conditions as may be specified therein, any wild animal specified in such permit, for the purpose of,-

(a) education;

(b) scientific research;

(bb) scientific management.

Explanation- For the purposes of clause (bb), the expression, "scientific management" means –

(i) translocation of any wild animals to an alternative suitable habitat; or

(ii) population management of wildlife, without killing or poisoning or destroying any wild animals;]

[(c) collection of specimens-

(i) for recognised zoos subject to the permission under section 38-I; or

(ii) for museums and similar institutions;

(d) derivation, collection or preparation of snake-venom for the manufacture of life-saving drugs;]

[Provided that no such permit shall be granted-

(a) in respect of any other wild animal specified in schedule I, except with the previous permission of the Central Government, and

(b) in respect of any other wild animal, except with the previous permission of the State Government;]

(d) derivation, collection, or preparation of snake-venom for the manufacture of life-saving drugs:]

13. [Suspension or cancellation of licence]- Omitted by the Wild Life (Protection) Amendment Act, 1991 (44 of 1991), s. 12 (w.e.f. 2-10-1991).

14. [Appeals].-Omitted by, s. 12, ibid. (w.e.f. 2-10-1991).

15. [Hunting of young and female of wild animals]-Omitted by, s. 12, ibid. (w.e.f. 2-10-1991).

16. [Declaration of closed time]. – Omitted by, s. 12, ibid. (w.e.f.2-10-1991)

17. [Restrictions on hunting]. - Omitted by s. 12, ibid. (w.e.f. 2-10-1991).

[CHAPTER IIIA

Protection of Specified Plants

17A. Prohibition of picking, uprooting, etc. of specified plant. - Save as otherwise provided in this Chapter, no person shall-

(a) wilfully pick, uproot, damage, destroy, acquire or collect any specified plant from any forest land and any area specified, by notification, by the Central Government;

(b) posses, sell, offer for sale, or transfer by way of gift or otherwise, or transport any specified plant, whether alive or dead, or part or derivative thereof:

Provided that nothing in this section shall prevent a member of a scheduled tribe, subject to the provisions of Chapter IV, from picking, collecting or possessing in the district he resides any specified plant or part or derivative thereof for his bonafide personal use.

17B. Grants of permit for special purposes- The Chief Wild Life Warden may, with the previous permission of the State Government, grant to any person a permit to pick, uproot, acquire or collect from a forest land or the area specified under section 17A or transport, subject to such conditions as may be specified therein, any specified plant for the purpose of-

(a) education;

(b) scientific research;

(c) collection, preservation and display in a herbarium of any scientific institution; or

(d) propagation by a person or an institution approved by the Central Government in this regard.

17C. Cultivation of specified plants without licence prohibited-(1) No person shall cultivate a specified plant except under and in accordance with a licence granted by the Chief Wild Life Warden or any other officer authorised by the State Government in this behalf:

Provided that nothing in this section shall prevent a person, who immediately before the commencement of the Wild Life (Protection)

(Amendment) Act, 1991 (44 of 1991), was cultivating a specified plant from carrying on such cultivation for a period of six months from such commencement or where he has made an application within that period for the grant of a licence to him, until the licence is granted to him or he is informed in writing that a licence cannot be granted to him.

(2) Every licence granted under this section shall specify the area in which and the conditions, if any, subject to which the licensee shall cultivate a specified plant.

17D. Dealing in specified plants without licence prohibited –(1) No person shall, except under and in accordance with a licence granted by the Chief Wild Life Warden or any other officer authorised by the state Government in this behalf, commence or carry on business or occupation as a dealer in a specified plant or part or derivate thereof:

Provided that nothing in this section shall prevent a person, who, immediately before the commencement of the Wild Life (Protection) (Amendment) Act, 1991 (44 of 1991), was carrying on such business or occupation, from carrying on such business or occupation for a period of sixty days from such commencement, or where he has made an application within that period for the grant of a licence to him, until the licence is granted to him or he is informed in writing that a licence cannot be granted to him.

(2) Every licence granted under this section shall specify the premises in which and the conditions, if any, subject to which the licensee shall carry on his business.

17E. Declaration of stock- (1) Every person cultivating, or dealing in, a specified plant or part or derivative thereof shall, within thirty days from the date of commencement of the Wild Life (Protection) (Amendment) Act, 1991 (44 of 1991) declare to the Chief Wild Life Warden or any other officer authorised by the State Government in this behalf, his stocks of such plants and part or derivative thereof, as the case may be, on the date of such commencement.

(2) The provisions of sub-sections (3) to (8) (both inclusive) of section 44, section 45, section 46 and section 47 shall, as far as may be, apply in relation to an application and a licence referred to in section 17C and section 17D as they apply in relation to the licence or business in animals or animal articles.

17F. Possession, etc., of plants by licensee- No licensee under this Chapter shall-

(a)   keep in his control, custody or possession-

i. any specified plant, or part or derivative thereof in respect of which a declaration under the provisions of section 17E has to be made but has not been made;

ii. any specified plant, or part or derivative thereof which has not been lawfully acquired under the provisions of this Act or any rule or order made thereunder;

(b) (i) pick, uproot, collect or acquire any specified plant, or

(iii) acquire, receive, keep in his control, custody or possession, or sell,offer for sale or transport any specified plant or part or derivative thereof,except in accordance with the conditions subject to which the licence has been granted and such rules as may be made under this Act.

17G. Purchase, etc., of specified plants- No person shall purchase, receive or acquire any specified plant or part or derivative thereof otherwise than from a licensed dealer:

Provided that nothing in this section shall apply to any person referred to in section 17B.

17H. Plants to be Government property- (1) Every specified plant or part or derivative thereof, in respect of which any offence against this Act or any rule or order made thereunder has been committed, shall be the property of the State Government, and, where such plant or part or derivative thereof has been collected or acquired from a sanctuary or National Park declared by the Central Government, such plant or part or derivative thereof has been collected or acquired from a sanctuary or National Park or derivative thereof shall be the property of the Central Government.

(2) The provisions of sub-sections (2) and (3) section 39 shall, as far as may be, apply in relation to the specified plant or part or derivative thereof or they apply in relation to wild animals and articles referred to in sub-section (1) of that section.]

CHAPTER IV

[Protected Areas]

Sanctuaries

18. Declaration of sanctuary- [(1) The State Government may, by notification, declare its intention to constitute any area other than an area comprised within any reserve forest or the territorial waters as a sanctuary if it considers that such area is of adequate ecological, faunal, floral, geomorphological, natural or zoological significance, for the purpose of protecting, propagating or developing wild life or its environment.]

(2) The notification referred to in sub-section (1) shall specify, as nearly as possible, the situation and limits of such area.

Explanation- For the purposes of this section, it shall be sufficient to be sufficient to describe the area by roads, rivers, ridges or other well-known or readily intelligible boundaries.

[**18A. Protection to sanctuaries-** (1) When the State Government declares its intention under sub-section (1) of section 18 to constitute any area, not comprised within any reserve forest or territorial waters under that sub-section, as a sanctuary, the provisions of sections 27 to 33 A (both inclusive) shall come into effect forthwith.

(2) Till such time as the rights of affected persons are finally settled under sections 19 to 24 (both inclusive), the State Government shall make alternative arrangements required for making available fuel, fodder and other forest produce to the persons affected, in terms of their rights as per the Government records.

18B. Appointment of Collectors- The State Government shall appoint, an officer to act as Collector under the Act, within ninety days of coming into force of the Wild Life (Protection) Amendment Act, 2002 (16 of 2003), or within thirty days of the issue of notification under section 18, to inquire into and determine the existence, nature and extent of rights of any person in or over the land comprised within the limits of the sanctuary which may be notified under sub-section (1) of section 18.]

19. Collector to determine rights – [When a notification has been issued under section 18,] the Collector shall inquire into, and determine, the existence, nature and extent of the rights of any person in or over the land comprised within the limits of the sanctuary.

20. Bar of accrual of rights- After the issue of a notification under section 18, no right shall be acquired in, on or over the land comprised within the limits of the area specified in such notification, except by succession, testamentary or intestate.

21. Proclamation by Collector – When a notification has been issued under section 18, the Collector shall [within a period of sixty days] publish in the regional language in every town and village in or in the neighbourhood of the area comprised therein, a proclamation-

(a) specifying, as nearly as possible, the situation and the limits of the sanctuary; and

(b) requiring any person, claiming any right mentioned in section 19, to prefer before the Collector, within two months from date of such proclamation, a written claim in the prescribed form, specifying the nature and extent of such right with necessary details and the amount and particulars of compensation, if any, claimed in respect thereof.

22. Inquiry by Collector- The Collector shall, after service of the prescribed notice upon the claimant, expeditiously inquire into-

   a) the claim preferred before him under clause (b) of section 21, and

   b) the existence of any right mentioned in section 19 and not claimed under clause (b) of section 21,

so far as the same maybe ascertainable from the records of the State Government and the evidence of any person acquainted with the same.

23. Powers of Collector – For the purpose of such inquiry, the Collector may exercise the following powers, namely:-

   (a) the power to enter in or upon any land and to survey, demarcate and make a map of the same or authorise any other officer to do so;

   (b) the same powers as are vested in a civil court for the trial of suits.

24. Acquisition of rights – (1) In the case of a claim to a right in or over any land referred to in section 19, the Collector shall pass an order admitting or rejecting the same in whole or in part.

(2) If such claim is admitted in whole or in part, the Collector may either-

   (a) exclude such land from the limits of the proposed sanctuary, or

   (b) proceed to acquire such land or rights, except where by an agreement between the owner of such land or holder of rights and the Government, the owner or holder of such rights has agreed to surrender his rights to the Government, in or over such land and on payment of such compensation, as it provided in the [Right to Fair Compensation and Transparency in Land Acquisition, Rehabilitation and Resettlement Act, 2013 (30 of 2013).]

   [(c) allow, in consultation with the Chief Wild Life Warden, the continuation of any right of any person in or over any land within the limits of the sanctuary.]

25. Acquisition proceedings- (1) For the purpose of acquiring such land, or rights in or over such land,-

   (a) the Collector shall be deemed to be a Collector, proceeding under [Right to Fair Compensation and Transparency in Land acquisition, Rehabilitation and Resettlement Act,2013 (30 of 2013);]

(b) the claimant shall be deemed to be a person interested and appearing before him in pursuance of a notice given under [section 21] of that Act;

(c) the provisions of the sections, preceding [section21] of that Act, shall be deemed to have been complied with;

(d) where the claimant does not accept the award made in his favour the matter of compensation, he shall be deemed, within the meaning of [section 64] of that Act, to be a person interested who has not accepted the award, and shall be entitled to proceed to claim relief against the award under the provisions of [Chapter VIII] of that Act;

(e) the Collector, with the consent of the claimant, or [the Authority], with the consent of both the parties, may award compensation in land or money or partly in land and partly in money; and

(f) in the case of the stoppage of a public way or a common pasture, the Collector may, with the previous sanction of the State Government, provide for an alternative public way or common pasture, as far as may be practicable or convenient.

[Explanation- The expression "Authority" referred to in clause (e), shall mean the Land Acquisition, Rehabilitation and Resettlement Authority established under section 51 of the Right to Fair Compensation and Transparency in Land Acquisition, Rehabilitation and Resettlement Act, 2013 (30 of 2013).]

(2) The acquisition under this Act of any land or interest therein shall be deemed to be acquisition for a public purpose.

[25A. Time-limit for completion of acquisition proceedings- (1) The Collector shall, as far as possible, complete the proceedings under sections 19 to 25 (both inclusive), within a period of two years from the date of notification of declaration of sanctuary under section 18.

(2) The notification shall not lapse if, for any reasons, the proceedings are not completed within a period of two years.]

26. Delegation of Collector's powers – The State Government may, by general or special order, direct that the powers exercisable or the functions to be performed by the Collector under section 19 to 25 (both inclusive) may be exercised and performed by such other officer as may be specified in the order.

[26A. Declaration of area as sanctuary-(1) When-

(a) a notification has been issued under section 18 and the period for preferring claims has elapsed, and all claims, if any, made in relation to any land in an area intended to be declared as a sanctuary, have been disposed of by the State Government; or

(b) any area comprised within any reserve forest or any part of the territorial waters, which is considered by the State Government to be of adequate ecological faunal floral geomorphological, natural or zoological significance for the purpose of protecting, propagating or developing wild life or its environment, is to be included in a sanctuary,

the State Government shall issue a notification specifying the limits of the area which shall be comprised within the sanctuary and declare that the said area shall be sanctuary on and from such date as may be specified in the notification:

Provided that where any part of the territorial waters is to be included, prior concurrence of the Central Government shall be obtained by the State Government:

Provided further that the limits of the area of the territorial waters to be included in the sanctuary shall be determined in consultation with the Chief Naval Hydrographer of the Central Government and after taking adequate measures to protect the occupational interests of the local fishermen.

(2) Notwithstanding anything contained in sub-section (1), the right of innocent passage of any vessel or boat through the territorial waters shall not be affected by the notification issued under sub-section (1).

[(3) No alteration of the boundaries of a sanctuary shall be made by the State Government except on a recommendation of the National Board.]

27. Restriction on entry in sanctuary – (1) No person other than,-

(a) a public servant on duty,

(b) a person who has been permitted by the Chief Wild Life Warden or the authorised officer to reside within the limits of the sanctuary,

(c) a person who has any right over immovable property within the limits of the sanctuary,

(d) a person passing through the sanctuary along a public highway, and

(e) the dependants of the person referred to in clause (a), clause (b), clause (c), shall enter or reside in the sanctuary, except under and in accordance with the conditions of a permit granted under section 28.

(2) Every person shall, so long, as he resides in the sanctuary, be bound-

(a) to prevent the commission, in the sanctuary, of an offence against this Act;

(b) where there is reason to believe that any such offence against this Act has been committed in such sanctuary, to help in discovering and arresting the offender;

(c) to report the death of any wild animal and to safeguard its remains until the Chief Wild Life Warden or the authorised officer takes charge thereof;

(d) to extinguish any fire in such sanctuary of which he has knowledge or information and to prevent from spreading, by any lawful means in his power, any fire within the vicinity of such sanctuary of which he has knowledge or information; and

(e) to assist any forest officer, Chief Wild Life, Warden, Wild Life Warden or police officer demanding his aid for preventing the commission of any offence against this Act or in the investigation of any such offence.

[(3) No person shall, with intent to cause damage to any boundary-mark of a sanctuary or to cause wrongful gain as defined in the Indian Penal Code, 1860 (45 of 1860), alter, destroy, move or deface such boundary-mark.

(4) No person shall tease or molest any wild animal or litter the grounds of sanctuary.]

28. Grant of permit- (1) The Chief Wild Life Warden may, on application, grant to any person a permit to enter or reside in a sanctuary for all or any of the following purposes, namely:-

(a) investigation or study of wild life and purposes ancillary or incidental thereto;

(b) photography [and film-making without making any change in the habitat or causing any adverse impact to the habitat or wild life;]

(c) scientific research;

(d) tourism;

(e) transaction of lawful business with any person residing in the sanctuary.

(2) A permit to enter or reside in a sanctuary shall be issued subject to such conditions and on payment of such fee as may be prescribed.

[29. Destruction, etc., in a sanctuary prohibited without a permit – No person shall destroy, exploit or remove any wild life including forest produce from a sanctuary or destroy or damage or divert the habitat of any wild animal by any act whatsoever or divert, stop or enhance the flow of water into or outside the sanctuary, except under and in accordance with a permit granted by the Chief Wild Life Warden, and no such permit shall be granted unless the State Government being satisfied in consultation with the [National Board] that such removal of wildlife from the sanctuary or the change in the flow of water into or outside the sanctuary is necessary for the improvement and better management of wild life therein, authorises the issue of such permit:

Provided that where the forest produce is removed from a sanctuary the same may be used for meeting the personal bona fide needs of the people living in and around the sanctuary and shall not be used for any commercial purpose.

[Explanation- For the purposes of this section, grazing or movement of livestock permitted under clause (d) of section 33, or hunting of wild animals under a permit granted under section 11 or hunting without violating the conditions of a permit to granted under section 12, or the exercise of any rights permitted to continue under clause (c) of sub-section (2) of section 24, including the bona fide use of drinking and household water by local communities until they are settled, shall not be deemed to be an act prohibited under this section.]

30. Causing fire prohibited- No person shall set fire to a sanctuary, or kindle any fire, or leave any fire burning, in a sanctuary, in such manner as to endanger such sanctuary.

31. Prohibition of entry into sanctuary with weapon- No person shall enter a sanctuary with any weapon except with the previous permissions in writing of the Chief wild Life Warden or the authorised officer.

32. Ban on use of injurious substances – No person shall use, in a sanctuary, chemicals, explosives or any other substances which may cause injury to, or endanger, any wild life in such sanctuary.

33. Control of sanctuaries- The Chief Wild Life Warden shall be the authority who shall control, [manage and protect all sanctuaries in accordance with such management plans for the sanctuary approved by him as per the guidelines issued by the Central Government and in case the sanctuary also falls under the Scheduled Areas or areas where the scheduled Tribes and Other Traditional Forest Dwellers (Recognition of Forest Rights) Act, 2006 (2 of 2007) is applicable, in accordance with the management plan for such sanctuary prepared after due consultation with the Gram Sabha concerned] and for that purpose, within the limits of any sanctuary,-

(a) may construct such roads, bridges, buildings, fences or barrier gates, and carry out such other works as he may consider necessary for the purposes of such sanctuary:

[Provided that no construction of [tourist lodges, including Government lodges, for commercial purposes], hotels, zoos and safari parks shall be undertaken inside a sanctuary except with the prior approval of the National Board.]

(b) shall take such steps as will ensure the security of wild animals in the sanctuary and the preservation of the sanctuary and wild animals therein;

(c) may take such measures, in the interests of wild life, as he may consider necessary for the improvement of any habitat;

(d) may regulate, control or prohibit, in keeping with the interests of wild life, the grazing or movement of [live-stock.]

***

[33A. immunisation of live-stock- (1) The Chief Wild Life Warden shall take such measures in such manner, as may be prescribed, for immunisation against communicable diseases of the live-stock kept in or within five kilometres of a sanctuary.

(2) No person shall take, or cause to be taken or grazed, any live-stock in a sanctuary without getting it immunised.]

[33B. Advisory Committee- (1) The State Government shall constitute an Advisory Committee consisting of the Chief Wild Life Warden or his nominee not below the rank Conservator of Forests as its head and shall include a member of the State Legislature within whose constituency the sanctuary is situated, three representatives of Panchayathi Raj Institutions, two representatives of non-governmental organisations and three individuals active in the field of wild life conservation, one representative each from departments dealing with Home and Veterinary matters, Honorary wild Life Warden, if any, and the officer- in charge of the sanctuary as Member-Secretary.

(2) The Committee shall render advice on measures to be taken for better conservation and management of the sanctuary including participation of the people living within and around the sanctuary.

(3) The Committee shall regulate its own procedure including quorum.]

34. Registration of certain persons in possession of arms- (1) Within three months from the declaration of any area as a sanctuary, every person residing in or within ten kilometres of any such sanctuary and holding a licence granted under the Arms Act, 1959 (54 of 1959), for the possession of arms or exempted from the provisions of that act and possessing arms, shall apply in such form, on payment of such fee and within such time as may be prescribed, to the Chief Wild Life Warden or the authorised officer, for the registration of his name.

(2) On receipt of an application under sub-section (1), the Chief Wild Life Warden or the authorised officer shall register the name of the applicant in such manner as may be prescribed.

[(3) No new licences under the Arms Act, 1959 (54 of 1959) shall be granted within a radius of ten kilometres of a sanctuary without the prior concurrence of the Chief Wild Life warden.]

[(4) No renewal of any licence under the Arms Act, 1959, (54 of 1959) shall be granted to any person residing within ten kilometres of a sanctuary except under the intimation to the Chief Wild Life warden or the authorised officer.]

National Parks

35. Declaration of National Parks- (1) Whenever it appears to the state Government that an area, whether within a sanctuary or not, is, by reason of its ecological, faunal, floral, geomorphological or zoological association or importance, needed to be constituted as a National Park for the purpose of protecting, propagating or developing wild life therein as a National Park for the purpose of protecting, propagating or developing wildlife therein or its environment, it may, by notification, declare its intention to constitute such area as a National Park.

[Provided that where any part of the territorial waters is proposed to be included in such National Park, the provision of section 26A shall, as far as may be, apply in relation to the declaration of a National Park as they apply in relation to the declaration of a sanctuary.]

(2) The notification referred to in sub-section (1) shall define the limits of the area which is intended to be declared as a National Park.

(3) Where any area is intended to be declared as a National Park, the provisions of sections [19 to 26A (both inclusive except clause (c) of sub-section (2) of section 24)] shall, as far as may, be, apply to the investigation and determination of claims, and extinguishment of rights, in relation to any land in such area as they apply to the said matters in relation to any land in sanctuary.

[(3A) When the State Government declares its intention under sub-section (1) to constitute any area as a National Park, the provisions of sections 27 to 33A (both inclusive), shall come into effect forthwith, until the publication of the notification declaring such National Park under sub-section (4).

(3B) Till such time as the rights of the affected persons are finally settled under sections 19 to 26A (both inclusive except clause(c) of sub-section (2) of section 24], the State Government shall make alternative arrangements required for making available fuel, fodder and other forest produce to the persons affected, in terms of their rights as per the Government records.]

(4) When the following events have occurred, namely,-

(a) the period for preferring claims has elapsed, and all claims, if any, made in relation to any land in an intended to be declared as a National Park, have been disposed of by the State Government, and

(b) all rights in respect of lands proposed to be included in the National Park have become vested in the State Government, the State Government shall publish a notification specifying the limits of the area which shall be comprised within the National Park and declare that the said area shall be a National Park on and from such date as may be specified in the notification.

[(5) No alteration of boundaries of a National Park by the State Government shall be made except on a recommendation of the National Board.

(6) No person shall destroy, exploit or remove any Wild Life including forest produce from a National Park or destroy or damage or divert the habitat of any wild animal by any act whatsoever or divert, stop or enhance the flow of water into or outside the National Park, except under and in accordance with a permit granted by the Chief Wild Life Warden, and no such permit shall be granted unless the State Government being satisfied in consultation with the National Board that such removal of wild life from the National Park or the change in the flow into or outside the National Park is necessary for the improvement and better management of wild life therein, authorises the issue of such permit;

Provided that where the forest produce is removed from a National Park, the same may be used for meeting the personal bona fide needs of the people living in and around the National Park and shall not be used for any commercial purpose.]

(7) No grazing of any [live-stock] shall be permitted in a National Park no [live-stock] shall be allowed to enter therein except where such [live-stock] is used as a vehicle by a person authorised to enter such National Park.

(8) The provisions of sections 27 and 28, sections 30 to 32 (both inclusive), and clauses (a), (b) and (c) of [section 33, section 33 A] shall, as far as may be, apply in relation to a National Park as they apply in relation to a sanctuary.

[Explanation- For the purposes of this section, in case of an area, whether within a sanctuary or not, where the rights have been extinguished and the land has become vested in the State Government under any Act or otherwise, such area may be notified by it, by a notification, as a National

Park and the proceedings under sections 19 to 26 (both inclusive) and the provisions of sub-sections (3) and (4) of this section shall not apply.]

***

36. [Declaration of game reserve.]- Omitted by the Wild Life (Protection) Amendment Act, 1991 (44 of 1991), s.24 (w.e.f.2-10-1991).

[**36A. Declaration and management of a conservation reserve-** (1) The State Government may, after having consultations with the local communities, declare any area owned by the Government, particularly the areas adjacent to National Parks and sanctuaries and those areas which link one protected area with another, as a conservation reserve for protecting landscapes, seascapes, flora and fauna and their habitat:

Provided that where the conservation reserve includes any land owned by the Central Government, its prior concurrence shall be obtained before making such declaration.

(2) The provisions of sub-section (2) of section 18, sub-sections (2), (3) and (4) of section 27, sections 30, 32 and clauses (b) and (c) of section 33 shall, as far as may be, apply in relation to a conservation reserve as they apply in relation to a sanctuary.

36B. Conservation reserve management committee – (1) The state Government shall constitute a conservation reserve management committee to advise the Chief Wild Life Warden to conserve, manage and maintain the conservation reserve.

(2) The committee shall consist of a representative of the forest or Wild Life Department, who shall be the Member-secretary of the Committee, one representative of each Village Panchayath in whose jurisdiction the reserve is located, three representatives of non-governmental organisations working in the field of wild life conservation and one representative each from the Department of Agriculture and Animal Husbandry.

(3) The Committee shall regulate its own procedure including the quorum.

36C. Declaration and management of community reserve- (1) The State Government may, where the community or an individual has volunteered to conserve wild life and its habitat, declare any private or community land not comprised within a National Park, sanctuary or conservation reserve, as a community reserve, for protecting fauna, flora and traditional or cultural conservation values and practices.

(2) The provision of sub-section (2) of section18, sub-sections(2), (3) and (4) of section 27, sections 30, 32 and clauses (b) and (c) of section 33 shall, as far as may be, apply in relation to community reserve as they apply in relation to a sanctuary.

(3) After the issue of notification under sub-section (1), no change in the land use pattern shall be made within the community reserve, except in accordance with a resolution passed by the management committee and approval of the same by the State Government.

36D. Community reserve management committee- (1) The State Government shall constitute a Community Reserve Management Committee, which shall be the authority responsible for conserving, maintaining and managing the community reserve.

(2) The committee shall consist of [not less than five representatives] nominated by the Village Panchayath or where such Panchayath does not exist by the members of Grama Sabha and one representative of the State Forests or Wild Life Department under whose jurisdiction the community reserve is located.

[(2A) Where a community reserve is declared on private land under sub-section (1) of section 36C, the community reserve management committee shall consist of the owner of the land, a representative of the State Forests or Wild Life Department under Whose jurisdiction the community reserve is located and also the representative of the Panchayat concerned or the tribal community, as the case may be.]

(3) The committee shall be the competent authority to prepare and implement the management plan for the community reserve and to take steps to ensure the protection of wild life and its habitat in the reserve.

(4) The committee shall elect a Chairman who shall also be the Honorary Wild Life Warden on the community reserve.

(5) The committee shall regulate its own procedure including the quorum.]

Closed Area

37. [Declaration of closed area-]- Omitted by the Wild Life (Protection) Amendment Act, 2002 (16 of 2003), s. 21 (w.e.f. 1-4- 2003).

Sanctuaries or National Parks declared by Central government

38. Power of Central Government to declare areas as sanctuaries or National Parks [or conservation reserves]- (1) Where the State Government leases or otherwise transfers any area under its control, not being an area within a sanctuary, to the Central Government, the Central Government may, if it is satisfied that the conditions specified in section 18 are fulfilled in relation to the area so transferred to it, declare such area, by notification, to be a sanctuary and the provisions of [sections 18 to 35] (both inclusive), 54 and 55 shall apply in relation to such sanctuary as they apply in relation to a sanctuary declared by the State Government.

(2) The Central Government may, if it is satisfied that the conditions specified in section 35 are fulfilled in relation to any area referred to in section (1), whether or not such area has been declared, to be a sub sanctuary by the Central Government or State Government, declare such area, by notification, to be a National Park and the provisions of sections 35, 54, and 55 shall apply in relation to such National Park as they apply in relation to a National Park declared by the State Government.

[(2A) The Central Government may, if it is satisfied that the conditions specified in sub-section (1) of section 36A are fulfilled in relation to any area referred to in sub-section (1), declare such area, by notification, to be a conservation reserve and the provisions of sections 36A and 36B shall apply in relation to such conservation reserve as they apply in relation to a conservation reserve declared by the State Government.]

(3) In relation to a sanctuary or National Park [or conservation reserve] declared by the Central Government, the powers and duties of the Chief Wild Warden under the sections referred to in [sub-sections (1), (2) and (2A)], shall be exercised and discharged by the Director or by such other officer as may be authorised by the Director in this behalf and references, in the sections aforesaid, to the State Government shall be construed as references to the Central Government and reference therein to the Legislature of the State shall be construed as a reference to Parliament.

[CHAPTER IV A

Central Zoo Authority and Recognition of Zoos

38A. Constitution of Central Zoo Authority-(1) The Central Government shall constitute a body to be known as the Central Zoo Authority (hereinafter in this Chapter referred to as the Authority), to exercise the powers conferred on, and to perform the functions assigned to it under this Act.

(2) The Authority shall consist of-

(a) chairperson;

(b) such number of members not exceeding ten; and

(c) Member- secretary,to be appointed by the Central Government.

38B. Term of office and conditions of service of Chairperson and members, etc.- (1) The chairperson and every member [other than the Member-Secretary] shall hold office for such period, not exceeding three years, as may be specified by the Central Government in this behalf.

(2) The Chairperson or a member may by writing under his hand addressed to the Central Government, resign from the office of chairperson or as the case may be, of the member.

(3) The Central Government shall remove a person from the office of chairperson or member referred to in sub-section (2) if that person –

(a) becomes an un discharged insolvent;

(b) gets convicted and sentenced to imprisonment for an offence which in the opinion of the Central government involves moral turpitude;

(c) becomes of unsound mind and stands so declared by a competent court;

(d) refuses to act or becomes incapable of acting;

(e) is, without obtaining leave of absence from the authority, absent from three consecutive meetings of the Authority; or

(f) in the opinion of the Central Government has so abused the position of chairperson or member as to render that person's continuance in office detrimental to the public interest:

Provided that no person shall be removed under this clause unless that person has been given a reasonable opportunity of being heard in the matter.

(4) A vacancy caused under sub-section (2) or otherwise shall be filled by fresh appointment.

(5) The salaries and allowances and other conditions of appointment of chairperson, members and Member-Secretary of the Authority shall be such as may be prescribed.

(6) The Authority shall, with previous sanction of the Central Government, employ such officers and other employees as it deems necessary to carry out the purposes of the authority.

(7) The terms and conditions of service of the officers and other employees of the Authority shall be such as may be prescribed.

(8) No act or proceeding of the Authority shall be questioned or shall be invalid on the ground merely of the existence of any vacancies or defect in the constitution of the Authority.

38C. Functions of the Authority- The Authority shall perform the following functions, namely:-

(a) specify the minimum standards for housing, upkeep and veterinary care of the animals kept in a zoo;

(b) evaluate and assess the functioning of zoos with respect to the standards or the norms as may be prescribed;

(c) recognise or derecognise zoos;

(d) identify endangered species of wild animals for purposes of captive breeding and assigning responsibility in this regard to a zoo;

(e) co-ordinate the acquisition, exchange and loaning of animals for breeding purposes;

(f) ensure maintenance of stud-books of endangered species of wild animals bred in captivity;

(g) identify priorities and themes with regard to display of captive animals in a zoo;

(h) co-ordinate training of zoo personnel in India and outside India;

(i) co-ordinate research in captive breeding and educational programmes for the purposes of zoos.

(j) provide technical and other assistance to zoos for their proper management and development on scientific lines;

(k) perform such other functions as may be necessary to carry out the purposes of this Act with regard to zoos.

38D. Procedure to be regulated by the Authority – (1) The Authority shall meet as and when necessary shall meet at such time and place as the chairperson may think fit.

(2) The Authority shall regulate its own procedure.

(3) All orders and decisions of the Authority shall be authenticated by the Member-Secretary or any other officer of the Authority duly authorised Member-Secretary in this behalf.

38E. Grants and loans to Authority and Constitution Fund-(1) the Central Government may, after due appropriation made by Parliament by law in this behalf, make to the Authority grants and loans such sums of money as that Government may consider necessary.

(2) There shall be constituted a Fund to be called Central Zoo Authority Fund and there shall be credited thereto any grants and loans made to the Authority by the Central Government, all fees and charges received by the Authority under this Act and all sums received by the Authority from such other sources as may be decided upon by the Central Government.

(3) The Fund referred to in sub-section (2) shall be applied for meeting salary, allowances and other remuneration of the members, officers and

other employees of the Authority and the expenses of the Authority in the discharge of its functions under this Chapter and expenses on objects and for purposes authorised by this Act.

(4) The Authority shall maintain proper accounts and other relevant records and prepare an annual statement of accounts in such form as may be prescribed by the Central Government in consultation with the Comptroller and Auditor-General of India.

(5) The accounts of the Authority shall be audited by the Auditor –General at such intervals as may be specified by him and any expenditure incurred in connection with such audit shall be payable by the Authority to the Comptroller and Auditor –General.

(6) The Comptroller and Auditor-General and any person appointed by him in connection with the audit of the accounts of the Authority under this Act shall have the same rights and privileges and the authority in connection with such audit as the Comptroller and Auditor-General generally has in connection with the audit of the Government accounts and, in particular, shall have the right to demand the production of books, accounts, connected vouchers and other documents and papers and to inspect any of the offices of the Authority.

(7) The accounts of the Authority, as certified by the Comptroller and Auditor-General or any other person appointed by him in this behalf, together with the audit report thereon, shall be forwarded annually to the Central Government by the Authority.

38F. Annual Report. – The Authority shall prepare in such form and at such time, for each financial year, as may be prescribed, its annual report, giving a full account of its activities during the previous financial year and forward a copy thereof to the Central Government.

38G. Annual report and audit report to be laid before Parliament- The Central Government shall cause the annual report together with a memorandum of action taken on the recommendations contained therein, in so far as they relate to the Central Government, and the reasons for the non-acceptance, if any, of any such recommendations and the audit report to be laid as soon as may be after the reports are received before each House of Parliament.

38H. Recognition of zoos.- (1) No zoo shall be operated without being recognised by the Authority:

Provided that a zoo being operated immediately before the date of commencement of the Wild Life (Protection) (Amendment) Act, 1991 (44 of 1991) may continue to operate without being recognised for a period of [eighteen months from the date of such commencement] and if the application seeking recognition is made within that period, the zoo may continue to be operated until the said application is financially decided or withdrawn and in case of refusal for a further period of six months from the date of such refusal.

[(1A) On and after the commencement of the Wild Life (Protection) Amendment Act, 2002 (16 of 2003) a zoo shall not be established without obtaining the prior approval of the Authority.]

(2) Every application for recognition of a zoo shall be made to the Authority in such form and on payment of such fee as may be prescribed.

(3) Every recognition shall specify the conditions, if any, subject to which the applicant shall operate the zoo.

(4) No recognition to a zoo shall be granted unless the authority, having due regard to the interests of protection and conservation of wild life, and such standards, norms and other matters as may be prescribed, is satisfied that recognition should be granted.

(5) No application for recognition of a zoo shall be rejected unless applicant has been given a reasonable opportunity of being heard.

(6) The Authority may, for reasons to be recorded by it, suspend or cancel any recognition granted under sub-section (4):

Provided that no such suspension or cancellation shall be made except after giving the person operating the zoo a reasonable opportunity of being heard.

(7) An appeal from an order refusing to recognise a zoo under sub-section (5) or an order suspending or cancelling a recognition under sub-section (6) shall lie to the Central Government.

(8) An appeal under sub-section (7) shall be preferred within thirty days from the date of communication to the applicant of the order appealed against:

Provided that the Central Government may admit any appeal preferred after the expiry of the period aforesaid if it is satisfied that the appellant had sufficient cause for not preferring the appeal in time.

[**38-I. Acquisition of animals by a zoo-** (1) Subject to the other provisions of this Act, no zoo shall acquire, sell or transfer any wild animal or captive animal specified in Schedules I ***except with the previous permission of the Authority.

(2) No zoo shall acquire, sell, or transfer any wild or captive animal except from or to a recognised zoo.]

[Provided that nothing in this sub-section shall apply to a conservation breeding centre.]

38J. Prohibition of teasing, etc., in a zoo- No person shall tease, molest, injure or feed any animal or cause disturbance to the animals by noise or otherwise, or litter the grounds in a zoo.]

[CHAPTER IVB

National Tiger Conservation Authority

38K. Definitions.- In this Chapter,-

a) "National Tiger Conservation Authority" means the Tiger Conservation Authority constituted under section 38L;

b) "Steering Committee" means the Committee constituted under section 38U;

c) "Tiger Conservation Foundation" means the foundation established under section 38X;

d) "Tiger Reserve State" means a State having tiger reserve;

e) "Tiger Reserve" means the areas notified as such under section 38V.

38L. Constitution of National Tiger Conservation Authority- (1) The Central Government shall constitute a body to be known as the National Tiger Conservation Authority (hereinafter in this Chapter referred to as the Tiger Conservation Authority), to exercise the powers conferred on, and to perform the functions assigned to it under this Act.

2) The Tiger conservation Authority shall consist of the following members, namely;-

a) the Minister in charge of the Ministry of Environment and Forests-Chairperson;

b) the Minister of State in the Ministry of Environment and Forests-Vice Chairperson;

c) three members of Parliament of whom two shall be elected by the House of the People and one by the Council of States;

d) eight experts or professionals having prescribed qualifications and experience in conservation of wild life and welfare of people living in tiger reserve out of which at least two shall be from the field of tribal development;

e) Secretary, Ministry of Environment and Forests;

f) Director General of Forests and Special Secretary, Ministry of Environment and Forests;

g) Director, Wild Life Preservation, Ministry of Environment and Forests;

h) six Chief Wild Life Wardens from the Tiger Reserve States in rotation for three years;

i) an officer not below the rank of Joint Secretary and Legislative Counsel from the Ministry of Law and justice;

j) Secretary, Ministry of Tribal Affairs;

k) Secretary, Ministry of Social Justice and Empowerment;

l) Chairperson, National Commission for the Scheduled Tribes;

m) Chairperson, National Commission for the Scheduled Castes;

n) Secretary, Ministry of Panchayati Raj;

o) [an officer not below the rank of Inspector General of Forests] having at least ten years experience in a tiger reserve or wildlife management, who shall be the Member-Secretary, to be notified by Central Government, in the Official Gazette.

1) It is hereby declared that the office of member of the Tiger Conservation Authority shall not disqualify its holder for being chosen as, or for being, a member of either House of Parliament.

38M. Term of office and conditions of service of members - 1) A member nominated under clause (d) of sub-section (2) of section 38L shall hold office for such period not exceeding three years:

Provided that a member may, by writing under his hand addressed to the Central Government, resign from his office.

2) The Central government shall remove a member referred to in clause (d) of sub-section (2) of section 38L, from office if he-

a) is, or at any time has been, adjudicated as insolvent;

b) has been convicted of an offence which, in the opinion of the Central Government, involves moral turpitude;

c) is of unsound mind and stands so declared by a competent court;

d) refuses to act or becomes incapable of acting;

e) is, without obtaining leave of absence from the Tiger Conservation Authority, absent from three consecutive meetings of the said Authority; or

f) has, in the opinion of the Central Government, so abused his position as to render his continuation in office detrimental to the public interest:

Provided that no member shall be removed under this sub-section unless he has been given a reasonable opportunity of being heard in the matter.

3) Any vacancy in the office of a member shall be filled by fresh appointment and such member shall continue for the remainder of the term of the member in whose place he is appointed.

2) The salaries and allowances and other conditions of appointment of the members of the Tiger Conservation Authority shall be such as may be prescribed.

3) No act or proceeding of the Tiger Conservation Authority shall be questioned or shall be invalid on the ground merely of the existence of any vacancy or defect in the constitution of the Tiger Conservation Authority.

38N. Officers and employees of Tiger Conservation Authority- (1) The Tiger Conservation Authority may, with the previous sanction of the Central Government, appoint such other officers and employees as it considers necessary for the efficient discharge of its functions under this Act:

Provided that the officers and employees holding office under the Directorate of Project Tiger and dealing with Project Tiger immediately before the date of constitution of the Tiger Conservation Authority shall continue to hold office in the said Authority by the same tenure and upon the same terms and conditions of service or until the expiry of the period of six months from that date if such employee opts not to be employee of that Authority.

(2) The terms and conditions of service of the officers and other employees of the Tiger Conservation Authority shall be such as may be prescribed.

38O. Powers and functions of Tiger conservation Authority- (1) The Tiger Conservation Authority shall have the following powers and perform the following functions, namely:-

a) to approve the Tiger Conservation Plan prepared by the State Government under sub-section (5) of section 38V of this Act;

b) evaluate and assess various aspects of sustainable ecology and disallow any ecologically unsustainable land use such as, mining, industry and other projects within the tiger reserves;

c) lay down normative standards for tourism activities and guidelines for Project Tiger from time to time for Tiger Conservation in the buffer and core area of tiger reserves and ensure their due compliance;

d) provide for management focus and measures for addressing conflicts of men and wild animals and to emphasise on co-existence in forest areas outside the National Parks, sanctuaries or tiger reserve, in the working plan code;

e) provide information on protection measures including future conservation plan, estimation of population of tiger and its natural prey species, status of habitats, disease surveillance, morality survey, patrolling, reports on untoward happenings and such other management aspects as it may deem fit including future plan conservation;

f) approve, co-ordinate research and monitoring on tiger, co-predators, prey, habitat, related ecological and socio-economic parameters and their evaluation;

g) ensure that the tiger reserves and areas linking one protected area or tiger reserve with another protected area or tiger reserve are not diverted for ecologically unsustainable uses, except in public interest and with the approval of the National Board for Wild Life and on the advice of Tiger Conservation Authority;

h) facilitate and support the tiger reserve management in the State for biodiversity conservation initiatives through eco-development and people's participation as per approved management plans and to support similar initiatives in adjoining areas consistent with the Central and State laws;

i) ensure critical support including scientific, information technology and legal support for better implementation of the tiger conservation plan;

j) facilitate on going capacity building programme for skill development of officers and staff of tiger reserves; and

k) perform such other functions as may be necessary to carry out the purposes of this Act with regard to conservation of tigers and their habitat.

2) The Tiger conservation authority may, in the exercise of its powers and performance of its functions under this Chapter, issue directions in writing to any person, officer or authority for the protection of tiger or tiger reserves and such person, officer or authority shall be bound to comply with the directions:

Provided that no such direction shall interfere with or affect the rights of local people particularly the Scheduled Tribes.

38P. Procedure to be regulated by Tiger Conservation Authority - (1) The Tiger Conservation Authority shall meet at such time and at such place as the Chairperson may think fit.

(2) The Chairperson or in his absence the Vice-Chairperson shall preside over the meetings of the Tiger Conservation Authority.

(3) The Tiger Conservation Authority shall regulate its own procedure.

(4) All orders and decisions of the Tiger Conservation Authority shall be authenticated by the Member-Secretary or any other officer of the said Authority duly authorised by the Member-Secretary in this behalf.

38Q. Grants and loans to Tiger Conservation Authority and Constitution of Fund- (1) the Central Government may, after due appropriation made by Parliament by law in this behalf, make to the Tiger Conservation Authority grants and loans of such sums of money as that Government may consider necessary.

(2) There shall be constituted a fund to be called the Tiger Conservation Authority Fund and there shall be credited thereto-

    i. any grants and loans made to the Tiger Conservation Authority by the Central Government;

    ii. all fees and charges received by the Tiger conservation authority under this Act; and

    iii. all sums received by the Authority from such other sources as may be decided upon by the Central Government.

(3) The Fund referred to in sub-section (2) shall be applied for meeting salary, allowances and other remuneration of the members, officers and other employees of the Tiger Conservation Authority and the expenses of the Tiger Conservation Authority incurred in the discharge of its functions under this Chapter.

38R. Accounts and audit of Tiger Conservation Authority - (1) The Tiger Conservation Authority shall maintain proper accounts and other relevant records and prepare an annual statement of accounts in such form as may be prescribed by the Central Government in consultation with the Comptroller and Auditor –General of India.

(2) The accounts of the Tiger Conservation Authority shall be audited by the Comptroller and Auditor –General of India at such intervals as may be specified by him and any expenditure incurred in connection with such audit shall be payable by the Tiger Conservation Authority to the Comptroller and Auditor-General of India.

(3) The comptroller and Auditor-General of India and any other person appointed by him in connection with the audit of the accounts of the Tiger Conservation Authority shall have the same rights and privileges and authority in connection with such audit as the Comptroller and Auditor-General generally has in connection with the audit of the Government accounts and, in particular, shall have the right to demand the production of books, accounts, connected vouchers and other documents and papers and to inspect the office of the Tiger Conservation Authority.

(4) The Accounts of the Tiger Conservation Authority as certified by the Comptroller and Auditor-General of India or any other person appointed by him in this behalf together with the audit report there on, shall be forwarded annually to the Central Government by the Tiger Conservation Authority.

38S. Annual report of Tiger Conservation Authority - The Tiger Conservation Authority shall prepare in such form and at such time, for each financial year, as may be prescribed, its annual report, giving a full account of its activities during the previous financial year and forward a copy there of the Central Government.

38T. Annual report and audit report to be laid before Parliament- The Central Government shall cause the annual report together with a memorandum of action taken on the recommendations contained there in, in so far as they relate to the Central Government, and the reasons for the non-acceptance, if any, of any of such recommendations, and the audit report to be laid, as soon as may be after the reports are received, before each House of Parliament.

38U. Constitution of Steering Committee- (1) The State Government may constitute a Steering Committee for ensuring co-ordination, monitoring, protection and conservation of tiger, co-predators and prey animals within the tiger range States.

(2) The Steering Committee shall consists of-

 (a) the Chief Minister – Chairperson;

 (b) the Minister in-charge of Wild Life – Vice-Chairperson;

 (c) such number of official members not exceeding five including at least Two Field Directors of Tiger Reserve or Director of National Park and one from the State Government's Departments dealing with tribal affairs;

 (d) three experts or professionals having qualifications and experience in conservation of wild life of which at least one shall be from the field of tribal development;

 (e) two members from the State's Tribal Advisory Council;

(f) one representative each from State Government's Departments dealing with Panchayathi Raj and Social Justice and Empowerment;

(g) Chief Wild Life warden of the State shall be the Member-Secretary, ex officio, to be notified by the State Government, in the Official Gazette.

38V. Tiger Conservation plan- (1) The State government shall, on the recommendation of the Tiger Conservation Authority, notify an area as a Tiger Reserve.

(2) The provisions of sub-section (2) of section 18, sub-sections (2),(3) and (4) of section 27, section 30, 32 and clauses (b) and (c) of section 33 of this Act shall, as far as may be, apply in relation to a Tiger Reserve as they apply in relation to a sanctuary.

(3) The State Government shall prepare a Tiger Conservation Plan including staff development and deployment plan for the proper management of each area referred to in sub-section (1), so as to ensure-

(a) protection of Tiger Reserve and providing site specific habitat inputs for a viable population of tigers co-predators and prey animals without distorting the natural prey-predator ecological cycle in the habitat;

(b) ecologically compatible land uses in the Tiger Reserves and areas linking one protected area or Tiger reserve with another for addressing the livelihood concerns of local people, so as to provide dispersal habitats and corridor for spill over population of wild animals from the designated core areas of Tiger Reserves or from tiger breeding habitats within other protected areas;

(c) the forestry operations of regular forest divisions and those adjoining Tiger Reserves are not incompatiable with the needs of Tiger Conservation.

(4) Subject to the provisions contained in this Act, the State Government shall while preparing a Tiger Conservation Plan, ensure the agricultural, livelihood, developmental and other interests of the people living in tiger bearing forests or a Tiger Reserve.

Explanation- For the purposes of this Section, the expression "tiger reserve" includes-

(i) core or critical tiger habitat areas of National Parks and Sanctuaries, where it has been established, on the basis of scientific and objective criteria, that such areas are required to be kept as inviolate for the purposes of tiger conservation, without affecting the rights of the Scheduled Tribes or such other forest dwellers, and notified as such by the State Government in consultation with an Expert Committee constituted for the purpose;

(ii) buffer or peripheral area consisting of the area peripheral to critical tiger habitat or core area, identified and established in accordance with the provisions contained in Explanation (i) above, where a lesser degree of habitat protection is required to ensure the integrity of the critical tiger habitat with adequate dispersal for tiger species, and which aim at promoting co-existence between wildlife and human activity with due recognition of the livelihood, developmental, social and cultural rights of the local people, wherein the limits of such areas are determined on the basis of scientific and objective criteria in consultation with the concerned Gram Sabha and an Expert Committee constituted for the purpose.

(5) Save as for voluntary relocation on mutually agreed terms and conditions, provided that such terms and conditions satisfy requirements laid down in this sub-section, no Scheduled Tribes or other forest dwellers shall be resettled or have their rights adversely affected for the purpose of creating in violate areas for tiger conservation unless-

(i) the process of recognition and determination of rights and acquisition of land or forest rights of the Scheduled Tribes and such other forest dwelling persons is complete;

(ii) the concerned agencies of the State Government, in exercise of their powers under this Act, establishes with the consent of the Scheduled Tribes and such other forest dwellers in the area, and in consultation with an ecological and scientist familiar with the area, that the activities of the Scheduled Tribes and other forest dwellers or the impact of their presence upon wild animals is sufficient to cause irreversible damage and shall threaten the existence of tigers and their habitat;

(iii) the State Government, after obtaining the consent of the Scheduled Tribes and other forest dwellers inhabiting the area, and in consultation with an independent ecological and social scientist familiar with the area, has come to a conclusion that other reasonable options of co-existence, are not available;

(iv) resettlement or alternative package has been prepared providing for livelihood for the affected individuals and communities and fulfils the requirements given in the National Relief and Rehabilitation Policy;

(v) the informed consent of the Gram Sabha concerned, and of the persons affected, to the resettlement programme has been obtained; and

(vi) the facilities and land allocation at the resettlement location are provided under the said programme, otherwise their existing rights shall not be interfered with.

38W. Alteration and de-notification of tiger reserves- (1) No alteration in the boundaries of a tiger reserve shall be made except on a recommendation of the Tiger Conservation Authority and the approval of the National Board for Wild Life.

(2) No State Government shall de-notify a tiger reserve, except in public interest with the approval of the Tiger Conservation Authority and the National Board for Wild Life.

38X. Establishment of Tiger Conservation Foundation - (1) The State Government shall establish a Tiger Conservation Foundation for tiger reserves within the State in order to facilitate and support their management for conservation of tiger and biodiversity and, to take initiatives in eco-development by involvement of people in such development process.

(2) The Tiger Conservation Foundation shall, inter alia have the following objectives:-

(a) to facilitate ecological, economic, social and cultural development in the tiger reserves;

(b) to promote eco-tourism with the involvement of local stakeholder communities and provide support to safeguard the natural environment in the tiger reserves;

(c) to facilitate the creation of, and or maintenance of, such assets as may be necessary for fulfilling the above said objectives;

(d) to solicit technical, financial, social, legal and other support required for the activities of the Foundation for the achieving the above said objectives;

(e) to augment and mobilise financial resources including recycling of entry and such other fees received in a tiger reserve, to foster stake-holder development and eco-tourism;

(f) to support research, environmental education and training in the above related fields.

[38X A. Provisions of Chapter to be in addition to provisions relating to sanctuaries and National Park- The provisions contained in this Chapter shall be in addition to, and not in derogation of, the provisions relating sanctuaries and National Parks (whether included and declared, or are in the process of being so declared) included in a tiger reserve under this Act.]

CHAPTER IVC

[Wild Life] Crime Control Bureau

38Y. Constitution of [WILD LIFE] Crime Control Bureau- The Central Government may, for the purposes of this Act, by order published in the Official Gazette, constitute a *** Wildlife Crime control Bureau consisting of-

a) the Director of Wildlife Preservation- Director ex-officio;

b) the Inspector General of Police- Additional Director;

c) the Deputy Inspector-General of Police- Joint Director;

d) the Deputy Inspector-General of Forest- Joint Director;

e) the Additional Commissioner (Customs and [Central Goods and Services Tax]- Joint Director and;

f) such other officers as may be appointed from amongst the officers covered under sections 3 and 4 of this Act.

38Z. Powers and functions of the Wildlife Crime Control Bureau - (1) Subject to the provisions of this Act, the Wildlife Crime Control Bureau shall take measures with respect to-

i) collect and collate intelligence related to organized wildlife crime activities and to disseminate the same to State and other enforcement agencies for the immediate action so as to apprehend the criminals and to establish a centralised wildlife crime data bank;

ii) co-ordination of actions by various officers, State Governments and other authorities in connection with the enforcement of the provisions of this Act, either directly or through regional and border units set up by the Bureau;

iii) implementation of obligations under the various International Conventions and protocols that are in force at present or which may be ratified or acceded to by India in future;

iv) assistance to concerned authorities in foreign countries and concerned International Organisations to facilitate co-ordination and universal action for Wildlife Crime Control;

v) develop infrastructure and capacity building for scientific and professional investigation into wildlife crimes and assist State Governments to ensure success in prosecutions related to wildlife crimes;

vi) advice the Government of India on issues relating to wildlife crimes having national and international ramifications, and suggest changes required in relevant policy and laws from time to time.

(2) The Wildlife Crime Control Bureau shall exercise-

(3) such powers as may be delegated to it under sub-section (1) of section 5; sub-section (1) and (8) of section 50 and section 55 of this Act; and

(4) such other powers as may be prescribed.]

CHAPTER V

Trade or Commerce in Wild Animals, Animal Articles and Trophies

39. Wild animals, etc., to be Government property-(1) Every –

(a) wild animal, other than vermin, which is hunted under section 11 or sub-section (1) of the section 29 or sub-section (6) of section 35 or kept or [bred in captivity or hunted] in contravention of any provision of this Act or any rule or order made thereunder or found dead, or killed*** or by mistake; and

(b) animal article, trophy or uncured trophy or meat derived from any wild animal referred to in clause (a) in respect of which any offence against this Act or any rule or order made thereunder has been committed,

[(c) ivory imported into India and an article made from such ivory in respect of which any offence against this Act or any rule or order made there under has been committed;

(d) vehicle, vessel, weapon, trap, or tool that has been used for committing an offence and has been seized under the provisions of this Act.]

shall be the property of the State Government, and, where such animal is hunted in a sanctuary or National Park declared by the Central Government, such animal or any animal article, trophy, uncured trophy or meat [derived from such animal or any vehicle or vessel, weapon, trap or tool used in such hunting] shall be the property of the Central Government.

(2) Any person who obtains, by any means, the possession of Central Government property, shall, within forty-eight hours from obtaining such possession, make a report as to obtaining of such possession to the, nearest police station or the authorised officer and shall, if so required, hand over such property to the officer- in- charge of such police station or such authorised officer, as the case may be.

(3) No person shall, without the previous permission in writing of the Chief Wild Life Warden or the authorised officer-

(a) acquire or keep in his possession, custody or control, or

(b) transfer to any person, whether by way of gift, sale or otherwise, or

(c) destroy or damage, such Government property.

[(4) Where any such Government property is a live animal, the State Government shall ensure that it is housed and cared for by a recognised zoo or rescue centre when it cannot be released to its natural habitat.

(5) Any animal article, trophy or uncured trophy or meat derived from any wild animal, as referred to in sub-sections (1) and (2) may be disposed of by the State Government or the Central Government, as the case may be, in such manner as may be prescribed by the Central Government:

Provided that such disposal shall not include any commercial sale or auction and no certificate of ownership shall be issued for such disposal]

40. Declaration –(1) Every person having at the commencement of this Act the control, custody or possession of any captive animal specified in schedule I ***,[or animal article, trophy or uncured trophy] derived from such animal or salted or dried skins of such animal or the musk of a musk deer or the horn of a rhinoceros, shall, within thirty days from the commencement of this Act, declare to the Chief Wild Life Warden or the authorised officer the number and description of the animal, or article of the foregoing description under his control, custody or possession and place where such animal or article is kept.

(2) No person shall, after the commencement of this Act, acquire, receive, keep in his control, custody or possession, sell, offer for sale or 420 otherwise transfer or transport any animal specified in Schedule I *** or any uncured trophy or meat derived from such animal, or the salted or dried skins of such animal or the musk of a musk deer or the horn of a rhinoceros, except with the previous permission in writing of the Chief Wild Life Warden or the authorised officer.

[(2A) No person other than a person having a certificate of ownership, shall, after the commencement of the Wild life (Protection) Amendment Act, 2002 (16 of 2003) acquire, receive, keep in his control, custody or possession in any captive animal, animal article, trophy or uncured trophy specified in Schedule I ***, except by way of inheritance.

(2B) Every person inheriting any captive animal, animal article, trophy or uncured trophy under sub-section (2A) shall, within ninety days of such inheritance make a declaration to the Chief Wild Warden or the authorised officer and the provisions of sections 41 and 42 shall apply as if the declaration had been made under sub-section (1) of section 40:

Provided that nothing in sub-sections (2A) and (2B) shall apply to the live elephant.]

[(3) Nothing in sub-section (1) or sub-section (2) shall apply to a recognised zoo subject to the provisions of section 38-I or to a public museum.]

(4) The State Government may, by notification, require any person to declare to the Chief Wild Life Warden or the authorised officer [any animal or animal article] or trophy (other than a musk of a musk deer or horn of a rhinoceros) or salted or dried skins derived from an animal specified in Schedule I*** in his control, custody or possession in such form, in such manner, and within such time, as may be prescribed.

[**40A. Immunity in certain cases.-** (1) Notwithstanding anything contained in sub-sections (2) and (4) of section 40 of this Act, the Central Government may, by notification, require any person to declare to the Chief Wild Life Warden or the authorised officer, any captive animal, animal article, trophy or uncured trophy derived from animals specified in schedule I*** in his control, custody or possession, in respect of which no declaration had been made under sub-section (1) or sub-section 40, in such manner and within such time as may be prescribed.

(2) Any action taken or purported to be taken for violation of section 40 of this Act at any time before the commencement of the Wild Life (Protection) Amendment Act, 2002 (16 of 2003) shall not be proceeded with and all pending proceedings shall stand abated.

(3) Any captive animal, animal article, trophy or uncured trophy declared under sub-section (1), shall be dealt with in such manner and subject to such conditions as may be prescribed.]

41. Inquiry and preparation of inventories – (1) On receipt of a declaration made under section 40, the Chief Wild Life Warden or the authorised officer may, after such notice, in such manner and at such time, as may be prescribed,-

    (a) enter upon the premises of a person referred to in section 40;

    (b) make inquiries and prepare inventories of animal articles, trophies, uncured trophies, salted and dried skins and captive animals specified in Schedule I *** and found thereon; and

    (c) affix upon the animal, animal articles, trophies or uncured trophies identification marks in such manner as may be prescribed.

(2) No person shall obliterate or counterfeit any identification mark referred to in this Chapter.

42. Certificate of ownership – The Chief Wild Life Warden may, for the purposes of section 40, issue a certificate of ownership in such form, as may be prescribed to any person who, in his opinion, is in lawful possession of any wild animal or any animal article, trophy, uncured trophy and may, where possible, mark, in the prescribed manner, such animal article, trophy or uncured trophy for purposes of identification.

[Provided that before issuing the certificate of ownership in respect of any captive animal, the Chief Wild Life Warden shall ensure that the applicant has adequate facilities for housing, maintenance and upkeep of the animal.]

[42A. Surrender of captive animals, animal article, etc.- (1) Any person having a certificate of ownership in respect of any captive animal, animal article, trophy or uncured trophy, meat or ivory imported into India or an article made from such ivory, and who is not desirous of keeping it in his control, custody or possession may, after giving notice of seven working days to the Chief Wild Warden, surrender the same to him and any such certificate of ownership shall stand cancelled from the date of such surrender.

(2) No compensation shall be payable to any person for surrender of any such animal, article, trophy, meat or ivory to the Chief Wild Life Warden under sub-section (1).

(3) Any such animal, article, trophy, meat or ivory surrendered under this section shall become the property of the State Government and the provisions of section 39 shall apply.]

[43. Regulation of transfer of animal, etc.- (1) No person having in his possession captive animal, animal article, trophy or uncured trophy in respect of which he has a certificate of ownership shall transfer by way of sale or offer for sale or by any other mode of consideration of commercial nature, such animal or article or trophy or uncured trophy.

(2) Where a person transfers or transports from the State in which he resides to another State or acquires by transfer from outside the State, any such animal, animal article, trophy or uncured trophy in respect of which he has a certificate of ownership, he shall, within thirty days of the transfer or transport, report the transfer or transport to the Chief Wild Life Warden or the authorised officer within whose jurisdiction the transfer or transport is effected.

[Provided that the transfer or transport of a captive elephant for a religious or any other purpose by a person having a valid certificate of ownership shall be subject to such terms and conditions as may be prescribed by the Central Government.]

(3) Nothing in this section shall apply-

(a) to tail feather of peacock and the animal article or trophies made therefrom;

(b) to transfer of captive animals between recognised zoos subject to the provisions of section 38-I , and transfer amongst zoos and public museums.]

44. Dealings in trophy and animal articles without licence prohibited.- (1) Subject to the provisions of Chapter VA, no person shall, except under and in accordance with, a licence granted under sub-section (4)]-

(a) commence or carry on the business as-

(i) a manufacture of or dealer in, any animal article; or

(ii) a taxidermist; or

(iii) a dealer in trophy or uncured trophy; or

(iv) a dealer in captive animals; or

(v) a dealer in meat; or

(b) cook or serve meat in any eating-house;

[(c) derive, collect or prepare or deal in snake venom;]

Provided that nothing in this sub-section shall prevent a person, who, immediately before the commencement of this Act was carrying on the business or occupation specified in this sub-section, from carrying on such business or occupation for a period of thirty days from such commencement, or where he has made an application within that period for the grant of a licence to him, until the licence is granted to him or he is informed in writing that a licence cannot be granted to him:

[Provided further that nothing in this sub-section shall apply to the dealers in tail feathers of peacock and articles made therefrom and the manufactures of such articles.]

Explanation.- For the purposes of this section, "eating-house" includes a hotel, restaurant or any other place where any eatable is served on payment, whether or not such payment is separately made for such eatable or is included in the amount charged for board and lodging.

(2) Every manufacture of, or dealer in, animal article, or every dealer in captive animals, trophies or uncured trophies, or every taxidermist shall, within fifteen days from the commencement of this Act, declare to the Chief

Wild Life Warden his stock of animals articles, captive animals, trophies and uncured trophies, as the case may be, as on the date of such declaration and the Chief Wild Life Warden or the Authorised officer may place an identification mark on every animal article, captive animal, trophy or uncured trophy, as the case may be.

(3) Every person referred to in sub-section (1) who intends to obtain a licence, shall*** make an application to the Chief Wild Life Warden or the authorised officer for the grant of a licence.

(4) (a) Every application referred to in sub-section (3) shall be made in such form and on payment of such fee as may be prescribed, to the Chief Wild Life Warden or the authorised officer.

[(b) No licence referred to in sub-section (1) shall be granted unless the Chief Wild Life Warden or the authorised officer having regard to the antecedents and pervious experience of the applicant, the implication which the grant of such licence would have on the status of wild life and to such other matters as may be prescribed in this behalf and after making such inquiry in respect of those matters as he may think fit, is satisfied that the licence should be granted.]

(5) Every licence granted under this section shall specify the premises in which and the conditions, if any, subject to, which the licensee shall carry on his business.

(6) Every licence granted under this section shall –

    (a) be valid for one year from the date of its grant;

    (b) not be transferable; and

    (c) be renewable for a period not exceeding one year at a time.

(7) No application for the renewal of a licence shall be rejected unless the Chief Wild Warden has been given a reasonable opportunity of presenting his case and unless the Chief Wild Warden or the authorised officer is satisfied that-

    (i) the application for such renewal has been made after the expiry of the period specified therefor, or

    (ii) any statement made by the applicant at the time of the grant or renewal of the licence was incorrect or false in material particulars, or

    (iii) the applicant has contravened any term or condition of the licence or any provision of this Act or any rule made thereunder, or

    (iv) the applicant does not fulfil the prescribed conditions.

(8) Every order granting or rejecting application for the grant or renewal of a licence shall be made in writing.

(9) Nothing in the foregoing sub-sections shall apply in relation to vermin.

45. Suspension or cancellation of licences.- Subject to any general or special order of the State government, the Chief Wild Life Warden or the authorised officer may, for reasons to be recorded by him in writing, suspend or cancel any licence granted or renewed under section 44:

Provided that no such suspension or cancellation shall be made except after giving the holder of the licence a reasonable opportunity of being heard.

46. Purchase.- (1) An appeal from an order refusing to grant or renew a licence under section 44 or an order suspending or cancelling a licence under section 45 shall lie-

(a) if the order is made by the authorised officer, to the chief Wild Life Warden; or

(b) if the order is made by the Chief Wild Life Warden, to the State Government.

(2) In the case of an order passed in appeal by the Chief Wild Life Warden under clause (a) of sub-section (1), a second appeal shall lie to the State Government.

(3) Subject as aforesaid, every order passed in appeal under this section shall be final.

(4) An appeal under this section shall be preferred within thirty days from the communication, to the applicant, of the order appealed against:

Provided that the appellate authority may admit any appeal preferred after the expiry of the period aforesaid if it is satisfied that the appellant had sufficient cause for not preferring the appeal in time.

47. Maintenance of records.- A licensee under this Chapter shall-

(a) keep records, and submit such returns of his dealings, as may be prescribed,-

(i) to the Director or any other officer authorised by him in this behalf, and

(ii) to the Chief Wild Life Warden or the authorised officer; and

(c) make such records available on demand for inspection by such officers.

48. Purchase of animals, etc., by licensee- No licensee under this Chapter shall-

(a) keep in his control, custody or possession,-

(i) any animal, animal article, trophy or uncured trophy in respect of which a declaration under the provisions of sub-section (2) of section 44 has to be made but has not been made;

(ii) any animal or animal article, trophy, uncured trophy or meat which has not been lawfully acquired under the provision of this Act or any rule or order made thereunder;

(b) (i) capture any wild animal, or

(ii) acquire, receive keep in his control, custody or possession, or sell, offer for sale or transport, any captive animal specified in Schedule I *** or any animal article trophy, uncured trophy or meat derived therefrom or serve such meat, or put under a process of taxidermy or make animal article containing part or whole of such animal, except in accordance with such rules as may be made under this Act;

Provided that where the acquisition or, possession, control or custody of such animal or animal article, trophy or uncured trophy entails the transfer or transport from one State to another, no such transfer or transport shall be effected except with the previous permission in writing of the Director or any other officer authorised by him in this behalf:

Provided further that no such permission under the foregoing proviso shall be granted unless the Director or the officer authorised by him is satisfied that the animal or article aforesaid has been lawfully acquired.

[48A. Restriction on transportation of wild life – No person shall accept any wild animal (other than vermin), or any animal article, or any specified plant or part or derivative thereof, for transportation except after exercising due care to ascertain that permission from the Chief Wild Life Warden or any other officer authorised by the State Government in this behalf has been obtained for such transportation.]

49. Purchase of captive animal, etc., by a person other than a licensee – No person shall purchase, receive or acquire any captive animal, wild animal, other than vermin, or any animal article, trophy, uncured trophy or meat derived therefrom otherwise than from a dealer or from a dealer or from a person authorised to sell or otherwise transfer the same under this Act:

[Provided that nothing in this section shall apply to a recognised zoo subject to the provisions of section 38-1 or to a public museum.]

[CHAPTER VA

Prohibition of Trade or Commerce in Trophies, Animal Articles, Etc., Derived from Certain Animals

49A. Definitions- In this Chapter,-

(a) "Scheduled animal" means an animal specified for the time being in Schedule I ***;

(b) "Scheduled animal article" means an article made from any Scheduled animal and includes an article or object in which the whole or any part of such animal [has been used but does not include tail feather of peacock, an article or trophy made therefrom and snake venom or its derivative.]

(c) "Specified date" means-

(i) in relation to a scheduled animal on the commencement of the Wild Life (Protection) (Amendment) Act, 1986, the date of expiry of two months from such commencement;***

(ii) in relation to any animal added or transferred to Scheduled I*** at any time after such commencement, the date of expiry of two months from such addition or transfer.

[(iii) in relation ivory imported into India or an article made from such ivory, the date of expiry of six months from the commencement of the Wild Life (Protection) (Amendment) Act, 1991 (44 of 1991)]

49B. Prohibition of dealings in trophies, animal articles, etc., derived from scheduled animals- (1) Subject to the other provisions of this section, on and after the specified date, no person shall,-

(a) commence or carry on the business as-

(i) a manufacturer of, or dealer in, scheduled animal articles; or

[(ia) a dealer in ivory imported into India or articles made therefrom or a manufacturer of such articles; or]

(ii) a taxidermist with respect to any scheduled animals or any parts of such animal; or

(iii) a dealer in trophy or uncured trophy derived from any scheduled animal; or

(iv) a dealer in any captive animals being scheduled animals; or

(v) a dealer in meat derived from any scheduled animal; or

(b) cook or serve meat derived from any scheduled animal in any eating-house.

Explanation – For the purposes of this sub-section,"eating-house" has the same meaning as in the Explanation below sub-section (1) of section 44.

(2) Subject to the other provisions of this section, no licence granted or renewed under section 44 before the specified date shall entitle the holder thereof or any other person to commence or carry on the business referred to in clause (a) of sub-section (1) of this section or the occupation referred to in clause (b) of that sub-section after such date.

(3) Notwithstanding anything contained in sub-section (1) or sub-section (2), where the Central Government is satisfied that it is necessary or expedient so to do in the public interest, it may, by general or special order published in the official Gazette, exempt, for purposes of export, any corporation owned or controlled by the Central Government (including a Government company within the meaning of section 617 of the Companies Act, 1956 (1 of 1956), or any society registered under the Societies Registration Act, 1860 (21 of 1860), or any other law for the time being in force, wholly or substantially financed by the Central Government, from the provisions of sub-sections (1) and (2).

(4) Notwithstanding anything contained in sub-section (1) or sub-section (2), but subject to any rules which may be made in this behalf, a person holding a licence under section 44 to carry on the business as a taxidermist may put under a process of taxidermy any scheduled animal or any part thereof –

(a) for or on behalf of the Government or any corporation or society exempted under sub-section (3), or

(b) with the previous authorisation in writing of the Chief Wild Life Warden, for and on behalf of any person for educational or scientific purposes.

49C. Declaration by dealers – (1) Every person carrying on the business or occupation referred to in sub-section (1) of section 49B shall, within thirty days from the specified date declare to the Chief Wild Life Warden or the authorised officer –

(a) his stocks, if any, as at the end of the specified date of-

(i) scheduled animal articles;

(ii) scheduled animals and parts thereof;

(iii) trophies and uncured trophies derived from scheduled animals;

(iv) captive animals being scheduled animals;

[(v) ivory imported into India or articles made therefrom;]

(b) the place or places at which the stocks mentioned in the declaration are kept; and

(c) the description of such of items, if any, the stocks mentioned in the declaration which he desires to retain with himself for his bona fide personal use.

(2) On receipt of a declaration under sub-section (1), the Chief Wild Life Warden or the authorised officer may take all or any of the measures specified in section 41 and for this purpose, the provisions of section 41 shall, so far as may be, apply.

(3) Where, in a declaration made under sub-section (1), the person making the declaration express his desire to retain with himself any of the items of the stocks specified in the declaration for his bona fide personal use, the Chief Wild Life Warden, with the prior approval of the Director, may, if he is satisfied that the person is in lawful possession of such items, issue certificates of ownership in favour of such person with respect to all, or as the case may be, such of items as in the opinion of the Chief Wild Life Warden, are required for the bona fide personal use of such person and affix upon such items identification marks in such manner as may be prescribed:

Provided that no such item shall be kept in any commercial premises.

(4) No person shall obliterate or counterfeit any identification mark referred to in sub-section (3).

(5) An appeal shall lie against any refusal to grant certificate of ownership under sub-section (3) and the provisions of sub-sections (2), (3) and (4) of section 46 shall, so far as may be, apply in relation to appeals under this sub-section.

(6) Where a person who has been issued a certificate of ownership under sub-section (3) in respect of any item-

(a) transfers such item to any person, whether by way of gift, sale or otherwise, or

(b) transfers or transports from the State in which he resides to another State any such item, he shall, within thirty days of such transfer or transport, report the transfer or transport to the Chief Wild Life Warden or the authorised officer within whose jurisdiction the transfer or transport is effected.

(7) No person, other than a person who has been issued a certificate of ownership under sub-section (3), shall on and after the specified date keep under his control, sell or offer for sale or transfer to any person [any scheduled animal, a scheduled animal article, or ivory imported into India or any article made therefrom.]

[CHAPTER VB

Regulation of International Trade in Endangered Species of Wild Fauna and Flora as Per Convention on International Trade in Endangered Species of Wild Fauna and Flora

49D. Definitions – In this Chapter, unless the context otherwise requires,-

(a) "artificially propagated" means plants which have been grown under controlled conditions from plant materials grown under similar conditions;

(b) "bred in captivity" means produced from parents in captivity;

(c) "Convention" means the Convention on International Trade in Endangered Species of Wild Fauna and Flora signed at Washington D. C., in the United States of America on the 3rd of March, 1973, and amended at Bonn on the 22nd of June , 1979, its appendices, decisions, resolutions and notifications made thereunder and its amendments, to the extent binding on India;

(d) "export" means export from India to any other country of a specimen;

(e) "import" means import into India from any other country of a specimen;

(f) "introduction from the sea " means transportation into India of specimens of any species which were taken from the marine environment not under the jurisdiction of India or any other country;

(g) " Management Authority " means the Management Authority designated under section 49E;

(h) "readily recognisable part or derivative" includes any specimen which appears from an accompanying document, the packaging or a mark or label, or from any other circumstances, to be a part or derivative of an animal or plant of a species listed in Schedule IV;

(i) "re-export" means export of any specimen that has previously been imported;

(j) "Scientific Authority" means a Scientific Authority designated under section 49F;

(k) "scheduled specimen" means any specimen of a species listed in Appendices I, II or III of the Convention and incorporated as such in Schedule IV;

(l) "species" means any species, sub-species, or geographically separate population thereof;

(m) "specimen" means-

(i) any animal or plant, whether alive or dead;

(ii) in the case of an animal,-

(A) for species included in appendices I and II of Schedule IV, any readily recognisable part or derivative thereof;

(B) for species included in Appendix III of Schedule IV, any readily recognisable part or derivative thereof specified in Appendix III of Schedule IV in relation to the species; and

(iii) in the case of a plant,-

(A) for species included in Appendix I of Schedule IV, any readily recognisable part or derivative thereof;

(B) for species included in Appendices II and III of Schedule IV, any readily recognisable part or derivative thereof specified in Appendices II and III of Schedule IV in relation to the species;

(n) "trade" means export, re-export, import and introduction from the sea.

49E. Designation of Management Authority- (1) The Central Government shall, by notification, designate an officer not below the rank of an Additional Director General of Forests as the Management Authority for discharging the functions and exercising the powers under this Act.

(2) The Management Authority shall be responsible for issuance of permits and certificates for trade of scheduled specimens in accordance with the Convention, submission of reports, and shall perform such other functions as may be necessary to implement the provisions of the Convention.

(3) The Management Authority shall prepare and submit annual and biennial reports to the Central Government.

(4) The Central Government may appoint such officers and employees as may be necessary to assist the Management Authority in discharging its functions or exercising its powers under this Chapter, on such terms and conditions of service including salaries and allowances as may be prescribed.

(5) The Management Authority may, with the prior approval of the Central Government, delegate its functions or powers, to such officers not below the rank of the Assistant Inspector General of Forests, as it may consider necessary for the purposes of this Chapter.

49F. Designation of scientific Authority- (1) The Central Government shall, by notification, designate one or more institutes engaged in research on species as Scientific Authority for the purposes of this chapter, for fulfilling the functions under the Convention.

(2) The designated scientific Authority shall advise the Management Authority in such matters as may be referred to it by the Management Authority.

(3) The Scientific Authority shall monitor the export permits granted for specimens of species listed in Appendix II of Schedule IV and the actual export of such specimens.

(4) Whenever a Scientific Authority is of the opinion that the export of specimens of such species requires to be limited in order to maintain that species throughout its range at a level consistent with its role in the eco systems in which it occurs and well above the level at which that species might become eligible for inclusion in Appendix I of the Convention, it shall advise the Management Authority to take such appropriate measures to limit the grant of export permits for specimens of that species as the Scientific Authority may deem necessary for said purpose.

49G. Directions of Central Government – The Management Authority and the Scientific Authorities, shall, while performing their duties and exercising powers under this Chapter, be subject to such general or special directions, as the Central Government may, from time to time, give.

49H. International trade in scheduled specimen and restriction in respect thereof- (1) No person shall engage in trade of scheduled specimens except as provided for under this Chapter.

(2) The Central Government shall prescribe the conditions and procedures by which the exemptions contained in Article VII of the Convention may be availed.

(3) Every person engaging in trade of a scheduled specimen shall report the details of the Scheduled specimen and the transaction to the Management

Authority or the officer authorised by it in such manner as may be prescribed.

(4) Every person engaging in trade of a scheduled specimen, shall present it for clearance to the Management Authority or the officer authorised by it or a customs officer only at the ports of exit and entry as may be specified by the Central Government.

(5) The form and manner of making an application for a permit or certificate to trade in a scheduled specimen, the fee payable therefor, the conditions subject to which the permit or certificate, shall be such as may be prescribed by the Central Government.

49 I. Conditions for export of scheduled specimens- (1) The export of any specimen of species included in Appendices I or II of schedule IV shall require the prior grant and presentation of an export permit.

(2) The export of any specimen of species included in Appendix III of Schedule IV shall require the prior grant and presentation of an export permit if the species has been listed in Appendix III of the Convention by India or a certificate of origin in other cases.

(3) An export permit shall not be granted unless-

    (a) the Management Authority is satisfied that the specimen concerned has not been obtained in contravention of any law for the time being in force relating to protection of fauna and flora;

    (b) the Management Authority is satisfied that any living specimen will be so prepared and shipped as to minimise the risk of injury, damage to health or cruel treatment;

    (c) in the case of a specimen of a species listed in Appendices I or II of schedule IV, the Scientific Authority has advised that the export will not be detrimental to the survival of that species; and

    (d) in the case of specimens of species listed in Appendix I of Schedule IV, an import permit has been granted by the competent authority of the country of destination.

49J. Conditions for import of scheduled specimens-(1) The import of any specimen of a species included in Appendix I of schedule IV shall require the prior grant and presentation of an import permit and either an export permit or a re-export certificate from the country of export.

(2) An import permit for a specimen of a species listed in Appendix I of Schedule IV shall not be granted unless-

(a) the Management Authority is satisfied that the specimen concerned will not be used for primarily commercial purposes;

(b) the Scientific Authority has advised that the import will be for purposes which are not detrimental to the survival of the species; and

(c) the Scientific Authority is satisfied that the proposed recipient of a living specimen is suitably equipped to house and care for it.

(3) The import of any specimen of a species included in Appendix II of Schedule IV shall require the prior presentation of either an export permit or a re-export certificate issued by the country of export.

(4) The import of any specimen of a species included in Appendix III of Schedule IV shall require the prior presentation of-

(a) a certificate of origin; or

(b) in the case where the import is from a country which has included the species in Appendix III of the Convention, an export permit; or

(c) a re- export certificate granted by the country of re-export.

49K. Conditions for re-export of scheduled specimens- (1)The re-export of any specimen of species included in Appendices I or II of Schedule IV shall require the prior grant and presentation of a re-export certificate.

(2) A re-export certificate shall not be granted unless-

(a) the Management Authority is satisfied that any specimen to be re-exported was imported in accordance with the provisions of this Chapter and of the Convention;

(b) the Management Authority is satisfied that any living specimen will be so prepared and shipped as to minimise the risk of injury, damage to health or cruel treatment; and

(c) in the case of any living specimen of species listed in Appendix I of Schedule IV, the Management Authority is satisfied that an import permit has been granted.

49L. Conditions for introduction from sea of scheduled specimens- (1) The introduction from the sea of a specimen of a species included in Appendices I or II of Schedule IV shall require the prior grant and presentation of a certificate of introduction from the sea.

(2) A certificate of introduction from the sea shall not be granted unless-

(a) the Scientific Authority has advised that the introduction of any specimen will not be detrimental to the survival of the species;

(b) in the case of a specimen of a species listed in Appendix I of Schedule IV, the Management Authority is satisfied that it is not to be used

for primarily commercial purposes and that the proposed recipient of any living specimen is suitably equipped to house and care for it; and

(c) in the case of a living specimen of a species listed in Appendix II of Schedule IV, the Management Authority is satisfied that it will be so handled as to minimise the risk of injury, damage to health or cruel treatment.

49M. Possession, transfer and breeding of living scheduled animal species- (1) Every person possessing a living specimen of an animal species listed in Schedule IV shall report the details of such specimen or specimens in his possession to the Management Authority or the authorised officer:

Provided that the Central Government may exempt one or more specimens of any animal species included in Schedule IV from such declaration for such quantity and for such period as it may deem fit.

(2) The Management Authority or the authorised officer may, on being satisfied that a person was in possession of a living specimen of an animal species listed in Schedule IV which had not been obtained in contravention of any law relating to protection of fauna and flora, issue a registration certificate allowing the owner to retain such specimen.

(3) Any person who transfers possession, by any means whatsoever, of any living specimen of an animal species listed in Schedule IV shall report the details to the Management Authority or the authorised officer.

(4) The Management Authority or the authorised officer shall register all transfers of living specimens of animal species listed in Schedule IV and issue the transferee with a registration certificate.

(5) Any person in possession of any living specimen of an animal species listed in Schedule IV which bears any offspring shall report the birth of such offspring to the Management Authority or the authorised officer.

(6) The Management Authority or the authorised officer shall on receipt of the report under sub-section (5) register any offspring born to any living specimen of an animal species listed in Schedule IV and issue the owner with a registration certificate.

(7) Any person in possession of any living specimen of an animal species listed in Schedule IV which dies shall report such death to the Management Authority or the authorised officer.

(8) No person shall possess, transfer or breed any living specimen of any animal species listed in Schedule IV except in conformity with this section and the rules made by the Central Government in this behalf.

(9) The form, manner and period for reporting possession, transfers, and births, deaths, and registration of the same under this section shall be as prescribed by the Central Government.

49N. Application for Licence by breeders of Appendix I species –(1) Every person who is engaged in breeding in captivity or artificially propagating any scheduled specimen listed in Appendix I of Schedule IV shall make, within a period of ninety days of the commencement of the Wild Life (Protection) Amendment act, 2022, an application for a licence to the Chief Wild Life Warden.

(2) The form and manner of the application to be made to the Chief Wild Life Warden under sub-section (1), the fee payable, the form of licence, the procedure to be followed in granting or cancelling the licence shall be such as may be prescribed by the Central Government.

49 O. Licence of breeders of Appendix I species,- (1) On receipt of application under sub-section (1) of section 49 N, the Chief Wild Life Warden shall, if-

(a) the application is in the prescribed form;

(b) the resolutions of the Convention relating to breeding in captivity or artificial propagation of species listed in Appendix I of Schedule IV are satisfied; and

(c) the provisions of the Act and rules made thereunder have been duly complied with, record an entry of the statement in a register and grant the applicant a licence.

(2) The Chief Wild Life Warden shall, if the provisions or resolutions of the Convention or this Act and any rules made hereunder have not been complied with, or if a false particular is furnished, refuse or cancel the licence as the case may be after providing the applicant with an opportunity of being heard.

(3) The licence under sub-section (1) shall be issued for a period of two years and may be renewed after two years on payment of such fee as may be prescribed.

(4) Any person aggrieved by the refusal of the Chief Wild Life Warden or cancellation of licence under sub-section (2) may prefer an appeal to the State Government within a period of sixty days in such manner as may be prescribed.

49P. Prohibition on alteration, etc.- No person shall alter, deface, erase or remove a mark of identification affixed upon the scheduled specimen or its package.

49Q. Species and scheduled specimens to be Government property – (1) Every species or scheduled specimen, in respect of which any office against this Act or rules made thereunder has been committed, shall become the property of the Central Government and the provisions of section 39 shall, without prejudice to the Customs Act, 1962 (52 of 1962), apply, mutatis mutandis, in relation to species and scheduled specimens as they apply in relation to wild animals, captive animals and animal articles.

(2) Where a living specimen of a species listed in Schedule IV has been seized under this Act or the Customs Act,1962 (52 of 1962) or any other law for the time being in force as a result of import into India in contravention of this Act, the Management Authority shall, after consultation with the country of export, return the specimen to that country at the expense of that country, or ensure that it is housed and cared for by a recognised zoo or rescue centre in case it cannot be returned to the country of export.

(3) The Management Authority may for such purposes consult the scientific Authority as it deems appropriate.

49R. Application of provisions of Act in respect of species listed in Schedule I or II and Schedule IV. –(1) Where the same species is listed in schedule I or II and schedule IV, then, the provisions of this Act applicable to such species listed in Schedule I or II and the rules made thereunder shall apply.

(2) Nothing in sections 49M, 49N or 49-O shall apply to a species listed in Schedule I or schedule II if the same species is also listed in Schedule IV.

(3) The provisions of this chapter shall be subject to the provisions of Chapters III, IIIA, IVA, V, VA and VIA and without prejudice to anything contained therein.]

CHAPTER VI

Prevention And Detention Of Offences

50. Power of entry, search, arrest and detention- (1) Notwithstanding anything contained in any other law for the time being in force, the Director or any other authorised by him in this behalf [or the Management Authority or any officer authorised by the Management Authority] or the Chief Wild Life Warden or the authorised officer or any forest officer or any police officer not below the rank of a sub-inspector [or any customs officer not below the rank of an inspector or any officer of the coast guard not below the rank of an Assistant Commandant], may, if he has reasonable grounds for believing that any person has committed an offence against this Act,-

(a) require any such person to produce for inspection any captive animal, wild animal, animal article, meat, trophy or [trophy, uncured trophy, specified plant or part or derivative thereof [or scheduled specimen] in his control, custody or possession, or any licence, permit or other document granted to him or required to be kept by him under the provisions of this Act;

(b) stop any vehicle or vessel in order to conduct search or inquiry or enter upon and search any premises, land, vehicle or vessel, in the occupation of such person, and open and search any baggage or other things in his possession;

[(c) seize any captive animal, wild animal, animal article, meat, trophy or uncured trophy, or any specified plant or part or derivative thereof [or scheduled specimen], in respect of which an offence against this Act appears to have been committed, in the possession of any person together with any trap, tool, vehicle, vessel or weapon used for committing any such offence and, unless he is satisfied that such person will appear and answer any charge which may be preferred against him, arrest him without warrant, and detain him:

Provided that where a fisherman, residing within ten kilometres of a sanctuary or National Park, inadvertently enters on a boat, not used for commercial fishing, in the territorial waters in that sanctuary or National Park, a fishing tackle or net on such boat shall not be seized.]

* * * *

(3) It shall be lawful for any of the officers referred to in sub-section (1) to stop and detainany person, whom he sees doing any act for which a licence or permit is required under the provisions of this Act, for the purposes of requiring such person to produce the licence or permits and if such person fails to produce the licence or permit, as the case may be, he may be arrested without warrant, unless he furnishes his name and address, and otherwise satisfies the officer arresting him that he will duly answer any summons or other proceedings which may be taken against him.

[(3A) Any officer of a rank not inferior to that of an Assistant Director of Wild Life Preservation or [an Assistant Conservator of Forest] who, or whose subordinate, has seized any captive animal or wild animal under clause (c) of sub-section (1) may give the same for custody on the execution by any person of a bond for the production of such animal if and when so required, before the Magistrate having jurisdiction to try the offence on account of which the seizure has been made.]

(4) Any person detained, or things seized under the foregoing power, shall forthwith be taken before a Magistrate to be dealt with according to law

[under intimation to the Chief Wild Life Warden or the officer authorised by him in this regard.]

(5) Any person who, without reasonable cause, fails to produce anything, which he is required to produce under this section, shall be guilty of an offence against this Act.

[(6) Where any meat, uncured trophy, specified plant or part or derivative thereof is seized under the provisions of this section, the Assistant Director of Wild Life Preservation or any other officer of a gazetted rank authorised by him in this behalf or the Chief Wild Life Warden or the authorised officer may arrange for the disposal of the same in such manner as may be prescribed.]

(7) Whenever any person is approached by any of the officers referred to in sub-section (1) for assistance in the prevention or detention of an offence against this Act, or in apprehending persons charged with the violation of this Act, or for seizure in accordance with clause (c) of sub-section (1), it shall be the duty of such person or persons to render such assistance.

[(8) Notwithstanding anything contained in any other law for the time being in force, any officer not below the rank of an Assistant Director of Wild Life Preservation or [an officer not below the rank of Assistant Conservator of Forests authorised by the State Government in this behalf] shall have the powers, for purposes of making investigation into any offence against any provision of this Act-

    (a) to issue a search warrant;

    (b) to enforce the attendance of witness;

    (c) to compel the discovery and production of documents and material objects; and

    (d) to receive and record evidence.

(9) any evidence recorded under clause (d) of sub-section (8) shall be admissible in any subsequent in any subsequent trial before a Magistrate provided that it has been taken in the presence of the accused person.]

51. Penalties – (1) any person who [contravenes any provision of this Act [(except Chapter VA and section 38J)] or any rule or order made thereunder or who commits a breach of any of the conditions of any licence or permit granted under this Act, shall be guilty of an offence against this Act, and shall, on conviction, be punishable with imprisonment for a term which may extend to [three years], or with fine which may extend to [one lakh rupees], or with both:

[Provided that where the offence committed is in relation to any animal specified in Schedule I ***or meat of any such animal or animal article, trophy or uncured trophy derived from such animal or where the offence relates to hunting in a sanctuary or a National Park or altering the boundaries of a sanctuary or a National Park [or where the offence relates to a specimen of a species listed on Appendix I of Schedule IV], such offence shall be punishable with imprisonment for a term which shall not be less than three years but may extend to seven years and also fine which shall not be less than [twenty-five thousand rupees]:

Provided further that in the case of a second or subsequent offence of the nature mentioned in this sub-section, the term of the imprisonment shall not be less than three years but may extend to seven years and also with fine which shall not be less than [one lakh rupees].]

[(1A) Any person who contravenes any provisions of Chapter VA, shall be punishable with imprisonment for a term which shall not be less than [three years] but which may extend to seven years and also with fine which shall not be less than [twenty-five thousand rupees].]

[(1B) Any person who contravenes the provisions of section 38J, shall be punishable with imprisonment for a term which may extend to six months, or with fine which may extend to two thousand rupees, or with both:

Provided that in the case of a second or subsequent offence the term of imprisonment may extend to one year or the fine may extend to five thousand rupees.]

(2) When any person is convicted of an offence against this Act, the Court trying the offence may order that any captive animal, wild animal, animal article, trophy, [uncured trophy, meat, ivory imported into India or an article made from such ivory, any specified plant, or part or derivative thereof] in respect of which the offence has been committed, and any trap, tool, vehicle, vessel or weapon, used in the commission of the said offence be forfeited to the State Government and that any licence or permit, held by such person under the provisions of this Act, be cancelled.

(3) Such cancellation of licence or permit or such forfeiture shall be in addition to any other punishment that may be awarded for such offence.

(4) Where any person is convicted of an offence against this Act, the Court may direct that the licence, if any, granted to such person under the Arms Act, 1959 (54 of 1959), for possession of any arm with which an offence against this Act has been committed, shall be cancelled and that such person shall not be eligible for a licence under the Arms act, 1959, for a period of five years from the date of conviction.

[(5) Nothing contained in section 360 of the Code of Criminal Procedure, 1973 (2 of 1974), or in the Probation of Offenders Act, 1958 (20 of 1958), shall apply to a person convicted of an offence with respect to hunting in a sanctuary or a National Park or of an offence against any provision of Chapter VA unless such person is under eighteen years of age.]

STATE AMENDMENTS

Assam

Amendment of section 51- In the principal Act, in section 51, in sub-section (1),

(i) in the first proviso,-

(a) in between the words "hunting in" and " a sanctuary" the words or "outside the boundary of" shall be inserted;

(b) for the words "three years", "seven years" and "ten thousand", the words "seven years", "ten years " and "fifty thousand" respectively shall be substituted.

(ii) in the second proviso, for the words "three years", "seven years" and "twenty five thousand", the words "ten years", "life imprisonment" and "seventy five thousand" respectively, shall be substituted.

[Vide Assam Act 31 of 2010, s.2]

[**51A. Certain conditions to apply while granting bail**- When any person accused of, the commission of any offence relating to Schedule I *** or offences relating to hunting inside the boundaries of National Park or wild life sanctuary or altering the boundaries of such parks and sanctuaries, is arrested under the provisions of the Act, then notwithstanding anything contained in the Code of Criminal Procedure, 1973 (2 of 1974) no such person who had been previously convicted of an offence under this Act shall, be released on bail unless-

(a) the Public Prosecutor has been given an opportunity of opposing the release on bail; and

(b) where the Public Prosecutor opposes the application, the Court is satisfied that there are reasonable grounds for believing that he is not guilty of such offence and that he is not likely to commit any offence while on bail.]

STATE AMENDMENTS

Assam

Insertion of section 51B- In the principal Act, after section 51A, the following new section 51B shall be inserted, namely:-

"**51B. Offences to be cognizable, non bailable and triable by the Court of Sessions-** (1) Every offence punishable under this Act shall be cognizable and non-cognizable within the meaning of the Code of Criminal Procedure, 1973.

(2) Notwithstanding anything contained in the Code of Criminal Procedure, 1973, no person accused of an offence punishable under this Act, shall be released on bail unless-

(a) the Public Prosecutor has been given an opportunity to oppose the application for such release; and

(b) where the Public Prosecutor opposes the application, the court is satisfied that there are reasonable grounds for believing that the accused is not likely to commit any offence while on bail.

(3) The offences under this Act, shall be triable by the Court of Sessions of the respective jurisdiction.

[Vide Assam Act 31 of 2010, s.3]

52. Attempts and abetment- Whoever attempts to contravene, or abets the contravention of, any of the provisions of this Act or of any rule or order made thereunder shall be deemed to have contravened that provision or rule or order, as the case may be.

53. Punishment for wrongful seizure- If any person, exercising powers under this Act, vexatiously and unnecessarily seizes the property of any other person on the pretence of seizing it for the reasons mentioned in section 50 he shall, on conviction, be punishable with imprisonment for a term which may extend to six months, or with fine which may extend to five hundred rupees, or with both.

[54. Power to compound offence- (1) The Central Government may, by notification, empower the Director of Wild Life Preservation or any other officer not below the rank of Assistant Director of Wild Life Warden and in the case of a State Government in the similar manner, empower the Chief Wild life Warden or any officer of a rank not below the rank of a Deputy Conservator of Forests, to accept from any person against whom a reasonable suspicion exists that he has committed an offence against this Act, payment of a sum of money by way of composition of the offence which such person is suspected to have committed.

(2) On payment of such sum of money to such officer, the suspected person, if in custody, shall be discharged and no further proceedings in respect of the offence shall be taken against such person.

(3) The officer compounding any offence may order the cancellation of any licence or permit granted under this Act to the offender, or if not empowered

to do so, may approach an officer so empowered, for the cancellation of such licence or permit.

(4) The sum of money accepted or agreed to be accepted as composition under sub-section (1) shall, in no case, exceed the sum of [five lakh rupees]:

Provided that no offence, for which a minimum period of imprisonment has been prescribed in section 51, shall be compounded.]

[55. Cognizance of offences – No court shall take cognizance of any offence against this Act on the complaint of any person other than-

(a) the Director of Wild Life Preservation or any other authorised in this behalf by the Central Government; or

[(aa) the Member-Secretary, Central Zoo Authority in matters relating to violation of the provisions of Chapter IVA; or]

[(ab) Member-Secretary, Tiger Conservation Authority; or

(ac) Director of the Concerned tiger reserve; or]

[(ad) the Management Authority or any officer, including an officer of the Wild Life Crime Control Bureau, authorised in this behalf by the Central Government; or]

(b) the Chief Wild Life Warden, or any other officer authorised in this behalf by the State Government [subject to such conditions as may be specified by that Government]; or

[(bb) the officer –in-charge of the zoo in respect of violation of provisions of section 38 J; or]

(c) any person who has given notice of not less than sixty days, in the manner prescribed, of the alleged offence and of his intention to make a complaint, to the Central Government or the State Government or the officer authorised as aforesaid.]

56. Operation of other laws not barred- Nothing in this Act shall be deemed to prevent any person from being prosecuted under any other law for the time being in force, for any act or omission which constitutes an offence against this Act or from being liable under such law to any higher punishment or penalty than that provided by this Act: Provided that no person shall be punished twice for the same offence.

57. Presumption to be made in certain cases- Where, in any prosecution for an offence against this Act, it is established that a person is in possession, custody or control of any [wild animal, captive animal], animal article, meat [trophy, uncured trophy, specified plant, or part or derivative thereof [or scheduled specimen] it shall be presumed, until the contrary is proved, the burden of proving which shall lie on the accused, that such person is in unlawful possession, custody or control of such [wild animal, captive animal], animal article, meat, [trophy, uncured trophy, specified plant, or part or derivative thereof [or scheduled specimen.]

58. Offences by Companies – (1) Where an offence against this Act has been committed by a company, every person who, at the time the offence was committed, was in charge of, and was responsible to, the company for the conduct of the business of the company as well as the company, shall be deemed to be guilty of the offence and shall be liable to be proceeded against and punished accordingly:

Provided that nothing contained in this sub-section shall render any such person liable to any punishment, if he proves that the offence was committed without his knowledge or that he exercised all due diligence to prevent the commission of such offence.

(2) Notwithstanding anything contained in sub-section (1), where an offence against this Act has been committed by a company and it is proved that the offence has been committed with the consent or connivance of, or is attributable to any neglect on the part of, any director, manager, secretary or other officer of the company, such director, manager, secretary or other officer shall also be deemed to be guilty of that offence and shall be proceeded against and punished accordingly.

Explanation – For the purposes of this section,-

(a) "company" means anybody corporate and includes a firm or other association of individuals; and

(b) "director", in relation to a firm, means a partner in the firm.

[CHAPTER VIA

Forfeiture of Property Derived from Illegal Hunting and Trade

58A. Application- The provisions of this Chapter shall apply only to the following persons, namely:-

(a) every person who has been convicted of an offence punishable under this Act with imprisonment for a term of three years or more;

(b) every associate of a person referred to in clause (a);

(c) any holder (hereafter in this clause referred to as the present holder) of any property which was at any time previously held by a person referred to in clause (a) or clause (b) unless the present holder or, as the case may be, anyone who held such property after such person and before the present holder, is or was a transferee in good faith for adequate consideration.

58B. Definitions- In this chapter, unless the context otherwise requires,-

(a) "Appellate Tribunal" means the Appellate Tribunal for Forfeited Property constituted under section 58N;

(b) "associate" in relation to a property is liable to be forfeited under this Chapter, includes-

(i) any individual who had been or is managing the affairs or keeping the accounts of such person;

(ii) any association of persons, body of individuals, partnership firm or private company within the meaning of the Companies Act, 1956 (1 of 1956) of which such person had been or is a member, partner or director;

(iii) any individual who had been or is a member, partner or director of an association of persons, body of individuals, partnership firm or private company referred to in sub-clause (ii) at any time when such person had been or is a member, partner or director of such association, body, partnership firm or private company;

(iv) any person, who had been or is managing the affairs, or keeping the accounts of any association of persons, body of individuals, partnership firm or private company referred to in sub-clause (iii);

(v) the trustee of any trust, where,-

(1) the trust has been created by such person; or

(2) the value of the assets contributed by such person (including the value of assets, if any, contributed by him earlier) to the trust amounts on the date on which contribution is made, to not less than twenty per cent of the value of the assets of the trust on that date;

(vi) where the competent authority, for reasons to be recorded in writing, considers that any properties of such person are held on his behalf by any other person, such other person;

(c) "competent authority" means an officer authorised under section 58D;

(d) "concealment" means the concealment or disguise of the nature, source, disposition, movement or ownership of property and includes the movement or conversion of such property by electronic transmission or by any other means;

(e) "freezing" means temporarily prohibiting the transfer, conversion, disposition movement of property by an order issued section 58F;

(f) "identifying" includes establishment of proof that the property was derived from, or used in, the illegal hunting and trade of wild life and its products;

(g) "illegally acquired property" in relation to any person to whom this Chapter applies, means,-

(i) any property acquired by such person, wholly or partly out of by means of any income, earnings or assets derived or obtained from or attributable to illegal hunting and trade of wild life and its products and derivatives;

(ii) any property acquired by such person, for a consideration or by any means, wholly or partly traceable to any property referred to in sub-clause (i) or the income or earning from such property,

and includes –

(A) any property held by such person which would have been, in relation to any previous holder thereof, illegally acquired property under this clause if such previous holder had not ceased to hold it, unless such person or any other person who held the property at any time after such previous holder or, where there are two or more such previous holders, the last of such previous holders is or was a transferee in good faith for adequate consideration;

(B) any property acquired by such person, for a consideration, or by any means, wholly or partly traceable to any property falling under item (A), or the income or earnings therefrom;

(h) "property" means property and assets of every description, whether corporeal or incorporeal, movable or immovable, tangible or intangible and deeds and instruments evidencing title to, or interest in, such property or assets, derived from the illegal hunting and trade of wild life and its products;

(i) "relative" means-

(1) spouse of the person;

(2) brother or sister of the person;

(3) brother or sister of the spouse of the person;

(4) any lineal ascendant or descendant of the person;

(5) any lineal ascendant or descendant of the spouse of the person;

(6) spouse of a person referred to in sub-clause (2), sub-clause (3), sub-clause (4) or sub-clause (5);

(7) any lineal descendant of a person referred to in sub-clause (2) or sub-clause (3);

(j) "tracing" means determining the nature, source, disposition, movement, title or ownership of property;

(k) "trust" includes any other legal obligation.

58C. Prohibition of holding illegally acquired property- (1) From the date of commencement of this chapter, it shall not be lawful for any person to whom this Chapter applies to hold any illegally acquired property either by himself or through any other person on his behalf.

(2) Where any person holds such property in contravention of the provisions of sub-section (1), such property shall be liable to be forfeited to the State Government concerned in accordance with the provisions of this Chapter:

Provided that no property shall be forfeited under this Chapter if such property was acquired by a person to whom this Act applies before a period of six years from the date on which he was charged for an offence relating to illegal hunting and trade of wild life and its products.

58D. Competent authority- The State Government may, by order published in the Official Gazette, authorise any officer not below the rank of Chief Conservator of Forests perform the functions of the competent authority under this Chapter in respect of such persons or classes of persons as the State Government may, direct.

58E. Identifying illegally acquired property –(1) An officer not below the rank of Deputy Inspector General of Police duly authorised by the Central Government or as the case may be, the State Government or as the case may be, the State Government, shall, on receipt of a complaint from the competent authority about any person having illegally acquired property, proceed to take all steps necessary for tracing and identifying any property illegally acquired by such person.

(2) The steps referred to in sub-section (1) may include any inquiry, investigation or survey in respect of any person, place, property, assets, documents, books of account in any bank or financial institution or any other relevant step as may be necessary.

(3) Any inquiry, investigation or survey referred to in sub-section (2) shall be carried out by an officer mentioned in sub-section (1) in accordance with such directions or guidelines as the competent authority may make or issue in this behalf.

58F. Seizure or freezing of illegally acquired property – (1) Where any officer conducting an inquiry or investigation under section 58E has reason to believe that any property in relation to which such inquiry or investigation is being conducted is an illegally acquired property and such property is likely to be concealed, transferred or dealt with in any manner which may result in frustrating any proceeding relating to forfeiture of such property under this Chapter, he may make an order for seizing such property and where it is not practicable to seize such property, he may make an order that such property shall not be transferred or otherwise dealt with, except with the prior permission of the officer making such order, or of the competent authority and a copy of such order shall be served on the person concerned:

Provided that a copy of such an order shall be sent to the competent authority within forty- eight hours of its being made.

(2) Any order made under sub-section (1) shall have no effect unless the said order is confirmed by an order of the competent authority within a period of thirty days of its being made.

Explanation – For the purposes of this section, "transfer of property" means any disposition, conveyance, assignment, settlement, delivery, payment or other alienation of property and, without limiting the generality of the foregoing, includes-

(a) the creation of a trust in property;

(b) the grant or creation of any lease, mortgage, charge, easement, licence, power, partnership or interest in property;

(c) the exercise of a power of appointment, of property vested in any person not the owner of the property, to determine its disposition in favour of any person other than the donee of the power; and

(d) any transaction entered into by any person with intent thereby to diminish directly or indirectly the value of his own property and to increase the value of the property of any other person.

58G. Management of properties seized or forfeited under this Chapter –(1) The State Government may, by order published in the Official Gazette, appoint as many of its officers (not below the rank of Conservator of Forests) as it thinks fit, to perform the functions of an Administrator.

(2) The administrator appointed under sub-section (1) shall receive and manage the property in relation to which an order has been made under sub-section (1) of section 58F or under section 58-I in such manner and subject to such conditions as may be prescribed.

(3) The Administrator shall also take such measures as the State Government may direct, to dispose of the property which is forfeited to the State Government.

58H. Notice of forfeiture of property. - (1) If having regard to the value of the properties held by any person to whom this Chapter applies, either by himself or through any other person on his behalf, his known sources of income, earnings or assets, and any other information or material available to it as a result of a report from any officer making an investigation under section 58E or otherwise, the competent authority for reasons to be recorded in writing believes that all or any of such properties are illegally acquired properties, it may serve a notice upon such person (hereinafter referred to as the person affected) calling upon him within a period of thirty days specified in the notice to show cause why all or any of such properties, as the case may be, should not be declared to be illegally acquired properties and forfeited to the State Government under this Chapter and in support of his case indicate the sources of his income, earnings or assets, out of which or by means of which he has acquired such property, the evidence on which he relies and other relevant information and particulars.

(2) Where a notice under sub-section (1) to any person specifies any property as being held on behalf of such person by any other person, a copy of the notice shall also be served upon such other person.

58 I. forfeiture of property in certain cases- (1) The competent authority may, after considering the explanation, if any, to the show cause notice issued under section 58H, and the materials available before it and after giving to the person affected and in a case where the person affected holds any property specified in the notice through any other person, also a reasonable opportunity of being heard, by order, record a finding whether all or any of the properties in question are illegally acquired properties:

Provided that if the person affected (and in a case where the person affected holds any property specified in the notice through any other person, such other person also), does not appear before the competent authority or represent his case before it within a period of thirty days specified in the show cause notice, the competent authority may proceed to record a finding under this sub-section ex parte on the basis of evidence available before it.

(2) Where the competent authority is satisfied that some of the properties referred to in the show cause notice are illegally acquired properties but it is not able to identify specifically such properties, then, it shall be lawful for the competent authority to specify the properties which, to the best of its judgement, are legally acquired properties and record a finding accordingly under sub-section (1) within a period of ninety days.

(3) Where the competent authority records a finding under this section to the effect that any property is illegally acquired property, it shall declare that such property shall, subject to the provisions of this Chapter stand forfeited to the State Government free from all encumbrances.

(4) In case the person affected establishes that the property specified in the notice issued under section 58 H is not an illegally acquired property and therefore not liable to be forfeited under the Act, the said notice shall be withdrawn and the property shall be released forthwith.

(5) Where any shares in a company stand forfeited to the State Government under this Chapter, the company shall, notwithstanding anything contained in the Companies Act, 1956, (1 of 1956) or the article of association of the company, forthwith register the State Government as the transferee of such shares.

58J. Burden of proof- In any proceedings under this Chapter, the burden of proving that any property specified in the notice served under section 58H is not illegally acquired property shall be on the person affected.

58K. Fine in lieu of forfeiture – (1) Where the competent authority makes a declaration that any property stands forfeited to the State Government under section 58- I and it is a case where the source of only a part of the illegally acquired property has not been proved to the satisfaction of the competent authority, it shall make an order giving option to the person affected to pay, in lieu of forfeiture, a fine equal to the market value of such part.

(2) Before making an order imposing a fine under sub-section (1), the person affected shall be given a reasonable opportunity of being heard.

(3) Where the person affected pays the fine due under sub-section (1), within such time as may be allowed in that behalf, the competent authority may, by order revoke the declaration of forfeiture under section 58-I and thereupon such property shall stand released.

58L. Procedure in relation to certain trust properties – In the case of any person referred to in sub-clause (vi) of clause (b) of section 58B, if the competent authority, on the basis of the information and materials available to it, for reasons to be recorded in writing believes that any property held in trust is illegally acquired property, it may serve a notice upon the author of the trust, or as the case may be, the contributor of the assets out of or by means of such property was acquired by the trust and the trustees, calling upon them within a period of thirty days specified in the notice, to explain the source of money or other assets out of or by means of which such property was acquired or, as the case may be, the source of money or other assets which were contributed to the trust for acquiring such property and thereupon such notice shall be deemed to be a notice served under section 58 H and all the other provisions of this Chapter shall apply accordingly.

Explanation- For the purposes of this section "illegally acquired property" in relation to any property held in trust, includes-

(i) any property which if it had continued to be held by the author of the trust or the contributor of such property to the trust would have been illegally acquired property in relation to such author or contributor;

(ii) any property acquired by the trust out of any contributions made by any person which would have been illegally acquired property in relation to such person had such person acquired such property out of such contributions.

58M. Certain transfers to be null and void - Where after the making of an order under sub-section (1) of section 58F or the issue of a notice under section 58H or under section 58L, any property referred to in the said order or notice is transferred by any mode whatsoever, such transfer shall, for the purposes of the proceedings under this Chapter, be ignored and if such property is subsequently forfeited to the State Government under section 58-I, then, the transfer of such property shall be deemed to be null and void.

58N. Constitution of Appellate Tribunal – (1) The State Government may, by notification in the Official Gazette, constitute an Appellate Tribunal to be called the Appellate Tribunal for Forfeited Property consisting of a Chairman, and such number of other members (being officers of the State Government not below the rank of a Principal Secretary to the Government), as the State Government thinks fit, to be appointed by that Government for hearing appeals against the orders made under section 58 F, section 58 I, sub-section (1) of section 58K or section 58L.

(2) The Chairman of the Appellate Tribunal shall be a person who is or has been or is qualified to be a Judge of a High Court.

(3) The terms and conditions of service of the Chairman and other members shall be such as may be prescribed.

58O. Appeals – (1) Any person aggrieved by an order of the competent authority made under section 58F, section 58-I, sub-section (1) of section 58K or section 58L may, within forty-five days from the date on which the order served on him prefer an appeal to the Appellate Tribunal:

Provided that the Appellate Tribunal may entertain an appeal after the said period of forty-five days, but not after sixty days, from the date aforesaid if it is satisfied that the appellant was prevented by sufficient cause from filing the appeal in time.

(2) On receipt of an appeal under sub-section (1), the Appellate Tribunal may, after giving an opportunity of being heard to the appellant, if he so desires, and after making such further inquiry as it deems fit, confirm, modify or set aside the order appealed against.

(3) The Appellate Tribunal may regulate its own procedure.

(4) On application to the Appellate Tribunal and on payment of the prescribed fee, the Appellate Tribunal may allow a party to any appeal or any person authorised in this behalf by such party to inspect at any time during office hours, any relevant records and registers of the Appellate Tribunal and obtain a certified copy or any part thereof.

58P. Notice or order not to be invalid for error in description – No notice issued or served, no declaration made, and no order passed under this Chapter shall be deemed to be invalid by reason of any error in the description of the property or person mentioned therein if such property or person is identifiable from the description so mentioned.

58Q. Bar of jurisdiction – No order passed or declaration made under this Chapter shall be appealable except as provided therein and no civil court shall have jurisdiction in respect of any matter which the Appellate Tribunal or any competent authority is empowered by or under this Chapter to determine, and no injunction shall be granted by any court or other authority in respect of any action taken or to be taken in pursuance of any power conferred by or under this chapter.

58R. Competent Authority and Appellate Tribunal to have powers of civil court.- The competent authority and the Appellate Tribunal shall have all the powers of a civil court while trying a suit under the Code of Civil Procedure, 1908 (5 of 1908) in respect of the following matters, namely:-

    (a) summoning and enforcing the attendance of any person and examining him on oath;

    (b) requiring the discovery and production of documents;

    (c) receiving evidence on affidavits;

    (d) requisitioning any public record or copy thereof from any court or office;

    (e) issuing commissions for examination of witnesses or documents;

    (f) any other matter which may be prescribed.

58S. Information to competent authority – (1) Notwithstanding anything contained in any other law for the time being in force, the competent authority shall have power to require any officer or authority of the Central Government or a State Government or a local authority to furnish information in relation to such persons, on points or matters as in the opinion of the competent authority will be useful for, or relevant to, the purposes of this Chapter.

(2) Every officer referred to in section 58 T may furnish suo motu any information available with him to the competent authority if in the opinion

of the officer such information will be useful to the competent authority for the purposes of this Chapter.

58T. Certain officers to assist Administrator, competent authority and Appellate Tribunal- For the purposes of any proceedings under this chapter, the following officers shall render such assistance as may be necessary to the Administrator appointed under section 58G, competent authority and the Appellate Tribunal, namely:-

(a) officers of Police;

(b) officers of the State Forest Departments;

(c) officers of the Central Economic Intelligence Bureau;

(d) officers of the Directorate of Revenue Intelligence;

(e) such other officers as specified by the State Government in this behalf by notification in the Official Gazette.

58U. Power to take possession- (1) Where any property has been declared to be forfeited to the State Government under this Chapter, or where the person affected has failed to pay the fine under sub-section (1) of section 58K within the time allowed therefor under sub-section (3) of that section, the competent authority may order the person affected as well as any other person who may be in possession of the property to surrender or deliver possession thereof to the Administrator appointed under section 58G or to any person duly authorised by him in this behalf within thirty days of the service of the order.

(2) If the person refuses or fails to comply with an order made under sub-section (1), the Administrator may take possession of the property and may for that purpose use such force as may be necessary.

(3) Notwithstanding anything contained in sub-section (2), the Administrator may, for the purpose of taking possession of any property referred to in sub-section (1) requisition the services of any police officer to assist him and it shall be the duty of such officer to comply with such requisition.

58V. Rectification of mistakes – With a view to rectifying any mistake apparent from record, the competent authority or the Appellate Tribunal, as the case may be, may amend any order made by it within a period of one year from the date of the order:

Provided that if any such amendment is likely to affect any person prejudicially and the mistake is not of a clerical nature, it shall not be made without giving to such person a reasonable opportunity of being heard.

58W. Findings under other laws not conclusive for proceedings under this Chapter – No finding of any officer or authority under any other law shall be conclusive for the purposes of any proceedings under this chapter.

58X. Service of notice and orders – Any notice or order issued or made under this Chapter shall be served,-

(a) by tendering the notice or order or sending it by registered post to the person for whom it is intended or to his agent;

(b) if the notice or order cannot be served in the manner provided in clause (a), then, by affixing it on a conspicuous place in the property in relation to which the notice or order is issued or made or on some conspicuous part of the premises in which the person for whom it is intended is known to have last resided or carried on business or personally worked for gain.

58Y. Punishment for acquiring property in relation to which proceedings have been taken under this Chapter – Any person who knowingly acquires, by any mode whatsoever, any property in relation to which proceedings are pending under this Chapter shall be punishable with imprisonment for a term which may extend to five years and with fine which may extend to fifty thousand rupees.]

CHAPTER VII

Miscellaneous

59. Officers to be public servants- Every officer referred to [in chapter II and the chairperson, members, member-secretary and other officers and employees referred to in Chapter IV A], [chapter IV B] and every other officer exercising any of the powers conferred by this Act shall be deemed to be a public servant within the meaning of section 21 of the Indian Penal code (45 of 1860).

60. Protection of action taken in good faith – (1) No-suit, prosecution or other legal proceeding shall lie against any officer or other employee of the Central Government or the State Government for anything which is in good faith done or intended to be done under this Act.

(2) No suit or other legal proceeding shall lie against the Central Government or the State Government or any of its officers or other employees for any damage caused or likely to be caused by anything which is in good faith done or intended to be done under this Act.

[(3) No suit or other legal proceeding shall lie against the Authority referred to in Chapter IVA [Chapter IVB] and its chairperson, members, member-secretary, officers and other employees for anything which is in good faith done or intended to be done under this Act.]

[**60A. Reward to persons-** (1) When a court imposes a sentence of fine or a sentence of which fine forms a part, the Court may, when passing judgement, order that the reward be paid to a person who renders assistance in the detention of the offence or the apprehension of the offenders out of the proceeds of fine not exceeding [fifty per cent. of such fine].

(2) Where a case is compounded under section 54, the officer compounding may order reward to be paid to a person who renders assistance in the detention of the offence or the apprehension of the offenders out of sum of money accepted by way of composition not exceeding [fifty per cent. of such money].

[**60B. Reward by State Government-** The State Government may empower the Chief Wild Life Warden to order payment of reward not exceeding ten thousand rupees to be paid to a person who renders assistance in the detention of the offence or the apprehension of the offender, from such fund and in such manner as may be prescribed.]

61. Power to alter entries in schedules- (1) The central Government may, if it is of opinion that it is expedient so to do, by notification, [[amend any Schedule or add] or delete any entry to or from any schedule] or transfer any entry from one part of a schedule to another Part of the same Schedule or from one Schedule to another.

* * * *

(3) On the issue of a notification under sub-section (1) ***, the relevant Schedule shall be deemed to be altered accordingly, provided that every such alteration shall be without prejudice to anything done or omitted to be done before such alteration.

* * * *

Provided that any such alteration made by the State Government, if it has been made with the previous consent of the Central Government, shall prevail in that State:

Provided further that nothing in the foregoing proviso shall prevent the Central Government from modifying or cancelling, at any time, the alteration made by the State Government.

62. Declaration of certain wild animals to be vermin – [The Central Government] may, by notification, declare any wild animal [specified in Schedule II] to be vermin for any area and for such period as may be specified therein and so long as such notification is in force, such wild animal shall be [deemed not to be included in Schedule II for such area and for such period as specified in the notification].

[62A. Regulation or prohibition of import, etc., of invasive alien species –(1) The Central Government may, by notification, regulate or prohibit the import, trade, possession or proliferation of invasive alien species which pose a threat to the wild life or habitat in India.

(2) The Central Government may authorise the Director or any other officer to seize and dispose of, including through destruction, the species referred to in the notification issued under sub-section (1).

62B. Power to issue directions – Notwithstanding any other provision of this Act, the Central Government may call for any information or report from a State Government or any such other agency or body or issue any direction to a State Government or any such other agency or body for effective implementation of the provisions of the Act for the protection, conservation and management of wild life in the country.]

63. Power of Central Government to make rules – [(1) the Central Government may, by notification, make rules for all or any of the following matters, namely:-

(a) Conditions and other matters subject to which a licensee may keep any specified plant in his custody or possession under section 17F;

[(ai) the term of office of members other than those who are members ex officio; the manner of filling vacancies, the procedure to be followed by the National Board under sub-section (2) and allowances of those members under sub-section (3) of section 5A;]

[(aa) the matters to be prescribed under clause (b) of sub-section (4) of section 44;]

(b) the salaries, allowances and other conditions of appointment of chairperson, members and member-secretary under sub-section (5) of section 38B;

(c) the terms and conditions of service of the officers and other employees of the Central Zoo Authority under sub-section (7) of section 38B;

(d) the form in which the annual statement of accounts of the Central Zoo Authority shall be prepared under sub-section (4) of section 38E;

(e) the form in which and the time at which the annual report of the Central Zoo Authority shall be prepared under section 38F;

(f) the form in which and the free required to be paid with the application for recognition of a zoo under sub-section (2) of section 38H;

(g) the standards, norms and other matters to be considered for granting recognition under sub-section (4) of section 38H;

[(gi) qualifications and experience of experts or professionals under clause (d) of sub-section (2) of section 38-I;

(gii) the salaries and allowances and other conditions of appointment of the members under sub-section (4) of section 38M;

(giii) the terms and conditions of service of the officers and other employees of the Tiger Conservation Authority under sub-section (2) of section 38N;

(giv) the form in which the annual statement of accounts of Tiger Conservation Authority shall be prepared under sub-section (1) of section 38R;

(gv) the form in which and the time at which the annual report of Tiger Conservation Authority shall be prepared under section 38S;

(gvi) other powers of the Wild Life Crime Control Bureau under clause (ii) of sub-section (2) of section 38Z.]

[(gvii) the manner of disposal of Government property under sub-section (5) of section 39;

(gviii) the terms and conditions of a transfer or transport of a captive elephant by a person having a valid certificate of ownership for a religious or any other purpose under the proviso to sub-section (2) of section 43;]

(h) the form in which declaration shall be made under sub-section (2) of section 44;

(i) the matters to be prescribed under Cl.(b) of sub-section (4) of section 44;

(j) the terms and conditions which shall govern transaction referred to in clause (b) of section 48;

[(ji) the terms and conditions of service including salaries and allowances for appointment of the officers and employees of the Management Authority under sub-section (4) of section 49 E;

(jii) the conditions and procedures subject to which any exemption provided for in Article VII of the Convention may be availed under sub-section (2) of section 49H;

(jiii) the reporting of details of scheduled specimens and the transaction as per sub-section (3) of section 49H;

(jiv) the form and manner of application, the fee payable, the conditions and the procedure to be followed under sub-section (5) of section 49H;

(jv) the matters provided for in sub-sections (8) and (9) of section 49M;

(jvi) the form and manner of the application, the fee payable, the form of licence and the procedure to be followed in granting or cancelling a licence as per sub-section (2) of section 49N;

(jvii) the fee payable for renewal of licence as per sub-section (3), and manner of making appeal under sub-section (4), of section 49-O;

(jviii) any other matter for proper implementation of the Convention as may be required under Chapter VB;]

(k) the manner in which notice may be given by a person under clause (c) of section 55;

(l) the matters specified in sub-section (2) of section 64 in so far as they relate to sanctuaries and National Parks declared by the Central Government.]

(2) Every rule made under this section shall be laid, as soon as may be after it is made, before each House of Parliament, while it is in session, for a total period of thirty days which may be comprised in one session or in two or more successive sessions, and if before the expiry of the session immediately following the session or the successive sessions aforesaid, both Houses agree in making any modification in the rule or both Houses agree that the rule should not be made, the rule shall thereafter have effect only in such modified form or be of no effect, as the case may be; so, however, that any such modification or annulment shall be without prejudice to the validity of anything previously done under that rule.

64. Power of State Government to make rules- (1) The State Government may, by notification, make rules for carrying out the provisions of this Act in respect of matters which do not fall within the purview of section 63.

(2) In particular and without prejudice to the generality of foregoing power, such rules may provide for all or any of the following matters, namely:-

[(a) the term of office of members other than those who are members, ex officio, the manner of filling vacancies and the procedure to be followed by the Board under sub-section (2) of section 6;

(b) allowances referred to in sub-section (3) of section 6;]

(c) the forms to be used for any application, certificate, claim, declaration, licence, permit, registration, return, or other document, made, granted, or submitted under the provisions of this Act and the fees, if any, therefor;

(d) the conditions subject to which any licence or permit may be granted under this Act;

[(dd) the conditions subject to which the offices will be authorised to file cases in the court;]

(e) the particulars of the record of wild animals (captured or killed) to be kept and submitted by the licensee;

[(ee) the manner in which measures for immunisation of live-stock shall be taken;]

(f) regulation of possession, transfer and the sale of captive animals, meat, animal articles, trophies and uncured trophies;

(g) regulation of taxidermy;

[(ga) the manner and conditions subject to which the Administrator shall receive and manage the property under sub-section (2) of section 58G;

(gb) the terms and conditions of service of the Chairman and other members under sub-section (3) of section 58N;

(gc) the fund from which and the manner in which payment of reward under section 60B shall be made;]

(h) any other matter which has to be, or may be, prescribed under this Act.

65. Rights of Scheduled Tribes to be protected- Nothing in this Act shall affect the hunting rights conferred on the Scheduled Tribes of the Nicobar Islands in the Union Territory of Andaman and Nicobar Islands by notification of the Andaman and Nicobar Administration, No.40/67/F, No.G 635,Vol.III,dated the 28th April,1967, published at pages 1 to 5 of the Extraordinary issue of the Andaman and Nicobar Gazette, dated the 28th April,1967.

66. Repeal and savings- (1) As from the commencement of this Act, every other Act relating to any matter contained in this Act and in force in a State shall, to the extent to which that Act or any provision contained therein corresponds, or is repugnant, to this Act or any provision contained in this Act, stand repealed;

Provided that such repeal shall not,-

(i) affect the previous operation of the Act so repealed, or anything duly done or suffered thereunder;

(ii) affect any right, privilege, obligation or liability, acquired or incurred under the Act so repealed;

(iii) affect any penalty, forfeiture or punishment incurred in respect of any offence committed against the Act so repealed; or

(iv) affect any investigation, legal proceeding or remedy in respect of any such right, privilege, obligation, liability, penalty, forfeiture, or punishment as aforesaid; and any such investigation, legal proceeding or remedy may be instituted, continued or enforced, and any such penalty, forfeiture and punishment may be imposed, as if the aforesaid Act had not been repealed.

(2) Notwithstanding such repeal,-

(a) anything done or any action taken under the Act so repealed, (including any notification, order, certificate, notice or receipt issued, application made, or permit granted) which is not inconsistent with the provisions of this Act, be deemed to have been done or taken under the corresponding provisions of this Act as, if this Act were in force at the time such thing was done or action was taken, and shall continue to be in force, unless and until superseded by anything done or any action taken under this Act;

(b) every licence granted under any Act so repealed and in force immediately before the commencement of this Act shall be deemed to have been granted under the corresponding provisions of this Act, continue to be in force for the unexpired portion of the period for which such licence had been granted.

(3) For the removal of doubts, it is hereby declared that any sanctuary or National Park declared by a State Government under any Act repealed under sub-section (1) shall be deemed to be a sanctuary or National Park, as, the case may be, declared by the State government under this Act and where any right in or over any land in any such National Parks which had not been extinguished under the said Act, at or before the commencement of this Act, the extinguishment of such rights shall be made in accordance with the provisions of this Act.

[(4) For the removal of doubts, it is hereby further declared that where any proceeding under any provision of section 19 to 25 (both inclusive) is pending on the date of commencement of the Wild Life (Protection) Amendment Act, 1991, (44 of 1991), any reserve forest or a part of territorial waters comprised within a sanctuary declared under section 18 to be a sanctuary before the date of such commencement shall be deemed to be a sanctuary declared under section 26A.]

* * *

[1][SCHEDULE I

(*See* sections 9, 11, 12, 38-I, 39, 40, 40A, 41, 42, 42A, 43, 48, 48A, 50, 51, 51A and 57 and

Chapter V-A) PART A: MAMMALS

Sl. No.	Common name	Scientific name
	ANTELOPES	
1.	Blackbuck	*Antilope cervicapra*
2.	Chinkara/Indian Gazelle	*Gazella bennettii*
3.	Four-horned Antelope	*Tetracerus quadricornis*
4.	Tibetan Antelope	*Pantholops hodgsonii*
5.	Tibetan Gazelle	*Procapra picticaudata*
	BADGERS	
6.	Greater Hog Badger	*Arctonyx collaris*
7.	Northern Hog Badger	*Arctonyx albogularis*
8.	Ratel / Honey Badger	*Mellivora capensis*
	BATS	
9.	Andaman Horseshoe Bat	*Rhinolophus cognatus*
10.	**Black-eared Flying Fox**	*Pteropus melanotus*
11.	Leafletted Leaf-nosed Bat/Kolar Leaf-nosed Bat	*Hipposideros hypophyllus*

12.	Nicobar Flying Fox	*Pteropus faunulus*
13.	Salim Ali's Fruit Bat	*Latidens salimalii*
14.	Wroughton's Free tailed Bat	*Otomops wroughtoni*

BEARS

15.	Asiatic Black Bear	*Ursus thibetanus*
16.	Brown Bear	*Ursus arctos*
17.	Sun Bear	*Helarctos malayanus*
18.	Sloth Bear	*Melursus ursinus*

BINTURONG

| 19. | Binturong | *Arctictis binturong* |

CANIDS

20.	Asiatic Wild Dog/Dhole	*Cuon alpinus*
21.	Grey Wolf	*Canis lupus*
22.	Jackal *Canis aureus*	

CAPRINES

23.	Argali/Nayan/Great Tibetan Sheep	*Ovis amnion*
24.	Bharal/Blue Sheep	*Pseudois nayaur*
25.	Chinese Goral	*Naemorhedus griseus*
26.	Himalayan Goral	*Naemorhedus goral*
27.	Himalayan Serow	*Capricornis sumatrenis*
28.	Markhor	*Copra falconeri*
29.	Red Goral	*Naemorhedus baileyi*
30.	Red Serow	*Capricornis rubidus*
31.	Siberian/Asiatic/Himalayan Ibex	*Copra sibirica*
32.	Takin	*Budorcas taxicolor*
33.	Urial	*Ovis vignei*

CATS

34.	Asiatic Golden Cat	*Catopuma temminckii*
35.	Asiatic Lion	*Panthera leo persica*
36.	Caracal	*Caracal caracal*
37.	Cheetah	*Acinonyx jubatus*
38.	Clouded Leopard	*Neofelis nebulosi*
39.	Desert Cat	*Felis silvestris*

40.	Eurasian Lynx	*Lynx lynx*
41.	Fishing Cat	*Prionailurus viverrinus*
42.	Jungle Cat	*Felis chaus*
43.	Leopard	*Panthera pardus*
44.	Leopard Cat	*Prionailurus bengalensis*
45.	Marbled Cat	*Pardofelis marmorata*
46.	Pallas's Cat	*Otocolobus manul*
47.	Rusty Spotted Cat	*Prionailurus rubiginosus*
48.	Snow Leopard	*Panthera uncia*
49.	Tiger	*Panthera tigris*

CIVETS

50.	Asian Palm Civet	*Paradoxurus hermaphroditus*
51.	Jerdon's Palm Civet	*Paradoxurus jerdoni*
52.	Large Indian Civet	*Viverra zibetha*
53.	Malabar Large-spotted Civet	*Viverra civettina*
54.	Masked Palm Civet	*Paguma larvata*
55.	Small Indian Civet	*Viverricula indica*
56.	Small-toothed Palm Civet	*Arctogalidia trivirgata*

DEER

57.	Alpine Musk Deer	*Moschus chrysogaster*
58.	Black Musk Deer	*Moschus fuscus*
59.	Himalayan Musk Deer	*Moschus leucogaster*
60.	Hog Deer	*Axis porcinus*
61.	Indian Chevrotain/Mouse Deer	*Moschiola indica*
62.	Kashmir Musk Deer	*Moschus cupreus*
63.	Kashmir Red Deer/Hangul	*Cervus hangul*
64.	Manipur Brow-antlered Deer/Thamin	*Rucervus eldii eldii*
65.	Sambar	*Rusa unicolor*
66.	Swamp Deer/Barasingha	*Rucervus duvaucelii*

67.	Northern Red Muntjak	*Muntiacus vaginalis*
68.	Leaf Muntjak	*Muntiacus putaoensis*
69.	Malabar Red Muntjak	*Muntiacus malabaricus*

DOLPHINS

70.	Fraser's Dolphin	*Lagenodelphis hosei*
71.	Gangetic/South Asian River Dolphin	*Platanista gangetica*
72.	Indo-Pacific Bottlenose Dolphin	*Tursiops aduncus*
73	Indo-Pacific hump-back Dolphin	*Sousa chinensis*
74.	Indus River Dolphin	*Platanista minor*
75.	Irrawady Dolphin	*Orcaella brevirostris*
76.	Pantropical Spinner Dolphin	*Stenella longirostris*
77.	Pantropical Spotted Dolphin	*Stenella attenuata*
78.	Risso's Dolphin	*Grampus griseus*
79.	Rough-toothed Dolphin	*Steno bredanensis*
80.	Short-beaked Saddleback Dolphin/Common Dolphin	*Delphinus delphis*
81.	Striped Dolphin	*Stenella coeruleoalba*

DUGONG

| 82. | Dugong/Sea Cow | *Dugong dugon* |

ELEPHANT

| 83. | Asiatic Elephant | *Elephas maximus* |

FOXES

84.	Bengal Fox	*Vulpes bengalensis*
85.	Red Fox	*Vulpes vulpes*
86.	Tibetan Sand Fox	*Vulpes ferrilata*

HARES

| 87. | Hispid Hare | *Caprolagus hispidus* |

HOGS
88. Pygmy Hog   *Porcula salvania*

HYAENA
89. Striped Hyaena   *Hyaena hyaena*

LINSANG
90. Spotted Linsang   *Prionodon pardicolor*

MARMOTS
91. Himalayan Marmot   *Marmota himalayana*
92. Long-tailed Marmot   *Marmota caudata*

MARTENS
93. Nilgiri Marten   *Martes gwatkinsii*
94. Stone/Beech Marten   *Maries foina*
95. Himalayan Yellow-throated Marten   *Martes flavigula*

MONGOOSES
96. Small Indian Mongoose   *Urva auropunctata*
97. Grey Mongoose   *Urva edwardsii*
98. Brown Mongoose   *Urva fuscu*
99. Javan Mongoose   *Urva javanica*
100. Ruddy Mongoose   *Urva smithii*
101. Crab-eating Mongoose   *Urva urva*
102. Stripe-necked Mongoose   *Urva vitticolla*

OTTERS
103. Eurasian Otter   *Lutra lutra*
104. Oriental Small-clawed Otter *Aonyx cinereal*
105. Smooth-coated Otter   *Lutrogale perspicillata*

OTHER RODENTS
106. Bonhote's Mouse   *Mus famulus*
107. Nilgiri Vandeleuria/Nilgiri Long-tailed Tree Mouse *Vandeleuria nilagirica*
108. Large Rock Rat/Elvira Rat   *Cremnomys Elvira*

109.	Hume's Hadromys/Hume's Rat	*Hadromys humei*
110.	Large Metad/Kondana Rat	*Millardia kondana*
111.	Miller's Nicobar Rat	*Rattus burrus*
112.	Ranjini's Rat	*Rattus ranjiniae*

PANGOLINS

113.	Indian Pangolin	*Manis crassicaudata*
114.	Chinese Pangolin	*Manis pentadactyla*

PIG

115.	Andaman Wild Pig	*Sus scrofa andamanensis*

PIKA

116.	Royle's Pika	*Ochotona roylei*

PORPOISE

117.	Finless Porpoise	*Neophocaena phocaenoides*

PORCUPINES

118.	Asiatic Brush-tailed Porcupine	*Atherurus macrourus*
119.	Himalayan Crestless Porcupine	*Hystrix brachyura*
120.	Indian Porcupine	*Hystrix indica*

PRIMATES

121.	Arunachal Macaque	*Macaca munzala*
122.	Assamese Macaque	*Macaca assamensis*
123.	Bengal Slow Loris	*Nycticebus bengalensis*
124.	Black-footed Gray Langur	*Semnopithecus hypoleucos*
125.	Bonnet Macaque	*Macaca radiata*
126.	Capped Langur	*Trachypithecus pileatus*
127.	Gee's Golden Langur	*Trachypithecus geei*
128.	Gray Slender Loris	*Loris lydekkerianus*
129.	Hoolock Gibbon	*Hoolock hoolock*
130.	Kashmir Gray Langur	*Semnopithecus ajax*

131.	Lion-Tailed Macaque	*Macaca Silenus*
132.	Nepal Gray Langur	*Semnopithecus schistaceus*
133.	Nicobar Long-tailed Macaque	*Macaca fascicularis umbrosus*
134.	Nilgiri Langur	*Semnopithecus johnii*
135.	Northern Pig-tailed Macaque	*Macaca leonine*
136.	Phayre's Leaf Monkey	*Trachypithecus phayrei*
137.	Sela macaque	*Macaca selai*
138.	Stump-tailed macaque	*Macaca arctoides*
139.	Tarai Gray Langur	*Semnopithecus hector*
140.	Tufted Gray Langur	*Semnopithecus priam*
141.	White-cheeked Macaque	*Macaca leucogenys*

RED PANDA

| 142. | Himalaya Red Panda | *Ailurus fulgens* |
| 143. | Chinese Red Panda | *Ailurus styani* |

RHINOCEROS

| 144. | Indian/Greater One-horned Rhinoceros | *Rhinoceros unicornis* |

SQUIRRELS

145.	Hairy-footed Flying Squirrel	*Belomys pearsonii*
146.	Namdhapa Flying Squirrel	*Biswamoyopterus biswasi*
147.	Woolly Flying Squirrels	*All species of the Genus Eupetaurus*
148.	Giant Flying Squirrels	*All species of the Genus Petaurista*
149.	Malabar/Indian Giant Squirrel	*Ratufa indica*
150.	Malayan Giant Squirrel	*Ratufa bicolor*
151.	Grizzled Giant Squirrel	*Ratufa macroura*
152.	Travancore Flying Squirrel	*Petinomys fuscocapillus*

SHREWS

| 153. | Andaman Shrew | *Crocidura andamanensis* |
| 154. | Day's Shrew | *Suncus dayi* |

155.	Himalayan Tahr	*Hemitragus jemlahicus*
156.	NilgiriTahr	*Nilgiritragus hylocrius*

TREESHREWS

157.	Nicobar Treeshrew	*Tupaia nicobarica*

WHALES

158.	Common Minke Whale	*Balaenoptera acutorostrata*
159.	Sei Whale	*Balaenoptera borealis*
160.	Bryde's Whale	*Balaenoptera edeni*
161.	Blue Whale	*Balaenoptera musculus*
162.	Fin Whale	*Balaenoptera physalus*
163.	Humpback Whale	*Megaptera novaeangliae*
164.	Pygmy Killer Whale	*Feresa attenuate*
165.	Short-finned Pilot Whale	*Globicephala macrorhynchus*
166.	Killer Whale	*Orcinus orca*
167.	Melon-headed Whale	*Peponocephala electra*
168.	False Killer Whale	*Pseudorca crassidens*
169.	Sperm Whale/Cachalot	*Physeter macrocephalus*
170.	Pygmy Sperm Whale	*Kogia breviceps*
171.	Dwarf Sperm Whale	*Kogia sima*
172.	Blainville's Beaked Whale	*Mesoplodon densirostris*
173.	Ginkgo-toothed Beaked Whale	*Mesoplodon ginkgodens*
174.	Cuvier's Beaked Whale	*Ziphius cavirostris*

WILD CATTLE

175.	Gaur/Indian Bison	*Bos gaurus*
176.	Wild Yak	*Bos mutus*
177.	Wild Water Buffalo	*Bubalus arnee*

WILD ASS

178.	Indian Wild Ass	*Equus hemionus*

| 179. | Tibetan Wild Ass | *Equus kiang* |

WEASELS

180.	Mountain Weasel	*Mustela altaica*
181.	Siberian Weasel	*Mustela sibirica*
182.	Yellow-bellied Weasel	*Mustela kathiah*
183.	Ermine or Short-tailed Weasel	Mustela erminea

PART B: BIRDS

Sl. No.	Common name	Scientific name

BARN OWLS

| 1. | Andaman Barn Owl | *Tyto deroepstorffi* |
| 2. | Common Barn Owl | *Tyto alba* |

BITTERNS, HERONS AND EGRETS

3.	Cinnamon Bittern	*Ixobrychus cinnamomeus*
4.	White-bellied Heron	*Ardea insignis*
5.	White-eared Night Heron	*Gorsachius magnificus*

BUNTINGS

| 6. | Yellow-breasted Bunting | *Emberiza aureola* |

BUSTARDS

7.	Bengal Florican	*Houbaropsis bengalensis*
8.	Great Indian Bustard	*Ardeotis nigriceps*
9.	Lesser Florican	*Sypheotides indicus*

| 10. | Little Bustard | *Tetrax tetrax* |
| 11. | Macqueen's Bustard | *Chlamydotis macqueenii* |

CISTICOLAS, PRINIAS, AND ALLIES
| 12. | Grey-crowned Prinia | *Prinia cinereocapilla* |
| 13. | Rufous-fronted Prinia | *Prinia buchanani* |

COURSERS AND PRATINCOLES
| 14. | Indian Courser | *Cursorius coromandelicus* |
| 15. | Jerdon's Courser | *Rhinoptilus bitorquatus* |

CRANES
16.	Black-necked Crane	*Grus nigricollis*
17.	Common Crane	*Grus grus*
18.	Demoiselle Crane	*Grus virgo*
19.	Hooded Crane	*Grus monachal*
20.	Sarus Crane	*Antigone antigone*
21.	Siberian Crane	*Leucogeranus leucogeranus*

CROWS AND ALLIES
| 22. | Andaman Treepie | *Dendrocitta bayleii* |

DUCKS, GEESE, AND SWANS
23.	Andaman Teal	*Anas albogularis*
24.	Baer's Pochard	*Aythya baeri*
25.	Common Pochard	*Aythya farina*
26.	Cotton Pygmy Goose	*Nettapus coromandelianus*
27.	Fulvous Whistling Duck	*Dendrocygna bicolor*

28.	Marbled Teal	*Marmaronetta angustirostris*
29.	Pink-headed Duck	*Rhodonessa caryophyllacea*
30.	White-headed Duck	*Oxyura leucocephala*
31.	White-winged Wood Duck	*Asarcornis scutulata*

FALCONS

32.	Amur Falcon	*Falco amurensis*
33.	Laggar Falcon	*Falco jugger*
34.	Peregrine Falcon	*Falco peregrinus*
35.	Red-necked Falcon	*Falco chicquera*
36.	Saker Falcon	*Falco cherrug*

FINFOOTS

37.	Masked Finfoot	*Heliopais personatus*

FLYCATCHERS, CHATS AND ALLIES

38.	Chinese Rubythroat	*Calliope tschebaiewi*
39.	Hodgson's Bushchat	*Saxicola insignis*
40.	Kashmir Flycatcher	*Ficedula subrubra*
41.	Large Blue Flycatcher	*Cyornis magnirostris*
42.	Nilgiri Sholakili	*Sholicola major*
43.	White-bellied Sholakili	*Sholicola albiventris*

FRIGATEBIRDS

44.	Christmas Island Frigatebird	*Fregata andrewsi*

FROGMOUTHS

45.	Hodgson's Frogmouth	*Batrachostomus hodgsoni*
46.	Sri Lanka Frogmouth	*Batrachostomus moniliger*

GULLS AND TERNS

47.	Black-bellied Tern	*Sterna acuticauda*
48.	Gull-billed Tern	*Gelochelidon nilotica*
49.	Indian Skimmer	*Rynchops albicollis*
50.	River Tern	*Sterna aurantia*

HORNBILLS

51.	Austen's Brown Hornbill	*Anorrhinus austeni*
52.	Great Hornbill	*Buceros bicornis*
53.	Malabar Grey Hornbill	*Ocyceros griseus*
54.	Malabar Pied Hornbill	*Anthracoceros coronatus*
55.	Narcondam Hornbill	*Rhyticeros narcondami*
56.	Oriental Pied Hornbill	*Anthracoceros albirostris*
57.	Rufous-necked Hornbill	*Aceros nipalensis*
58.	Wreathed Hornbill	*Rhyticeros undulatus*

IBISBILL

59.	Eurasian Spoonbill	*Platalea leucorodia*
60.	Ibisbill	*Ibidorhyncha Struthersii*

KINGFISHERS

61.	Blyth's Kingfisher	*Alcedo hercules*

KITES, HAWKS, EAGLES AND VULTURES

62.	Andaman Serpent Eagle	*Spilornis elgini*
63.	Bearded Vulture	*Gypaetus barbatus*
64.	Besra	*Accipiter virgatus*
65.	Black Baza	*Aviceda leuphotes*
66.	Black Eagle	*Ictinaetus malaiensis*
67.	Bonelli's Eagle	*Aquila fasciata*
68.	Booted Eagle	*Hieraaetus pennatus*
69.	Brahminy Kite	*Haliastur indus*
70.	Changeable Hawk Eagle	*Nisaetus cirrhatus*
71.	Chinese Sparrowhawk	*Accipiter soloensis*
72.	Cinereous Vulture	*Aegypius monachus*
73.	Common Buzzard	*Buteo buteo*
74.	Crested Goshawk	*Accipiter trivirgatus*
75.	Crested Serpent Eagle	*Spilomis cheela*

76.	Eastern Imperial Eagle	*Aquila heliacal*
77.	Eastern Marsh Harrier	*Circus spilonotus*
78.	Egyptian Vulture	*Neophron percnopterus*
79.	Eurasian Sparrowhawk	*Accipiter nisus*
80.	Golden Eagle	*Aquila chrysaetos*
81.	Greater Spotted Eagle	*Clanga clanga*
82.	Grey-faced Buzzard	*Butastur indicus*
83.	Grey-headed Fish Eagle	*Haliaeetus ichthyaetus*
84.	Griffon Vulture	*Gyps.fulvus*
85.	Hen Harrier	*Circus cyaneus*
86.	Himalayan Buzzard	*Buteo refectus*
87.	Himalayan Vulture	*Gyps himalayensis*
88.	Indian Spotted Eagle	*Clanga hastata*
89.	Indian Vulture	*Gyps indicus*
90.	Japanese Sparrowhawk	*Accipiter gularis*
91.	Jerdon's Baza	*Avicedajerdoni*
92.	Lesser Fish Eagle	*Icthyophaga humilis*
93.	Long-legged Buzzard	*Buteo rufinus*
94.	Montagu's Harrier	*Circuspygargus*
95.	Mountain Hawk Eagle	*Nisaetus nipalensis*
96.	Nicobar Serpent Eagle	*Spilomis klossi*
97.	Nicobar Sparrowhawk	*Accipiter butleri*
98.	Northern Goshawk	*Accipiter gentilis*
99.	Pallas's Fish Eagle	*Haliaeetus leucoryphus*
100.	Pallid Harrier	*Circus macrourus*
101.	Pied Harrier	*Circus melanoleucos*
102.	Red Kite	*Milvus milvus*
103.	Red-headed Vulture	*Sarcogyps calvus*
104.	Rufous-bellied Eagle	*Lophotriorchis kienerii*

105.	Shikra	*Accipiter badius*
106.	Short-toed Snake Eagle	*Circaetus gallicus*
107.	Slender-billed Vulture	*Gyps tenuirostris*
108.	Steppe Eagle	*Aquila nipalensis*
109.	Tawny Eagle	*Aquila rapax*
110.	Upland Buzzard	*Buteo hemilasius*
111.	Western Marsh Harrier	*Circus aeruginosus*
112.	White-bellied Sea Eagle	*Haliaeetus leucogaster*
113.	White-eyed Buzzard	*Butastur teesa*
114.	White-rumped Vulture	*Gyps bengalensis*
115.	White-tailei Sea Eagle	*Haliaeetus albicilla*

LAUGIDNGTHRUSHES AND LARGE

BABBLERS

116.	Ashambu Laughingthrush	*Montecincla*
117.	Banasura Laughingthrush	*meridionalis Montecinclajerdoni*
118.	Bar-winged Wren Babbler	*Spelaeornis*
119.	Brown-capped Laughingthrush	*troglodytoides Trochalopteron austeni*
120.	Bugun Liocichla	*Liocichla bugunorum*
121.	Chestnut-backed Laughingthrush	*Pterorhinus nuchalis*
122.	Grey-sided Laughingthrush	*Pterorhinus caerulatus*
123.	Jerdon's Babbler	*Chrysomma altirostre*
124.	Moustached Laughingthrush	*Ianthocincla cineracea*
125.	Nilgiri Laughingthrush	*Montecincla*
126.	Sikkim Wedge-billed Babbler	*cachinnans Stachyris humei*

127.	Slender-billed Babbler	*Argya longirostris*
128.	Snowy-throated Babbler	*Stachyris oglei*
129.	Tawny-breasted Wren Babbler	*Spelaeornis longicaudatus*

LOCUSTELLA WARBLERS AND ALLIES

130.	Bristled Grassbird	*Schoenicola striatus*
131.	Broad-tailed Grassbird	*Schoenicola platyurus*
132.	West Himalayan Bush Warbler	*Locustella kashmirensis*

MEGAPODES

133.	Nicobar Megapode	*Megapodius Nicobariensis*

MINIVETS AND CUCKOOSHRIKES

134.	Small Minivet	*Pericrocotus cinnamomeus*

MUNIAS

135.	Green Munia	*Amandava Formosa*

NUTHATCHES

136.	Beautiful Nuthatch	*Sitta formosa*

OSPREY

137.	Osprey	*Pandion haliaetus*

OWLS

138.	Brown Fish Owl	*Ketupa zeylonensis*
139.	Brown Wood Owl	*Strix leptogrammica*
140.	Buffy Fish Owl	*Ketupa ketupu*

141.	Eurasian Eagle Owl	*Bubo bubo*
142.	Forest Owlet	*Athene blewitti*
143.	Indian Eagle Owl	*Bubo bengalensis*
144.	Mottled Wood Owl	*Strix ocellate*
145.	Northern Long-eared Owl	*Asio otus*
146.	Short-eared Owl	*Asio flammeu*
147.	Spot-bellied Eagle Owl	*Bubo nipalensis*
148.	Tawny Fish Owl	*Ketupa flavipes*

PARROTBILLS AND ALLIES

149.	Black-breasted Parrotbill	*Paradoxornis flavirostris*

PARROTS & PARAKEETS

150.	Lord Derby's Parakeet	*Psittacula derbiana*
151.	Red-breasted Parakeet	*Psittacula alexandri*

PARTRIDGES, QUAILS, AND PHEASANTS

152.	Blood Pheasant	*Ithaginis cruentus*
153.	Blyth's Tragopan	*Tragopan blythii*
154.	Cheer Pheasant	*Catretts wallichii*
155.	Chestnut-breasted Partridge	*Arborophila mandellii*
156.	Green Peafowl	*Pavo muticus*
157.	Grey Junglefowl	*Gallus sonneratii*
158.	Grey Peacock Pheasant	*Polyplectron bicalcaratum*
159.	Himalayan Monal	*Lophophorus impejanus*
160.	Himalayan Quail	*Ophrysia superciliosa*
161.	Indian Peafowl	*Pavo cristatus*
162.	Kalij Pheasant	*Lophura leucomelanos*
163.	Manipur Bush Quail	*Perdicula manipurensis*
164.	MountaiWBamboo Partridge	*Bambusicola fytchii*
165.	Mrs Hume's Pheasant	*Syrmaticus humiae*

166.	Satyr Tragopan	*Tragopan satyra*
167.	Sclater's Monal	*Lophophorus sclateri*
168.	Swamp Francolin	*Francolinus gularis*
169.	Temminck's Tragopan	*Tragopan temminckii*
170.	Tibetan Ear Pheasant	*Crossoptilon harmani*
171.	Tibetan Partridge	*Perdix hodgsoniae*
172.	Tibetan Snowcock	*Tetraogallus tibetanus*
173.	Western Tragopan	*Tragopan melanocephalus*

PIGEONS AND DOVES

174.	Andaman Green Pigeon	*Treron chloropterus*
175.	Nicobar Pigeon	*Caloenas nicobarica*
176.	Nilgiri Wood Pigeon	*Columba elphinstonii*
177.	Pale-capped Pigeon	*Columba punicea*
178.	Yellow-eyed Pigeon	*Columba eversmanni*

PIPITS AND WAGTAILS

179.	Forest Wagtail	*Dendronanthus indicus*
180.	Nilgiri Pipit	*Anthus nilghiriensis*

PLOVERS AND LAPWINGS

181.	Pacific Golden Plover.	*Pluvialis falva*
182.	Sociable Lapwing	*Vanellus gregarious*

SANDPIPERS

183.	Common Greenshank.	*Tringa nebularia*
184.	Great Knot	*Calidris tenuirostris*
185.	Spoon-billed Sandpiper	*Calidris pygmaea*
186.	Wood Snipe	*Gallinago nemoricola*

SCIMITAR BABBLERS AND ALLIES

187.	Mishmi Wren Babbler	*Spelaeornis badeigularis*
188.	Naga Wren Babbler	*Spelaeornis chocolatinus*

SMALL BABBLERS, FULVETTAS AND ALLIES

189.	Marsh Babbler	*Pellomeum palustre*
190.	Rufous-vented Grass Babbler	*Laticilla burnesii*
191.	Swamp Grass Babbler	*Laticilla cinerascens*

STARLINGS AND MYNA

192.	Common Hill Myna	*Gracula religiosa*
193.	Southern Hill Myna	*Gracula indica*

STORKS

194.	Greater Adjutant	*Leptoptilos dubius*
195.	Lesser Adjutant	*Leptoptilos javanicus*
196.	White Stork	*Ciconia Ciconia*

SWIFTS

197.	Crested Treeswift	*Hemiprocne coronata*
198.	Dark-rumped Swift	*Apus acuticauda*
199.	Glossy Swiftlet	*Collocalia esculenta*
200.	Indian Swiftlet	*Aerodramus unicolor*

THRUSHES AND ALLIES

201.	Nilgiri Thrush	*Zoothera neilgherriensis*

TROGONS

202.	Ward's Trogon	*Harpactes wardi*

TITS

203.	White-naped Tit	*Machlolophus nuchalis*

WEAVERS

204.	Finn's Weaver	*Ploceus Megarhynchus*

WOODPECKERS AND ALLIES

205. Andaman Woodpecker — *Dryocopus hodgei*

206. Great Slaty Woodpecker — *Mulleripicus pulverulentus*

207. Heart-spotted Woodpecker — *Hemicircus canente*

208. Yellow-crowned Woodpecker — *Leiopicus Mahrattensis*

PART C: REPTILES

S.No.	Common Name	Scientific Name
	BOAS	
1.	Red Sand Boa	*Eryx johnii*
2.	Whitaker's Boa	*Eryx whitakeri*
	CROCODILES	
3.	Gharial	*Gavialis gangeticus*
4.	Marsh Crocodile	*Crocodylus palustris*
5.	Saltwater Crocodile	*Crocodylus porosus*
	CHAMELEON	
6.	Indian Chameleon	*Chamaeleo zeylanicus*
	GECKOS	
7.	Andaman Giant gecko	*Gekko verreauxi*
8.	Bangalore Geckoella	*Cyrtodactylus srilekhae*
9.	Horsfield's Gliding Gecko	*Gekko horsfieldii*
10.	Indian Golden Gecko	*Calodactylodes aureus*

11.	Jeypore Ground Gecko	*Cyrtodactylus jeyporensis*
12.	Leopard Geckos / Eyelid Geckos	All species of the Genus *Eublepharis*
13.	Nicobar Gliding Gecko	*Gekko nicobarensis*
14.	Rishi Valley Geckoella	*Cyrtodactylus rishivalleyensis*
15.	Smith's Green-eyed Gecko	*Gekko smithii*
16.	Smooth-backed Gliding Gecko	*Gekko lionotum*
17.	Tokay Gecko	*Gekko gecko*

KING COBRA

18..	Indian Cobras	All species of the Genus *Naja*
19.	King Cobra	All species of the Genus *Ophiophagus*

LIZARDS

20.	Indian Spiny Tailed Lizard	*Saara hardwickii*

MONITORS

21.	Bengal Monitor	*Varanus bengalensis*
22.	Desert Monitor	*Varanus griseus*
23.	Water Monitor	*Varanus salvator*
24.	Yellow Monitor	*Varanus␣flavescens*

OTHER SNAKES

25.	Checkered Keelback	*Fowlea piscator*
26.	Dhaman or Indian Rat Snake	*Ptyas mucosa*

#	Common Name	Scientific Name
27.	Dog-faced Water Snake	*Cerberus rynchops*
28.	Indian Egg Eating Snake	*Boiga westennanni*
29.	Olive Keelback Water Snake	*Atretium schistosum*
30.	Russell's Viper	*Daboia russelii*

PYTHONS

#	Common Name	Scientific Name
31.	Pythons	All species of the Genus *Python*
32.	Reticulated Python	*Malayopython reticulates*

TURTLES & TORTOISES

#	Common Name	Scientific Name
33.	Arnboina Box Turtle	*Cuora amboinensis*
34.	Asian Giant Softshell Turtle	*Pelochelys cantorii*
35.	Asian Giant Tortoise	*Manouria emys*
36.	Asiatic Softshell Turtle	*Amyda cartilaginea*
37.	Assam Roofed Turtle	*Pangshura sylhetensis*
38.	Black Softshell Turtle	*Nilssonia nigricans*
39.	Cochin Forest Cane Turtle	*Vijayachelys silvatica*
40.	Crowned River Turtle	*Hardella thurjii*
41.	Green Sea Turtle	*Chelonia mydas*
42.	Hawksbill Turtle	*Eretmochelys imbricata*
43.	Indian EyedTurtle	*Morenia petersi*
44.	Indian Flap Shell Turtle	*Lissemys punctata*
45.	Indian Narrow-headed Softshell Turtle	*Chitra indica*
46.	Indian Roofed Turtle	*Pangshura tecta*
47.	Indian Softshell Turtle	*Nilssonia gangetica*
48.	Indian Star Tortoise	*Geochelone elegans*
49.	Indian Tent Turtle	*Pangshura tentoria*
50.	Keeled box Turtle	*Cuora mouhotii*
51.	Leatherback Turtle	*Dermochelys coriacea*

No.	Common Name	Scientific Name
52.	Leith's Softshell Turtle	*Nilssonia leithii*
53.	Loggerhead Turtle	*Caretta caretta*
54.	Northern River Terrapin	*Batagur baska*
55.	Olive Ridley Sea Turtle	*Lepidochelys olivacea*
56.	Peacock Softshell Turtle	*Nilssonia hurum*
57.	Red-crowned Roofed Turtle	*Batagur kachuga*
58.	Sal forest Tortoise	*Indotestudo elongata*
59.	Spotted Pond Turtle	*Geoclemys amiltonii*
60.	Three-striped Roofed Turtle	*Batagur dhongoka*
61.	Travancore Tortoise	*Indotestudo travancorica*
62.	Tricarinate Hill Turtle	*Melanochelys tricarinata*

PART D: AMPHIBIANS

No.	Common Name	Scientific Name
1.	Crocodile Newt	*Tylototriton verrucosus*
2.	Himalayan Salamander	*Tylototriton himalayanus*
3.	Koyna Toad	*Xanthophryne koynayensis*
4.	Purple Frogs	All species of the Genus *Nasikabatrachus*

PART E: FISHES

No.	Common Names	Scientific Name
GROUPER		
1.	Giant Grouper	*Epinephelus lanceolatus*
SEAHORSES		
2.	Seahorses and Pipefishes	All species in the Family *Syngnathidae*
RAYS		
3.	Bottlenose Wedgefish	*Rhynchobatus australiae*
4.	Bowmouth Guitarfish	*Rhina ancylostoma*

5.	Clubnose Guitarfish	*Glaucostegus thouin*
6.	Ganges Stingray	*Himantura fluviatilis*
7.	Giant Freshwater Whipray	*Urogymnus polylepis*
8.	Giant Guitarfish	*Rhynchobatus djiddensis*
9.	Giant Manta	*Mobula birostris*
10.	Porcupine Whipray	*Urogymnus asperrimus*
11.	Reef Manta	*Mobula alfredi*
12.	Smoothnose Wedgefish	*Rhynchobatus laevis*
13.	Widenose Guitarfish	*Glaucostegus obtusus*

SAWFISHES

14.	Common sawfish	*Pristis pristis*
15.	Dwarf sawfish	*Pristis clavata*
16.	Green Sawfish	*Pristis zijsron*
17.	Nanuw Sawfish	*Anoxypristis cuspidate*

SHARKS

18.	Gangetic Shark	*Glyphis gangeticus*
19.	Pondicherry Shark	*Carcharhinus hemiodon*
20.	Whale Shark	*Rhincodon typus*

PART F: ECHINODERMATA

No.	Common Name	Scientific Name
1.	Sea Cucumber	All species of the Class *Holothuroidea*

PART G: MOLLUSCA

No.	Common Name	Scientific Name

CLAMS

| 1. | Auted Giant Clam | *Tridacna squamosa* |
| 2. | Horse's Hoof Clam | *Hippopus hippopus* |

3. Small Giant Clam *Tridacna maxima*

CONES

4. Glory of India *Conus milneedwardsi*

HELMET SHELLS

5. Homed Helmet Shell/ King Shell *Cassis comuta*

NAUTILUS

6. Emperor Nautilus/ Chambered nautilus *Nautilus pompilius*

SHELLS

7. Bull Mouth Helmet/ Queenshell *Cypraecassis rufa*

TRUMPETS

8. Triton's Trumpet shell *Charania tritonis*

SPIRALS

9. Spiral Tudicla *Tudicla spirillus*

PART H: ARTHROPODS (OTHER THAN INSECTS)

No.	Common Name	Scientific Name
1.	Coconut or Robber Crab	*Birgus latro*

PART I: BUTTERFLIES(LEPIDOPTERA)

No.	Common name Family	Scientific name

Lycaenidae

1. Andaman Tailless *Arhopala zeta*

Oakblue

2. Blue Posy *Drupadia scaeva*
3. Broad banded *Simiskina phalena*

Brilliant

4. Cachar Mandarine *Charana cepheis*

Blue

5. Chapman's Hedge *Notarthrinus binghami*

Blue

6. Chestnut-and-plack *Tajuria yajna*

Royal

7. Chinese Hairstreak *Amblopala avidiena*
8. Chocolate Bushblue *Arhopala ariel*
9. Comic Oak.blue *Arhopala comica*
10. Ferrar's Cerulean *Jamides ferrari*
11. Ferruginous *Ahlbergia leechii*

Hairstreak

12. Great Brownie *Gerydus symethus*
13. Great Dark.ie *Allotinus drumila*
14. Hybrid Sapphire *Heliophorus hybrida*
15. Kanara Oakblue *Arhopala alea*
16. Mackwood 's *Strymon mackwoodi*

Hairstreak

17. Moth Butterfly *Liphyra brassolis*
18. Naga Hedge Blue *Oreolyce dohertyi*
19. Opal Oakblue *Arhopala opalina*
20. Paona Hairstreak *Shirozuozephyrus paona*
21. Peacock Hairstreak *Euaspa pavo*
22. Plain Tailless Oak.blue *Arhopala asopia*
23. Purple-brown Tailless *Arhopala arvina*

Oak.blue

24. Tytler's Dull Oakblue *Arhopala ace*
25. Watson's Hairstreak *Theda letha*
26. Watson's Mottle *Logania watsoniana*

Family Nympbalidae

27.	Andaman King Crow	*Euploea midamus roepstorffi*
28.	Bamboo Tree Brown	*Letheeuropa*
29.	Banded Duffer	*Discophora deo*
30.	Bhutan Sergeant	*Athyma jina*
31.	Bhutan Treebrown	*Lethemargaritae*
32.	Blue Baron	*Euthalia telchinia*
33.	Blue Begam	*Prothoe franck regalis*
34.	Blue Duke	*Euthalia durga*
35.	Blue Nawab	*Polyura schreiber*
36.	Branded Yeoman	*Algiafasciata*
37.	Camberwell Beauty	*Nymphalis antiopa yedanula*
38.	Chestnut Rajah	*Charaxes dumfordi*
39.	Commc;)ll Duffer	*Discophora sondaica*
40.	Dark Wall	*Lasiommata menava*
41.	Dismal Mystic	*Letheocellata*
42.	Dull Forester	*Lethegulnihal*
43.	Eastern Courtier	*Sophisa chandra*
44.	Empress	*Sasakia funebris*
45.	Freak	*Calinaga buddha*
46.	Fuliginous Sailer	*Neptisebusa ebusa*
47.	Golden Emperor	*Dillpamorgiana*
48.	Grand Duke	*Euthalia iva*
49.	Hockeystick Sailer	*Neptisnycteus*
50.	Hockeystick Sailer	*Phaedyma aspasia*
51.	Malay Staff Sergeant	*Athyma reta moorei*

52.	Malayan Nawab	*Polyura moori sandakana*
53.	Manipur Fivering	*Ypthima persimilis*
54.	Mottled Argus	*Loxerebia narasirigha*
55.	Naga Duke	*Euthalia curvifascia*
56.	Northern Jungle Queen	*Stichophthalma camadeva*
57.	Orchid Tit	*Chlioria othona*
58.	Pallid Forester	*Lethe satyavati*
59.	Peal's Palmfly	*Elymnias peali*
60.	Pointed Palmfly	*Elymnias penaga*
61.	Purple Bushbrown	*Mycalesis orseis*
62.	Scarce Blue Tiger	*Tirumala gautama*
63.	Scarce Catseye	*Coelites nothis*
64.	Scarce Jester	*Symbrenthia silana*
65.	Scarce Lilacfork	*Lethe dura*
66.	Scarce Red Forester	*Lethe distans*
67.	Scarce Siren	*Hestina nicevillei*
68.	Scarce White Commodore	*Sumalia zulema*
69.	Single Silverstripe	*Lethe ramadeva*
70.	Spotted Black Crow	*Euploea crameri*
71.	Tawny Emperor	*Chitoria ulupi*
72.	Tytler's Emperor	*Eulaceura manipurensis*
73.	Tytler's Treebrown	*Lethe gemina*
74.	White Emperor	*Helcyra hemina*
75.	White Spot Fritilliary	*Argynnis hegmone*

Family Papilionidae

76.	Banded Apollo	*Parnassius delphius*
77.	Black Windmill	*Byasa crassipes*
78.	Chinese Windmill	*Byasa plutonius*
79.	Common Clubtail	*Losaria coon*
80.	de Niceville's Windmill	*Byasa polla*
81.	Hannyngton Apollo	*Pamassius hannyngtoni*
82.	Himalayan Bhutan Glory	*Bhutanitis lidderdalii*
83.	Imperial Apollo	*Pamassius imperator*
84.	Kaiser-i-Hind	*Teinopalpus imperialis*
85.	Krishna Peacock	*Papilio krishna*
86.	Ladak Banded Apollo	*Parnassius stoliczkanus*
87.	Malabar Banded Swallowtail	*Papilio liomedon*
88.	Mystical Bhutan	*Bhutanitis ludlowi*Glory
89.	Nevill's Windmill	*Byasa nevilli*
90.	Varnished Apollo	*Parnassius acco*
91.	Yellow-crested Spangle	*Papilio elephenor*

Family Pieridae

92.	Butler's Dwarf	*Baltia butleri*
93.	Dwarf Clouded Yellow	*Colias dubia*
94.	Green Banded White	*Pieris krueperi*

| 95. | Lemon Clouded Yellow | *Colias thrasibulus* |
| 96. | Pale Jezabel | *Delias sanaca.* |

PART J: ODONATA (DRAGONFLY)

No.	Common name	Scientific name
1.	Himalayan Relict Dragonfly	*Epiophlebia laidlawi*

PART K : CORALS

No.	Common name	Scientific name
1.	Black Coral	All species of the Order *Antipatharia*
2.	Blue Coral	All species from the following Families in the Order *Helioporacea: Aulopsammiidae, Helioporidae,* and *Lithotelestidae*
3.	False Corals	All species of the Order *Corallimorpharia*
4.	Fire Coral	All species of the Genus *Millepora*
5.	Organ Pipe Coral	*Tubipora musica*
6.	Sea Anemones	All species from the following Families in the Order *Actiniaria: Actinernidae, Halcuriidae,* and *Edwardsiidae*
7.	Sea Pens	All species from the following Families in the Order *Pennatulacea: Anthoptilidae, Chunellidae, Echinoptilidae, Funiculinidae, Kophobelemnidae, Protoptilidae, Pse udumbell ulidae, Renillidae, Scleroptilidae, Stachyptilidae, Umbellutidae, Veretiltidae, Balticinidae, Pennatulidae,* and *Virgulariidae*
8.	Soft Corals	All species from the following Families in the Order *Alcyonacea:Acanthoaxiidae, Chelidonisididae, Pa rasphaerascleridae, Nephtheidae, Alcyoniidae, Clavulariidae, Xeniidae, Cornulariidae, Subergorgiidae, Pleaxauridae, Ellisellidae, Melithaeidae,* and *Briareidae*
9.	Stony Coral	All species of the Order *Scleractinia*
10.	Tube-dwelling	All species of the

following Families of the Anemones *Pennatulidae, Anthoptilidae,* Order *Penicillaria* :

Scleroptilidae, Halipteridae, and *Protoptilidae*

11. Tube-dwelling
        Anemones

All species of the Order *Spirularia*

12. Zoanthids   All species of the Order *Zooantharia*

SCHEDULE II

(*See* Sections 9, 11, 12, 38-1, 39, 44, 45, 46, 47, 48, 48A, 49, 50, 51, 54 and 57) PART A: MAMMALS

No.	Common Name	Scientific Name
ANTELOPE		
1.	Nilgai	*Boselaphus tragocamelus*
BADGERS		
2.	Burmese/Large toothed Ferret Badger	*Melogale personal a*
3.	Chinese/Small-toothed Ferret Badger	*Melogale moschata*
BATS		
4.	Durga Das's Leaf-nosed Bat	*Hipposideros durgadasi*
5.	Indian Flying Fox	*Pteropus giganteus*
6.	Mitred Horseshoe Bat	*Rhinolophus mitratus*
7.	Peters's Tubenosed Bat	*Harpiola grisea*
8.	Rainforest Tube-nosed Bat	*Murina pluvialis*
9.	Sombre Bat	*Eptesicus tatei*
CETACEANS		
10.	Cetacean species	All species of the Infraorder *Cetacea* other than those listed in Schedule I
DEER		
11.	Spotted Deer/Chital	*Axis axis*

HARES

12.	Desert Hare	*Lepus tibetanus*
13.	Indian Hare	*Lepus nigricollis*
14.	Woolly Hare	*Lepus oiostolus*

HEDGEHOGS

15.	Bare-bellied Hedgehog	*Paraechinus nudiventris*
16.	Indian Hedgehog	*Paraechinus micropus*
17.	Indian Long-eared Hedgehog	*Hemiechinus collaris*

OTHER RODENTS

18.	Andaman Rat	*Rattus stoicus*
19.	Car Nicobar Rat	*Rattus palmarum*
20.	Cutch Rock Rat	*Cremnomys cutchicus*
21.	Royle's Mountain Vole	*Alticola roylei*
22.	Sahyadris Forest Rat	*Rattus satarae*

PIG

23.	Wild Pig	*Sus scrofa*

PRIMATES

24.	Northern Plains Gray/Hanuman Langur	*Semnopithecus entellus*

SHREWS

25.	Andaman Spiny Shrew	*Crocidura hispida*
26.	Assam Mole Shrew	*Anourosorex assamensis*
27.	Indian Highland Shrew	*Suncus niger*
28.	Jenkin's Shrew	*Crocidura jenkinsi*
29.	Madras Treeshrew	*Anathema ellioti*
30.	Narcondam Shrew	*Crocidura narcondamica*

31.	Nicobar Shrew	*Crocidura nicobarica*

SQUIRRELS

32.	Jungle Palm Squirrel	*Funambulus tristriatus*
33.	Orange-bellied Himalayan Squirrel	*Dremomys lokriah*

TREE MICE

34.	Spiny Tree Mouse	*Platacanthomys lasiurus*

PART B: BIRDS

Sl. No.	Common Name	Scientific Name

ACCENTORS

1.	Alpine Accentor	*Prunella collaris*
2.	Altai Accentor	*Prunella himalayana*
3.	Black-throated Accentor	*Prunella atrogularis*
4.	Brown Accentor	*Prunella fulvescens*
5.	Maroon-backed Accentor	*Prunella immaculata*
6.	Robin Accentor	*Prunella rubeculoides*
7.	Rufous-breasted Accentor	*Prunella strophiata*

BARBETS

8.	Blue-eared Barbet	*Psilopogon duvaucelii*
9.	Blue-throated Barbet	*Psilopogon asiaticus*
10.	Brown-headed Barbet	*Psilopogon zeylanicus*
11.	Coppersmith Barbet	*Psilopogon haemacephalus*
12.	Golden-throated Barbet	*Psilopogon franklinii*
13.	Great Barbet	*Psilopogon virens*
14.	Lineated Barbet	*Psilopogon lineatus*
15.	Malabar Barbet	*Psilopogon malabaricus*
16.	White-cheeked Barbet	*Psilopogon viridis*

BARN OWLS

17.	Eastern Grass Owl	*Tyto longimembris*
18.	Oriental Bay Owl	*Phodilus badius*
19.	Sri Lanka Bay Owl	*Phodilus assimilis*

BEE-EATERS

20.	Blue-bearded Bee-eater	*Nyctyornis athertoni*
21.	Blue-cheeked Bee-eater	*Merops persicus*
22.	Blue-tailed Bee-eater	*Merops philippinus*
23.	Blue-throated Bee-eater	*Merops viridis*
24.	Chestnut-headed Bee-eater	*Merops leschenaulti*
25.	European Bee-eater	*Merops apiaster*
26.	Green Bee-eater	*Merops orientalis*

BITTERNS, HERONS AND EGRETS

27.	Black Bittern	*Ixobrychus flavicollis*
28.	Black-crowned Night Heron	*Nycticorax nycticorax*
29.	Cattle Egret	*Bubulcus ibis*
30.	Chinese Egret	*Egretta eulophotes*
31.	Chinese Pond Heron	*Ardeola bacchus*
32.	Goliath Heron	*Ardea goliath*
33.	Great Bittern	*Botaurus stellaris*
34.	Great Egret	*Ardea alba*
35.	Grey Heron	*Ardea cinerea*
36.	Indian Pond Heron	*Ardeola grayii*
37.	Intermediate Egret	*Ardea intermedia*
38.	Javan Pond Heron	*Ardeola speciosa*
39.	Little Bittern	*Ixobrychus minutus*
40.	Little Egret	*Egretta garzetta*
41.	Malayan Night Heron	*Gorsachius melanolophus*
42.	Pacific Reef Egret	*Egretta sacra*

43.	Purple Heron	*Ardea purpurea*
44.	Striated Heron	*Butorides striata*
45.	Western Reef Egret	*Egretta gularis*
46.	Yellow Bittern	*Ixobrychus sinensis*

NORTHERN STORM-PETRELS

| 47. | Swinhoe's Storm-petrel | *Oceanodroma monorhis* |

BROADBILLS

| 48. | Long-tailed Broadbill | *Psarisomus dalhousiae* |
| 49. | Silver-breasted Broadbill | *Serilophus lunatus* |

BULBULS

50.	Andaman Bulbul	*Brachypodius fuscoflavescens*
51.	Ashy Bulbul	*Hemixos flavala*
52.	Black Bulbul	*Hypsipetes leucocephalus*
53.	Black-crested Bulbul	*Rubigula flaviventris*
54.	Black-headed Bulbul	*Brachypodius melanocephalos*
55.	Cachar Bulbul	*Iole cacharensis*
56.	Crested Finchbill	*Spizixos canifrons*
57.	Flame-throated Bulbul	*Rubigula gularis*
58.	Flavescent Bulbul	*Pycnonotus flavescens*
59.	Grey-headed Bulbul	*Brachypodius priocephalus*
60.	Himalayan Bulbul	*Pycnonotus leucogenis*
61.	Mountain Bulbul	*Ixos mcclellandii*
62.	Nicobar Bulbul	*Ixos nicobariensis*
63.	Red-vented Bulbul	*Pycnonotus cafer*
64.	Red-whiskered Bulbul	*Pycnonotus jocosus*
65.	Square-tailed Bulbul	*Hypsipetes ganeesa*
66.	Striated Bulbul	*Alcurus striatus*

67.	White-browed Bulbul	*Pycnonotus luteolus*
68.	White-eared Bulbul	*Pycnonotus leucotis*
69.	White-throated Bulbul	*Alophoixus flaveolus*
70.	Yellow-browed Bulbul	*Acritillas indica*
71.	Yellow-throated Bulbul	*Pycnonotus xantholaemus*

BUNTINGS

72.	Black-faced Bunting	*Emberiza spodocephala*
73.	Black-headed Bunting	*Emberiza melanocephala*
74.	Chestnut Bunting	*Emberiza rutila*
75.	Chestnut-eared Bunting	*Emberiza fucata*
76.	Crested Bunting	*Emberiza lathami*
77.	Eurasian Reed Bunting	*Emberiza schoeniclus*
78.	Godlewski's Bunting	*Emberiza godlewskii*
79.	Grey-necked Bunting	*Emberiza buchanani*
80.	Little Bunting	*Emberiza pusilia*
81.	Ortolan Bunting	*Emberiza hortulana*
82.	Pine Bunting	*Emberiza leucocephalos*
83.	Red-headed Bunting	*Emberiza bruniceps*
84.	Rock Bunting	*Emberiza cia*
85.	Rustic Bunting	*Emberiza rustica*
86.	Striolated Bunting	*Emberiza striolata*
87.	Tristram's Bunting	*Emberiza tristrami*
88.	White-capped Bunting	*Emberiza steward*
89.	Yellow-browed Bunting	*Emberiza chrysophrys*
90.	Yellowhammer	*Emberiza citrinella*

BUTTONQUAILS

91.	Barred Buttonquail	*Turnix suscitator*
92.	Small Buttonquail	*Turnix sylvaticus*
93.	Yellow-legged Buttonquail	*Turnix tanki*

CANARY-FLYCATCHERS AND ALLIES

94.	Grey-headed Canary-flycatcher	*Culicicapa ceylonensis*
95.	Yellow-bellied Fantail	*Chelidorhynx hypoxanthus*

CETTIA WARBLERS AND ALLIES

96.	Aberrant Bush Warbler	*Horornis flavolivaceus*
97.	Ashy-throated Warbler	*Phylloscopus maculipennis*
98.	Asian Stubtail	*Urosphena squameiceps*
99.	Black-faced Warbler	*Abroscopus schisticeps*
100.	Booted Warbler	*Iduna caligata*
101.	Broad-billed Warbler	*Tickellia hodgsoni*
102.	Brooks's Leaf Warbler	*Phylloscopus subviridis*
103.	Brownish-flanked Bush Warbler	*Horornis fortipes*
104.	Buff-barred Warbler	*Phylloscopus puleher*
105.	Buff-throated Warbler	*Phylloscopus subaffinis*
106.	Cetti's Warbler	*Cettia cetti*
107.	Chestnut-crowned Bush Warbler	*Cettia major*
108.	Chestnut-headed Tesia	*Cettia castaneocoronata*
109.	Chinese Leaf Warbler	*Phylloscopus yunnanensis*
110.	Common Chiffchaff	*Phylloscopus collybita*
111.	Crested Tit Warbler	*Leptopoecile elegans*
112.	Dusky Warbler	*Phylloscopus fuscatus*
113.	Green Warbler	*Phylloscopus nitidus*
114.	Green-crowned Warbler	*Phylloscopus burkii*
115.	Greenish Warbler	*Phylloscopus trochiloides*
116.	Grey-bellied Tesia	*Tesia cyaniventer*
117.	Grey-cheeked Warbler	*Phylloscopus poliogenys*
118.	Grey-crowned Warbler	*Phylloscopus tephrocephalus*

119.	Grey-sided Bush Warbler	*Cettia brunnifrons*
120.	Hume's Bush Warbler	*Horornis brunnescens*
121.	Hume's Warbler	*Phylloscopus humei*
122.	Lanceolated Warbler	*Locustella lanceolata*
123.	Large-billed Leaf Warbler	*Phylloscopus magnirostris*
124.	Lemon-rumped Warbler	*Phylloscopus chloronotus*
125.	Manchurian Bush Warbler	*Horornis cantunans*
126.	Mountain Chiffchaff	*Phylloscopus sindianus*
127.	Mountain Tailorbird	*Phyllergates cucullatus*
128.	Pale-footed Bush Warbler	*Urosphena pallidipes*
129.	Pale-legged Leaf Warbler	*Phylloscopus tenellipes*
130.	Plain Leaf Warbler	*Phylloscopus neglectus*
131.	Rufous-faced Warbler	*Abroscopus albogularis*
132.	Rusty-rumped Warbler	*Helopsaltes certhiola*
133.	Sakhalin Leaf Warbler	*Phylloscopus borealoides*
134.	Sichuan Leaf Warbler	*Phylloscopus forresti*
135.	Slaty-bellied Tesia	*Tesia olivea*
136.	Smoky Warbler	*Phylloscopus fuligiventer*
137.	Sulphur-bellied Warbler	*Phylloscopus griseolus*
138.	Sykes's Warbler	*Iduna rama*
139.	Thick-billed Warbler	*Arundinax aedon*
140.	Tickell's Leaf Warbler	*Phylloscopus affinis*
141.	Two-barred Warbler	*Phylloscopus plumbeitarsus*
142.	Whistler's Warbler	*Phylloscopus whistleri*
143.	White-browed Tit Warbler	*Leptopoecile sophiae*
144.	White-spectacled Warbler	*Phylloscopus intermedius*
145.	Willow Warbler	*Phylloscopus trochilus*
146.	Wood Warbler	*Phylloscopus sibilatrix*

147.	Yellow-bellied Warbler	*Abroscopus superciliaris*
148.	Yellow-browed Warbler	*Phylloscopus inornatus*

CISTICOLAS, PRINIAS, AND ALLIES

149.	Ashy Prinia	*Prinia socialis*
150.	Black-throated Prinia	*Prinia atrogularis*
151.	Common Tailorbird	*Orthotomus sutorius*
152.	Dark-necked Tailorbird	*Orthotomus atrogularis*
153.	Golden-headed Cisticola	*Cisticola exilis*
154.	Graceful Prinia	*Prinia gracilis*
155.	Grey-breasted Prinia	*Prinia hodgsonii*
156.	Hill Prinia	*Prinia superciliaris*
157.	Jungle Prinia	*Prinia sylvatica*
158.	Plain Prinia	*Prinia inornata*
159.	Rufescent Prinia	*Prinia rufescens*
160.	Striated Prinia	*Prinia crinigera*
161.	Yellow-bellied Prinia	*Prinia flaviventris*
162.	Zitting Cisticola	*Cisticola juncidis*

CORMORANTS

163.	Great Cormorant	*Phalacrocorax car bo*
164.	Indian Cormorant	*Phalacrocorax fuscicollis*
165.	Little Cormorant	*Microcarbo niger*

COURSERS AND PRATINCOLES

166.	Collared Pratincole	*Glareola pratincola*
167.	Cream-coloured Courser	*Cursorius cursor*
168.	Oriental Pratincole	*Glareola maldivarum*
169.	Small Pratincole	*Glareola lactea*

CRAB-PLOVER

170.	Crab-plover	*Dromas ardeola*

CROWS AND ALLIES

171. Black-headed Jay — *Garrutus lanceolatus*
172. Carrion Crow — *Corvus corone*
173. Collared Treepie — *Dendrocitta frontalis*
174. Common Green Magpie — *Cissa chinensis*
175. Common Raven — *Corvus corax*
176. Eurasian Jackdaw — *Corvus monedula*
177. Eurasian Jay — *Garrulus glandarius*
178. Eurasian Magpie — *Pica pica*
179. Grey Treepie — *Dendrocitta formosae*
180. Hooded Crow — *Corvus comix*
181. Large-billed Crow — *Corvus macrorhynchos*
182. Large-spotted Nutcracker — *Nucifraga multipunctata*
183. Pied Crow — *Corvus albus*
184. Red-billed Blue Magpie — *Urocissa erythroryncha*
185. Red-billed Chough — *Pyrrhocorax pyrrhocorax*
186: Rook — *Corvus frugilegus*
187. Rufous Treepie — *Dendrocitta vagabunda*
188. Spotted Nutcracker — *Nucifraga caryocatactes*
189. White-bellied Treepie — *Dendrocitta leucogastra*
190. Yellow-billed Blue Magpie — *Urocissa flavirostris*
191. Yellow-billed Chough — *Pyrrhocorax graculus*

CUCKOOS

192. Andaman Coucal — *Centropus andamanensis*
193. Asian Emerald Cuckoo — *Chrysococcyx maculatus*
194. Asian Koel — *Eudynamys scolopaceus*

195.	Banded Bay Cuckoo	*Cacomantis sonneratii*
196.	Blue-faced Malkoha	*Phaenicophaeus viridirostris*
197.	Chestnut-winged Cuckoo	*Clamator coromandus*
198.	Common Cuckoo	*Cuculus canorus*
199.	Common Hawk Cuckoo	*Hierococcyx varius*
200.	Fork-tailed Drongo Cuckoo	*Surniculus dicruroides*
201.	Greater Coucal	*Centropus sinensis*
202.	Green-billed Malkoha	*Phaenicophaeus tristis*
203.	Grey-bellied Cuckob	*Cacomantis passerinus*
204.	Hodgson's Hawk Cuckoo	*Hierococcyx nisicolor*
205.	Horsfield's Bronze Cuckoo	*Chrysococcyx basalis*
206.	Indian Cuckoo	*Cuculus micropterus*
207.	Large Hawk Cuckoo	*Hierococcyx sparverioides*
208.	Lesser Coucal	*Centropus bengalensis*
209.	Lesser Cuckoo	*Cuculus poliocephalus*
210.	Oriental Cuckoo	*Cuculus optatus*
211.	Pied Cuckoo	*Clamator jacobinus*
212.	Plaintive Cuckoo	*Cacomantis merulinus*
213.	Sirkeer Malkoha	*Taccocua leschenaultii*
214.	Square-tailed Drongo Cuckoo	*Surniculus lugubris*
215.	Violet Cuckoo	*Chrysococcyx xanthorhynchus*

DARTERS

| 216. | Oriental Darter | *Anhinga melanogaster* |

DIPPERS

| 217. | Brown Dipper | *Cinclus pallasii* |
| 218. | White-throated Dipper | *Cinclus cinclus* |

DIVERS

219.	Black-throated Diver	*Gavia arctica*
220.	Red-throated Diver	*Gavia stellata*

DRONGOS

221.	Andaman Drongo	*Dicrurus andamanensis*
222.	Ashy Drongo	*Dicrurus leucophaeus*
223.	Black Drongo	*Dicrurus macrocercus*
224.	Bronzed Drongo	*Dicrurus aeneus*
225.	Crow-billed Drongo	*Dicrurus annectens*
226.	Greater Racket-tailed Drongo	*Dicrurus paradiseus*
227.	Hair-crested Drongo	*Dicrurus hottentottus*
228.	Lesser Racket-tailed Drongo	*Dicrurus retnifer*
229.	White-bellied Drongo	*Dicrurus caerulescens*

DUCKS, GEESE, AND SWANS

230.	Baikal Teal	*Sibirionetta formosa*
231.	Bar-headed Goose	*Anser indicus*
232.	Bean Goose	*Anser fabcdis*
233.	Common Goldeneye	*Bucephala clangula*
234.	Common Merganser	*Mergus merganser*
235.	Common Shelduck	*Tadorna tadorna*
236.	Common Teal	*Anas crecca*
237.	Eastern Spot-billed Duck	*Anas zonorhyncha*
238.	Eurasian Wigeon	*Mareca penelope*
239.	Falcated Duck	*Mareca falcata*
240.	Ferruginous Duck	*Aythya nyroca*
241.	Gadwall	*Mareca strepera*
242.	Garganey	*Spatula querquedula*
243.	Greater Scaup	*Aythya marila*
244.	Greater White-fronted Goose	*Anser albifrons*
245.	Greylag Goose	*Anser anser*

246.	Indian Spot-billed Duck	*Anas poecilorhyncha*
247.	Knob-billed Duck	*Sarkidiornis melanotos*
248.	Lesser Whistling Duck	*Dendrocygna javanica*
249.	Lesser White-fronted Goose	*Anser erythropus*
250.	Long tailed Duck	*Clangula hyemalis*
251.	Mallard	*Anas platyrhynchos*
252.	Mandarin Duck	*Aix galericulata*
253.	Mute Swan	*Cygnus olor*
254.	Northern Pintail	*Anas acuta*
255.	Northern Shoveler	*Spatula clypeata*
256.	Red-breasted Goose	*Branta ruficollis*
257.	Red-breasted Merganser	*Mergus senator*
258.	Red-crested Pochard	*Netta rufina*
259.	Ruddy Shelduck	*Tadorna ferruginea*
260.	Smew	*Mergellus albellus*
261.	Tufted Duck	*Aythya fuligula*
262.	Tundra Swan	*Cygnus columbianus*
263.	Whooper Swan	*Cygnus cygnus*

ELACHURA

264.	Spotted Elachura	*Elachura formosa*

FAIRY-BLUEBIRDS

265.	Asian Fairy-bluebird	*Irena pueila*

FALCONS

266.	Collared Falconet	*Microhierax caerulescens*
267.	Common Kestrel	*Falco tinnunculus*
268.	Eurasian Hobby	*Falco subbuteo*
269.	Lesser Kestrel	*Falco naumanni*
270.	Merlin	*Falco columbarius*
271.	Oriental Hobby	*Falco severus*

| 272. | Pied Falconet | *Microhierax melanoleucos* |
| 273. | Red-footed Falcon | *Falco vespertinus* |

FANTAILS

274.	Spot-breasted Fantail	*Rhipidura albogularis*
275.	White-browed Fantail	*Rhipidura aureola*
276.	White-throated Fantail	*Rhipidura albicollis*

FINCHES

277.	Black-and-yellow Grosbeak	*Mycerobas icterioides*
278.	Black-headed Greenfinch	*Chloris ambigua*
279.	Blanford's Rosefinch	*Agraphospiza rubescens*
280.	Blyth's Rosefinch	*Carpodacus grandis*
281.	Brambling	*Fringilla montifringilla*
282.	Brandt's Mountain Finch	Leucosticte brandti
283.	Brown Bullfinch	*Pyrrhula nipalensis*
284.	Chinese White-browed Rosefinch	*Carpodacus dubius*
285.	Collared Grosbeak	*Mycerobas affinis*
286.	Common Chaffinch	*Fringilla coelebs*
287.	Common Linnet	*Linaria cannabina*
288.	Common Rosefinch	*Carpodacus erythrinus*
289.	Crimson-browed Finch	*Carpodacus subhimachalus*
290.	Crimson-winged Finch	*Rhodopechys sanguineus*
291.	Dark-breasted Rosefinch	*Procarduelis nipalensis*
292.	Dark-rumped Rosefinch	*Carpodacus edwardsii*
293.	Desert Finch	*Rhodospiza obsoleta*
294.	Eurasian Siskin	*Spinus spinus*
295.	European Goldfinch	*Carduelis carduelis*
296.	Fire-fronted Serin	*Serinus pusillus*
297.	Gold-naped Finch	*Pyrrhoplectes epauletta*
298.	Great Rosefinch	*Carpodacus rubicilla*

299.	Grey-headed Bullfinch	*Pyrrhula erythaca*
300.	Hawfinch	*Coccothraustes coccothraustes*
301.	Himalayan Beautiful Rosefinch	*Carpodacus pulcherrimus*
302.	Himalayan White-browed Rosefmch	*Carpodacus thura*
303.	Mongolian Finch	*Bucanetes mongolicus*
304.	Orange Bullfinch	*Pyrrhula aurantiaca*
305.	Pale Rockfinch	*Carpospiza brachydactyla*
306.	Pale Rosefinch	*Carpodacus stoliczkae*
307.	Pink-browed Rosefinch	*Carpodacus rodochroa*
308.	Pink-rumped Rosefinch	*Carpodacus waltoni*
309.	Plain Mountain Finch	*Leucosticte nemoricola*
310.	Red Crossbill	*Loxia curvirostra*
311.	Red-fronted Rosefinch	*Carpodacus puniceus*
312.	Red-headed Bullfinch	*Pyrrhula erythrocephala*
313.	Scarlet Finch	*Carpodacus sipahi*
314.	Sillem's Rosefinch	*Carpodacus sillemi*
315.	Spectacled Finch	*Callacanthis burtoni*
316.	Spot-winged Grosbeak	*Mycerobas melanozanthos*
317.	Spot-winged Rosefinch	*Carpodacus rodopeplus*
318.	Streaked Rosefinch	*Carpodacus rubicilloides*
319.	Three-banded Rosefinch	*Carpodacus trifasciatus*
320.	Tibetan Siskin	*Spinus thibetanus*
321.	Trumpeter Finch	*Bucanetes githagineus*
322.	Twite	*Linaria flavirostris*
323.	Vinaceous Rosefinch	*Carpodacus vinaceus*
324.	White-winged Grosbeak	*Mycerobas carnipes*
325.	Yellow-breasted Greenfinch	*Chtoris spinoides*

FLAMINGOS

| 326. | Greater Flamingo | *Phoenicopterus roseus* |

327. Lesser Flamingo *Phoeniconaias minor*

FLOWERPECKERS

328. Andaman Flowerpecker *Dicaeum virescens*
329. Fire-breasted Flowerpecker *Dicaeum ignipectus*
330. Nilgiri Flowerpecker *Dicaeum concolor*
331. Pale-billed Flowerpecker *Dicaeum erythrorhynchos*
332. Plain Flowerpecker *Dicaeum minullum*
333. Scarlet-backed Flowerpecker *Dicaeum cruentatum*
334. Thick-billed Flowerpecker *Dicaeum agile*
335. Yellow-bellied Flowerpecker *Dicaeum melanozanthum*
336. Yellow-vented Flowerpecker *Dicaeum chrysorrheum*

FLYCATCHERS, CHATS AND ALLIES

337. Andaman Shama *Copsychus albiventris*
338. Asian Brown Flycatcher *Muscicapa dauurica*
339. Black Redstart *Phoenicurus ochruros*
340. Black-and-orange Flycatcher *Ficedula nigrorufa*
341. Black-backed Forktail *Enicurus immaculatus*
342. Blue Rock Thrush *Monticola solitarius*
343. Blue Whistling Thrush *Myophonus caeruleus*
344. Blue-and-white Flycatcher *Cyanoptila cyanomelana*
345. Blue-capped Redstart *Phoenicurus coeruleocephala*
346. Blue-capped Rock Thrush *Monticola cinclorhyncha*
347. Blue-fronted Redstart *Phoenicurus frontalis*
348. Blue-fronted Robin *Cinclidium frontale*
349. Bluethroat *Luscinia svecica*
350. Blue-throated Flycatcher *Cyornis rubeculoides*
351. Brown Rock Chat *Oenanthe fusca*
352. Brown-breasted Flycatcher *Muscicapa muttui*
353. Chestnut-bellied Rock Thrush *Monticola rufiventris*

354.	Common Redstart	*Phoenicurus phoenicurus*
355.	Dark-sided Flycatcher	*Muscicapa sibirica*
356.	Daurian Redstart	*Phoenicurus auroreus*
357.	Desert Wheatear	*Oenanthe deserti*
358.	Eversmann's Redstart	*Phoenicurus erythronotus*
359.	Ferruginous Flycatcher	*Muscicapa ferruginea*
360.	Finsch's Wheatear	*Oenanthe finschii*
361.	Firethroat	*Calliope pectardens*
362.	Golden Bush Robin	*Tarsiger chrysaeus*
363.	Gould's Shortwing	*Heteroxenicus stellatus*
364.	Grey Bushchat	*Saxicola ferreus*
365.	Hill Blue Flycatcher	*Cyornis banyumas*
366.	Himalayan Bush Robin	*Tarsiger rufilatus*
367.	Himalayan Rubythroat	*Calliope pectoralis*
368.	Himalayan Shortwing	*Brachypteryx cruralis*
369.	Hodgson's Redstart	*Phoenicurus hodgsoni*
370.	Hume's Wheatear	*Oenanthe albonigra*
371.	Indian Blue Robin	*Larvivora brunnea*
372.	Indian Robin	*Copsychus fulicatus*
373.	Isabelline Wheatear	*Oenanthe isabellina*
374.	Jerdon's Bushchat	*Saxicola jerdoni*
375.	Large Niltava	*Niltava grandis*
376.	Lesser Shortwing	*Brachypteryx leucophris*
377.	Little Forktail	*Enicurus scouleri*
378.	Little Pied Flycatcher	*Ficedula westermanni*
379.	Malabar Whistling Thrush	*Myophonus horsfieldii*
380.	Mugimaki Flycatcher	*Ficedula mugimaki*
381.	Nicobar Jungle Flycatcher	*Cyornis nicobaricus*
382.	Nilgiri Flycatcher	*Eumyias albicaudatus*

383.	Northern Wheatear	*Oenanthe oenanthe*
384.	Oriental Magpie Robin	*Copsychus saularis*
385.	Pale Blue Flycatcher	*Cyornis unicolor*
386.	Pale-chinned Flycatcher	*Cyornis poliogenys*
387.	Pied Bushchat	*Saxicola caprata*
388.	Pied Wheatear	*Oenanthe pleschanka*
389.	Plumbeous Water Redstart	*Phoenicurus fuliginosus*
390.	Pygmy Blue Flycatcher	*Ficedula hodgsoni*
391.	Red-breasted Flycatcher	*Ficedula parva*
392.	Red-flanked Bush Robin	*Tarsiger cyanurus*
393.	Red-tailed Wheatear	*Oenanthe chrysopygia*
394.	Rufous-bellied Niltava	*Niltava Sundara*
395.	Rufous-breasted Bush Robin	*Tarsiger hyperythrus*
396.	Rufous-gorgeted Flycatcher	*Ficedula strophiata*
397.	Rufous-tailed Rock Thrush	*Monticola saxatilis*
398.	Rufous-tailed Scrub Robin	*Cercotrichas galactotes*
399.	Rusty-bellied Shortwing	*Brachypteryx hyperythra*
400.	Rusty-tailed Flycatcher	*Ficedula ruficauda*
401.	Sapphire Flycatcher	*Ficedula sapphira*
402.	Siberian Blue Robin	*Larvivora cyane*
403.	Siberian Rubythroat	*Calliope calliope*
404.	Siberian Stonechat	*Saxicola maurus*
405.	Slaty-backed Flycatcher	*Ficedula erithacus*
406.	Slaty-backed Forktail	*Enicurus schistaceus*
407.	Slaty-blue Flycatcher	*Ficedula tricolor*
408.	Small Niltava	*Niltava macgrigoriae*
409.	Snowy-browed Flycatcher	*Ficedula hyperythra*
410.	Spotted Flycatcher	*Muscicapa striata*
411.	Spotted Forktail	*Enicurus maculatus*

412.	Stoliczka's Bushchat	*Saxicola macrorhynchus*
413.	Taiga Flycatcher	*Ficedula albicilla*
414.	Tickell's Blue Flycatcher	*Cyornis tickelliae*
415.	Ultramarine Flycatcher	*Ficedula superciliaris*
416.	Variable Wheatear	*Oenanthe picata*
417.	Verditer Flycatcher	*Eumyias thalassinus*
418.	Vivid Niltava	*Niltava vivida*
419.	White-bellied Blue Flycatcher	*Cyornis pallidipes*
420.	White-bellied Redstart	*Luscinia phaenicuroides*
421.	White-browed Bush Robin	*Tarsiger indicus*
422.	White-capped Redstart	*Phoenicurus leucocephalus*
423.	White-crowned Forktail	*Enicurus leschenaulti*
424.	White-gorgeted Flycatcher	*Anthipes monileger*
425.	White-rumped Shama	*Copsychus malabaricus*
426.	White-tailed Blue Flycatcher	*Cyornis concretus*
427.	White-tailed Robin	*Myiomela leucura*
428.	White-tailed Stonechat	*Saxicola leucurus*
429.	White-throated Redstart	*Phoenicurus schisticeps*
430.	White-winged Redstart	*Phoenicurus erythrogastrus*
431.	Yellow-rumped Flycatcher	*Ficedula zanthopygia*
432.	Zappey's Flycatcher	*Cyanoptila cumatilis*

FRIGATEBIRDS

433.	Great Frigatebird	*Fregata minor*
434.	Lesser Frigatebird	*Fregata ariel*

GANNETS AND BOOBIES

435.	Brown Booby	*Sula leucogaster*
436.	Masked Booby	*Sula dactylatra*
437.	Red-footed Booby	*Sula sula*

GOLDCRESTS

438.	Goldcrest	*Regulus regulus*

GREBES

439.	Black-necked Grebe	*Podiceps nigricollis*
440.	Great Crested Gyebe	*Podiceps cristatus*
441.	Horned Grebe	*Podiceps auratus*
442.	Little Grebe	*Tachybaptus ruficollis*
443.	Red-necked Grebe	*Podiceps grisegena*

GULLS AND TERNS

444.	Arctic Tern	*Sterna paradisaea*
445.	Black Noddy	*Anous minutus*
446.	Black Tern	*Chlidonias niger*
447.	Black-headed Gull	*Chroicocephalus ridibundus*
448.	Black-legged Kittiwake	*Rissa tridactyla*
449.	Black-naped Tern	*Sterna sumatrana*
450.	Bridled Tern	*Onychoprion anaethetus*
451.	Brown Noddy	*Anous stolidus*
452.	Brown-headed Gull	*Chroicocephalus brunnicephalus*
453.	Caspian Gull	*Larus cachinnans*
454.	Caspian Tern	*Hydroprogne caspia*
455.	Common Tern	*Sterna hirundo*
456.	Franklin's Gull	*Leucophaeus pipixcan*
457.	Greater Crested Tern	*Thalasseus bergii*
458.	Lesser Black-backed Gull	*Larus fuscus*
459.	Lesser Crested Tern	*Thalasseus bengalensis*
460.	Lesser Noddy	*Anous tenuirostris*
461.	Little Gull	*Hydrocoloeus minutus*
462.	Little Tern	*Sternula albifrons*

463.	Mew Gull	*Larus canus*
464.	Mongolian Gull	*Larus smithsonianus mongolicus*
465.	Pallas's Gull	*Ichthyaetus ichthyaetus*
466.	Roseate Tern	*Sterna dougallii*
467.	Sabine's Gull	*Xema sabini*
468.	Sandwich Tern	*Thalasseus sandvicensis*
469.	Saunders's Tern	*Sternula saundersi*
470.	Slender-billed Gull	*Chroicocephalus genei*
471.	Sooty Gull	*Ichthyaetus hemprichii*
472.	Sooty Tern	*Onychoprion fuscatus*
473.	Whiskered Tern	*Chlidonias hybrid*
474.	White Tern	*Gygis alba*
475.	White-cheeked Tern	*Sterna repressa*
476.	White-eyed Gull	*Ichthyaetus leucophthalmus*
477.	White-winged Tern	*Chlidonias leucopterus*

HONEYGUIDES

478.	Yellow-rumped Honeyguide	*Indicator xanthonotus*

HOOPOES

479.	Common Hoopoe	*Upupa epops*

HORNBILLS

480.	Indian Grey Hornbill	*Ocyceros birostris*

HYPOCOLIUS

481.	Grey Hypocolius	*Hypocolius ampelinus*

IBISES AND SPOONBILLS

482.	Black-headed Ibis	*Threskiornis melanocephalus*
483.	Glossy Ibis	*Plegadis falcinellus*

484. Red-naped Ibis *Pseudibis papillosa*

IORAS

485. Common Iora *Aegithina tiphia*

456. Marshall's Iora *Aegithina nigrolutea*

JACANAS

487. Bronze winged Jacana *Metopidius indicus*

488. Pheasant-tailed Jacana *Hydrophasianus chirurgus*

KINGFISHERS

489. Black-capped Kingfisher *Halcyon pileata*

490. Blue-eared Kingfisher *Alcedo meninting*

491. Brown-winged Kingfisher *Pelargopsis amauroptera*

492. Collared Kingfisher *Todiramphus chloris*

493. Common Kingfisher *Alcedo atthis*

494. Crested Kingfisher *Megaceryle lugubris*

495. Oriental Dwarf Kingfisher *Ceyx erithaca*

496. Pied Kingfisher *Ceryle rudis*

497. Ruddy Kingfisher *Halcyon coromanda*

498. Stork-billed Kingfisher *Pelargopsis capensis*

499. White-throated Kingfisher *Halcyon smymensis*

KITES, HAWKS AND EAGLES

500. Black Kite *Milvus migrans*

501. Black-winged Kite *Elanus caeruleus*

502. European Honey Buzzard *Pernis apivorus*

503. Legge's Hawk Eagle *Nisaetus kelaarti*

504. Oriental Honey Buzzard *Pernis ptilorhynchus*

505. Rough-legged Buzzard *Buteo lagopus*

LARKS

506. Ashy-crowned Sparrow Lark *Eremopterix griseus*

507.	Bengal Bushlark	*Mirafra assamica*
508.	Bimaculated Lark	*Melanocorypha bimaculata*
509.	Black-crowned Sparrow Lark	*Eremopterix nigriceps*
510.	Crested Lark	*Galerida cristata*
511.	Desert Lark	*Ammomanes deserti*
512.	Eurasian Skylark	*Alauda arvensis*
513.	Greater Hoopoe Lark	*Alaemon alaudipes*
514.	Greater Short-toed Lark	*Calandrella brachydactyla*
515.	Horned Lark	*Eremophila alpestris*
516.	Hume's Short-toed Lark	*Calandrella acutirostris*
517.	Indian Bushlark	*Mirafra erythroptera*
518.	Jerdon's Bushlark	*Mirafra affinis*
519.	Lesser Short-toed Lark	*Alaudala rufescens*
520.	Malabar Lark	*Galerida malabarica*
521.	Oriental Skylark	*Alauda gulgula*
522.	Rufous-tailed Lark	*Ammomanes phoenicura*
523.	Sand Lark	*Alaudala raytal*
524.	Singing Bushlark	*Mirafra cantillans*
525.	Sykes's Lark	*Galerida deva*
526.	Sykes's Short-toed Lark	*Calandrella dukhunensis*
527.	Tibetan Lark	*Melanocorypha maxima*

LAUGHINGTHRUSHES AND LARGE BABBLERS

528.	Assam Laughingthfush	*Trochalopteron chrysopterum*
529.	Beautiful Sibia	*Heterophasia pulchella*
530.	Bhutan Laughingthrush	*Trochalopteron imbricatum*
531.	Black-faced Laughingthrush	*Trochalopteron affine*
532.	Blue-winged Laughingthrush	*Trochalopteron squamatum*
533.	Blue-winged Minla	*Actinodura cyanouroptera*
534.	Brown-cheeked Fulvetta	*Alcippe poioicephala*

535.	Chestnut-crowned Laughingthrush	*Trochalopteron erythroeephalum*
536.	Chestnut-tailed Minla	*Actinodura strigula*
537.	Common Babbler	*Argya caudata*
538.	Elliot's Laughingthrush	*Trochalopteron elliotii*
539.	Greater Necklaced Laughingthrush	*Pterorhinus pectoralis*
540.	Grey Sibia	*Heterophasia gracilis*
541.	Himalayan Cutia	*Cutia nipalensis*
542.	Hoary-throated Barwing	*Actinodura nipalensis*
543.	Jungle Babbler	*Argya striata*
544.	Large Grey Babbler	*Argya malcolmi*
545.	Lesser Necklaced Laughingthrush	*Garrulax monileger*
546.	Long-tailed Sibia	*Heterophasia picaoides*
547.	Mount Victoria Babax	*Pterorhinus woodi*
548.	Nepal Fulvetta	*Alcippe nipalensis*
549.	Palani Laughingthrush	*Montecincla fairbanki*
550.	Red-billed Leiothrix	*Leiothrix lutea*
551.	Red-faced Liocichla	*Liocichla phoenicea*
552.	Red-tailed Minla	*Minla ignotincta*
553.	Rufous Babbler	*Argya subrufa*
554.	Rufous Sibia	*Heterophasia capistrata*
555.	Rufous-backed Sibia	*Leioptila annectens*
556.	Rufous-chinned Laughingthrush	*Ianthocincla rufogularis*
557.	Rufous-necked Laughingthrush	*Pterorhinus ruficollis*
558.	Rufous-vented Laughingthrush	*Pterorhinus gularis*
559.	Rusty-fronted Barwing	*Actinodura egertoni*
560.	Scaly Laughingthrush	*Trochalopteron subunicolor*
561.	Silver-eared Mesia	*Leiothrix argentauris*

562.	Spot-breasted Laughingthrush	*Garrulax merulinus*
563.	Spotted Laughingthrush	*Ianthocincla ocellata*
564.	Streaked Laughingthrush	*Trochalopteron lineatum*
565.	Streak-throated Barwing	*Actinodura waldeni*
566.	Striated Babbler	*Argya earlei*
567.	Striated Laughingthrush	*Grammatoptila striata*
568.	Striped Laughingthrush	*Trochalopteron virgatum*
569.	Variegated Laughingthrush	*Trochalopteron variegatum*
570.	Wayanad Laughingthrush	*Pterorhinus delesserti*
571.	White-browed Laughingthrush	*Pterorhinus sannio*
572.	White-crested Laughingthrush	*Garrulax leucolophus*
573.	White-throated Laughingthrush	*Pterorhinus albogularis*
574.	Yellow-billed Babbler	*Argya affinis*
575.	Yellow-throated Laughingthrush	*Pterorhinus galbanus*

LEAF WARBLERS

576.	Arctic Warbler	*Phylloscopus borealis*
577.	Blyth's Leaf Warbler	*Phylloscopus reguloides*
578.	Chestnut-crowned Warbler	*Phylloscopus castaniceps*
579.	Claudia's Leaf Warbler	*Phylloscopus claudiae*
580.	Grey-hooded Warbler	*Phylloscopus xanthoschistos*
581.	Tytler's Leaf Warbler	*Phylloscopus tytleri*
582.	Western Crowned Warbler	*Phylloscopus occipitalis*
583.	Yellow-vented Warbler	*Phylloscopus cantator*

LEAFBIRDS

584.	Blue-winged Leafbird	*Chloropsis cochinchinensis*
585.	Golden-fronted Leafbird	*Chloropsis aurifrons*
586.	Jerdon's Leafbird	*Chloropsis jerdoni*
587.	Orange-bellied Leafbird	*Chloropsis hardwickii*

LOCUSTELLA WARBLERS AND ALLIES

588.	Baikal Bush Warbler	*Locustella davidi*
589.	Brown Bush Warbler	*Locustella luteoventris*
590.	Chinese Bush Warbler	*Locustella tacsanowskia*
591.	Grasshopper Warbler	*Locustella naevia*
592.	Long-billed Bush Warbler	*Locustella major*
593.	Russet Bush Warbler	*Locustella mandelli*
594.	Spotted Bush Warbler	*Locustella thoracica*
595.	Striated Grassbird	*Megalurus palustris*

LONG-TAILED TITS

596.	Black-browed Tit	*Aegithalos iouschistos*
597.	Black-throated Tit	*Aegithalos concinnus*
598.	White-cheeked Ti$	*Aegithalos leucogenys*
599.	White-throated Tit	*Aegithalos niveogularis*

MINIVETS AND CUCKOOSHRIKES

600.	Andaman Cuckooshrike	*Coracina dobsoni*
601.	Ashy Minivet	*Pericrocotus divaricatus*
602.	Black-headed Cuckooshrike	*Lalage melanoptera*
603.	Black-winged Cuckooshrike	*Lalage melaschistos*
604.	Grey-chinned Minivet	*Pericrocotus Solaris*
605.	Large Cuckooshrike	*Coracina macei*
606.	Long-tailed Minivet	*Pericrocotus ethologus*
607.	Orange Minivet	*Pericrocotus flammeus*
608.	Pied Triller	*Lalage nigra*
609.	Rosy Minivet	*Pericrocotus roseus*
610.	Scarlet Minivet	*Pericrocotus speciosus*

611.	Short-billed Minivet	*Pericrocotus brevirostris*
612.	Swinhoe's Minivet	*Pericrocotus cantonensis*
613.	White-bellied Minivet	*Pericrocotus erythropygius*

MONARCHS

614.	Amur Paradise-flycatcher	*Terpsiphone incei*
615.	Black-naped Monarch	*Hypothymis azurea*
616.	Blyth's Paradise-flycatcher	*Terpsiphone affinis*
617.	Indian Paradise-flycatcher	*Terpsiphone paradisi*

MUNIAS

618.	Black-throated Munia	*Lonchura kelaarti*
619.	Chestnut Munia	*Lonchura atricapilla*
620.	Indian Silverbill	*Euodice malabarica*
621.	Red Munia	*Amandava amandava*
622.	Scaly-breasted Munia	*Lonchura punctulata*
623.	Tricoloured Munia	*Lonchura malacca*
624.	White-rumped Munia	*Lonchura striata*

NIGHTJARS

625.	Andaman Nightjar	*Caprimulgus andamanicus*
626.	European Nightjar	*Caprimulgus europaeus*
627.	Great Eared Nightjar	*Lyncornis macrotis*
628.	Grey Nightjar	*Caprimulgus jotaka*
629.	Indian Nightjar	*Caprimulgus asiaticus*
630.	Jerdon's Nightjar	*Caprimulgus atripennis*
631.	Jungle Nightjar	*Caprimulgus indicus*
632.	Large-tailed Nightjar	*Caprimulgus macrurus*
633.	Savanna Nightjar	*Caprimulgus affinis*
634.	Sykes's Nightjar	*Caprimulgus mahrattensis*

NUTHATCHES

635.	Chestnut-bellied Nuthatch	*Sitta cinnamoventris*
636.	Chestnut-vented Nuthatch	*Sitta nagaensis*
637.	Indian Nuthatch	*Sitta castanea*
638.	Kashmir Nuthatch	*Sitta cashmirensis*
639.	Velvet-fronted Nuthatch	*Sitta frontalis*
640.	White-cheeked Nuthatch	*Sitta leucopsis*
641.	White-tailed Nuthatch	*Sitta himalayensis*
642.	Yunnan Nuthatch	*Sitta yunnanensis*

ORIOLES

643.	Black-hooded Oriole	*Oriolus xanthornus*
644.	Black-naped Oriole	*Oriolus chinensis*
645.	Eurasian Golden Oriole	*Oriolus oriolus*
646.	Indian Golden Oriole	*Oriolus kundoo*
647.	Maroon Oriole	*Oriolus traillii*
648.	Slender-billed Oriole	*Oriolus tenuirostris*

OWLS

649.	Andaman Hawk Owl	*Ninox affinis*
650.	Andaman Scops Owl	*Otus balli*
651.	Asian Barred Owlet	*Glaucidium cuculoides*
652.	Boreal Owl	*Aegolius funereus*
653.	Brown Hawk Owl	*Ninox scutulata*
654.	Collared Owlet	*Taenioptynx brodiei*
655.	Collared Scops Owl	*Otus lettia*
656.	Dusky Eagle Owl	*Bubo coromandus*
657.	Eurasian Scops Owl	*Otus scops*
658.	Himalayan Owl	*Strix nivicolum*
659.	Hume's Hawk Owl	*Ninox obscura*
660.	Indian Scops Owl	*Otus bakkamoena*

661.	Jungle Owlet	*Glaucidium radiatum*
662.	Little Owl	*Athene Noctua*
663.	Mountain Scops Owl	*Otus spilocephalus*
664.	Nicobar Scops Owl	*Otus alius*
665.	Oriental Scops Owl	*Otus sunia*
666.	Pallid Scops Owl	*Otus brucei*
667.	Spotted Owlet	*Athene brama*
668.	Tawny Owl	*Strix aluco*

OYSTERCATCHERS

669.	Eurasian Oystercatcher	*Haematopus ostralegus*

PAINTED-SNIPES

670.	Greater Painted-snipe	*Rostratula benghalensis*

PARROTBILLS AND ALLIES

671.	Black-throated Parrotbill	*Suthora nipalensis*
672.	Brown Parrotbill	*Cholornis unicolor*
673.	Brown-throated Fulvetta	*Fulvetta ludlowi*
674.	Fire-tailed Myzornis	*Myzornis pyrrhoura*
675.	Fulvous Parrotbill	*Suthora fulvifrons*
676.	Golden-breasted Fulvetta	*Lioparus chrysotis*
677.	Great Parrotbill	*Conostoma demodium*
678.	Grey-headed Parrotbill	*Psittiparus gularis*
679.	Lesser Rufous-headed Parrotbill	*Chleuasicus atrosuperciliaris*
680.	Manipur Fulvetta	*Fulvetta manipurensis*
681.	Rufous-headed Parrotbill	*Psittiparus bakeri*
682.	Spot-breasted Parrotbill	*Paradoxornis guttaticollis*
683.	White-breasted Parrotbill	*Psittiparus ruficeps*
684.	White-browed Fulvetta	*Fulvetta vinipectus*
685.	Yellow-eyed Babbler	*Chrysomma sinense*

PARROTS

686.	Alexandrine Parakeet	*Psittacula eupatria*
687.	Blossom-headed Parakeet	*Psittacula roseata*
688.	Grey-headed Parakeet	*Psittacula finschii*
689.	Long-tailed Parakeet	*Psittacula longicauda*
690.	Malabar Parakeet	*Psittacula columboides*
691.	Nicobar Parakeet	*Psittacula caniceps*
692.	Plum-headed Parakeet	*Psittacula cyanocephala*
693.	Rose-ringed Parakeet	*Psittacula krameri*
694.	Slaty-headed Parakeet	*Psittacula himalayana*
695.	Vernal Hanging Parrot	*Loriculus vernalis*

PARTRIDGES, QUAILS, AND PHEASANTS

696.	Black Francolin	*Francolinus francolinus*
697.	Blue-breasted Quail	*Synoicus chinensis*
698.	Chinese Francolin	*Francolinus pintadeanus*
699.	Chukar Partridge	*Alectoris chukar*
700.	Common Quail	*Coturnix coturnix*
701.	Grey Francolin	*Francolinus pondicerianus*
702.	Hill Partridge	*Arborophila torqueola*
703.	Himalayan Snowcock	*Tetraogallus himalayensis*
704.	Japanese Quail	*Coturnix japonica* (excluding birds of the farm bred variety)
705.	Jungle Bush Quail	*Perdicula asiatica*
706.	Koklass Pheasant	*Pucrasia macrolopha*
707.	Painted Bush Quail	*Perdicula erythrorhyncha*
708.	Painted Francolin	*Francolinus pictus*
709.	Painted Spurfowl	*Galloperdix lunulata*
710.	Rain Quail	*Coturnix coromandelica*
711.	Red Junglefowl	*Gallus gallus*

712.	Red Spurfowl	*Galloperdix spadicea*
713.	Rock Bush Quail	*Perdicula argoondah*
714.	Rufous-throated Partridge	*Arborophila rufogularis*
715.	Snow Partridge	*Lerwa lerwa*
716.	White-cheeked Partridge	*Arborophila atrogularis*

PELICANS

717.	Dalmatian Pelican	*Pelecanus crispus*
718.	Great White Pelican	*Pelecanus onocrotalus*
719.	Spot-billed Pelican	*Pelecanus philippensis*

PENDULINE TITS

720.	White-crowned Penduline Tit	*Remiz coronatus*

PETRELS AND SHEARWATERS

721.	Barau's Petrel	*Pterodroma baraui*
722.	Cory's Shearwater	*Calonectris borealis*
723.	Flesh-footed Shearwater	*Ardenna carneipes*
724.	Jouanin's Petrel	*Bulweria fallax*
725.	Persian Shearwater	*Puffinus persicus*
726.	Short-tailed Shearwater	*Ardenna tenuirostris*
727.	Streaked Shearwater	*Calonectris leucomelas*
728.	Tropical Shearwater	*Puffinus bailloni*
729.	Wedge-tailed Shearwater	*Ardenna pacifica*

PIGEONS AND DOVES

730.	Andaman Cuckoo Dove	*Macropygia rufipennis*
731.	Andaman Wood Pigeon	*Columba palumboides*
732.	Ashy Wood Pigeon	*Columba pulchricollis*
733.	Ashy-headed Green Pigeon	*Treron phayrei*
734.	Asian Emerald Dove	*Chalcophaps indica*
735.	Barred Cuckoo Dove	*Macropygia unchall*
736.	Common Wood Pigeon	*Columba palumbus*

737.	Eurasian Collared Dove	*Streptopelia decaocto*
738.	European Turtle Dove	*Streptopelia turtur*
739.	Green Imperial Pigeon	*Ducula aenea*
740.	Grey-fronted Green Pigeon	*Treron affinis*
741.	Hill Pigeon	*Columba rupestris*
742.	Laughing Dove	*Streptopelia senegalensis*
743.	Mountain Imperial Pigeon	*Ducula badia*
744.	Namaqua Dove	*Oena capensis*
745.	Nicobar Imperial Pigeon	*Ducula nicobarica*
746.	Orange-breasted Green Pigeon	*Treron bicinctus*
747.	Oriental Turtle Dove	*Streptopelia orientalis*
748.	Pied Imperial Pigeon	*Ducula bicolor*
749.	Pin-tailed Green Pigeon	*Treron apicauda*
750.	Red Collared Dove	*Streptopelia tranquebarica*
751.	Snow Pigeon	*Columba leuconota*
752.	Speckled Wood Pigeon	*Columba hodgsonii*
753.	Spotted Dove	*Streptopelia chinensis*
754.	Thick-billed Green Pigeon	*Treron curvirostra*
755.	Wedge-tailed Green Pigeon	*Treron sphenurus*
756.	Yellow-footed Green Pigeon	*Treron phoenicopterus*

PIPITS AND WAGTAILS

757.	Blyth's Pipit	*Anthus godlewskii*
758.	Buff-bellied Pipit	*Anthus rubescens*
759.	Citrine Wagtail	*Motacilla citreola*
760.	Eastern Yellow Wagtail	*Motacilla tschutschensis*
761.	Grey Wagtail	*Motacilla cinerea*
762.	Long-billed Pipit	*Anthus similis*
763.	Meadow Pipit	*Anthus pratensis*
764.	Olive-backed Pipit	*Anthus hodgsoni*

765.	Paddyfield Pipit	*Anthus rufulus*
766.	Red-throated Pipit	*Anthus cervinus*
767.	Richard's Pipit	*Anthus richardi*
768.	Rosy Pipit	*Anthus roseatus*
769.	Tawny Pipit	*Anthus campestris*
770.	Tree Pipit	*Anthus trivialis*
771.	Upland Pipit	*Anthus sylvanus*
772.	Water Pipit	*Anthus spinoletta*
773.	Western Yellow Wagtail	*Motacilla flava*
774.	White Wagtail	*Motacilla alba*
775.	White-browed Wagtail	*Motacilla maderaspatensis*

PITTAS

776.	Blue Pitta	*Hydrorhis cyaneus*
777.	Blue naped Pitta	*Hydrornis nipalensis*
778.	Blue-winged Pitta	*Pitta moluccensis*
779.	Hooded Pitta	*Pitta sordida*
780.	Indian Pitta	*Pitta brachyura*
781.	Mangrove Pitta	*Pitta megarhyncha*

PLOVERS AND LAPWINGS

782.	American Golden Plover	*Pluvialis dominica*
783.	Caspian Plover	*Charadrius asiaticus*
784.	Common Ringed Plover	*Charadrius hiaticula*
785.	Eurasian Golden Plover	*Pluvialis apricaria*
786.	Greater Sand Plover	*Charadrius leschenaultii*
787.	Grey Plover	*Pluvialis squatarola*
788,	Grey-headed Lapwing	*Vanellus cinereus*
789.	Kentish Plover	*Charadrius alexandrinus*
790.	Lesser Sand Plover	*Charadrius mongolus*
791.	Little Ringed Plover	*Charadrius dubius*

792.	Long-billed Plover	*Charadrius placidus*
793.	Northern Lapwing	*Vanellus vanellus*
794.	Oriental Plover	*Charadrius veredus*
795.	Red-wattled Lapwing	*Vanellus indicus*
796.	River Lapwing	*Vanellus duvaucelii*
797.	White-tailed Lapwing	*Vanellus leucurus*
798.	Yellow-wattled Lapwing	*Vanellus malabaricus*

RAILS AND COOTS

799.	Andaman Crake	*Rallina canningi*
800.	Baillon's Crake	*Zapornia pusilla*
801.	Black-tailed Crake	*Zapornia bicolor*
802.	Brown Crake	*Zapornia akool*
803.	Brown-cheeked Rail	*Rallus indicus*
804.	Common Moorhen	*Gallinula chloropus*
805.	Corncrake	*Crex crex*
806.	Eurasian Coot	*Fulica atra*
807.	Grey-headed Swamphen	*Porphyrio poliocephalus*
808.	Little Crake	*Zapornia parva*
809.	Ruddy-breasted Crake	*Zapornia fusca*
810.	Slaty-breasted Rail	*Lewinia striata*
811.	Slaty-legged Crake	*Rallina eurizonoides*
812.	Spotted Crake	*Porzana porzana*
813.	Water Rail	*Rallus aquaticus*
814.	Watercock	*Gallicrex cinerea*
815.	White-breasted Waterhen	*Amaurornis phoenicurus*
816.	White-browed Crake	*Poliolimnas cinereus*

REED WARBLERS AND ALLEES

817.	Black-browed Reed Warbler	*Acrocephalus bistrigiceps*
818.	Blunt-winged Warbler	*Acrocephalus concinens*

819.	Blyth's Reed Warbler	*Acrocephalus dumetorum*
820.	Clamorous Reed Warbler	*Acrocephalus stentoreus*
821.	Great Reed Warbler	*Acrocephalus arundinaceus*
822.	Large-billed Reed Warbler	*Acrocephalus orinus*
823.	Moustached Warbler	*Acrocephalus melanopogon*
824.	Oriental Reed Warbler	*Acrocephalus orientalis*
825.	Paddyfield Warbler	*Acrocephalus agricola*
826.	Sedge Warbler	*Acrocephalus schoenobaenus*

ROLLERS

827.	Dollarbird	*Eurystomus orientalis*
828.	European Roller	*Coracias garrulus*
829.	Indian Roller	*Coracias benghalensis*
830.	Indochinese Roller	*Coracias affinis*

SANDGROUSES

831.	Black-bellied Sandgrouse	*Pterocles orientalis*
832.	Chestnut-bellied Sandgrouse	*Pterocles exustus*
833.	Painted Sandgrouse	*Pterocles indicus*
834.	Pallas's Sandgrouse	*Syrrhaptes paradoxus*
835.	Pin-tailed Sandgrouse	*Pterocles alchata*
836.	Spotted Sandgrouse	*Pterocles senegallus*
837.	Tibetan Sandgrouse	*Syrrhaptes tibetanus*

SANDPIPERS

838.	Asian Dowitcher	*Limnodromus semipalmatus*
839.	Bar-tailed Godwit	*Limosa lapponica*
840.	Black-tailed Godwit	*Limosa limosa*
841.	Broad-billed Sandpiper	*Calidris falcinellus*
842.	Buff-breasted Sandpiper	*Calidris subruficollis*

843.	Common Redshank	*Tringa totanus*
844.	Common Sandpiper	*Actitis hypoleucos*
845.	Common Snipe	*Gallinago gallinago*
846.	Curlew Sandpiper	*Calidris ferruginea*
847.	Dunlin	*Calidris alpina*
848.	Eurasian Curlew	*Numenius arquata*
849.	Eurasian Woodcock	*Scolopax rusticola*
850.	Great Snipe	*Gallinago media*
851.	Green Sandpiper	*Tringa ochropus*
852.	Grey-tailed Tattler	*Tringa brevipes*
853.	Jack Snipe	*Lymnocryptes minimus*
854.	Little Stint	*Calidris minuta*
855.	Long-billed Dowitcher	*Limnodromus scolopaceus*
856.	Long-toed Stint	*Calidris subminuta*
857.	Marsh Sandpiper	*Tringa stagnatilis*
858.	Pectoral Sandpiper	*Calidris melanotos*
859.	Pintail Snipe	*Gallinago stenura*
860.	Red Knot	*Calidris canutus*
861.	Red Phalarope	*Phalaropus fulicarius*
862.	Red-necked Phalarope	*Phalaropus lobatus*
863.	Red-necked Stint	*Calidris ruficollis*
864.	Ruddy Turnstone	*Arenaria interpres*
865.	Ruff	*Calidris pugnax*
866.	Sanderling	*Calidris alba*
867.	Sharp-tailed Sandpiper	*Calidris acuminata*
868.	Solitary Snipe	*Gallinago solitaria*
869.	Spotted Redshank	*Tringa erythropus*
870.	Swinhoe's Snipe	*Gallinago megala*
871.	Temminck's Stint	*Calidris temminckii*

872.	Terek Sandpiper	*Xenus cinereus*
873.	Whimbrel	*Numenius phaeopus*
874.	Wood Sandpiper	*Tringa glareola*

SCIMITAR BABBLERS AND ALLIES

875.	Black-chinned Babbler	*Cyanoderma pyrrhops*
876.	Buff-chested Babbler	*Cyanoderma ambiguum*
877.	Cachar Wedge-billed Babbler	*Stachyris roberti*
878.	Chestnut-capped Babbler	*Timalia pileata*
879.	Chin Hills Wren Babbler	*Spelaeornis oatesi*
880.	Coral-billed Scimitar Babbler	*Pomatorhinus ferruginosus*
881.	Dark-fronted Babbler	*Dumetia atriceps*
882.	Golden Babbler	*Cyanoderma chrysaeum*
883.	Grey-bellied Wren Babbler	*Spelaeornis reptatus*
884.	Grey-throated Babbler	*Stachyris nigriceps*
885.	Indian Scimitar Babbler	*Pomatorhinus horsfieldii*
886.	Large Scimitar Babbler	*Erythrogenys hypoleucos*
887.	Pin-striped Tit Babbler	*Mixornis gularis*
888.	Red-billed Scimitar Babbler	*Pomatorhinus ochraceiceps*
889.	Rufous-capped Babbler	*Cyanoderma ruficeps*
890.	Rufous-throated Wren Babbler	*Spelaeornis caudatus*
891.	Rusty-cheeked Scimitar Babbler	*Erythrogenys erythrogenys*
892.	Slender-billed Scimitar Babbler	*Pomatorhinus superciliaris*
893.	Spot-breasted Scimitar Babbler	*Erythrogenys mcclellandi*
894.	Streak-breasted Scimitar Babbler	*Pomatorhinus ruficollis*
895.	Tawny-bellied Babbler	*Dumetia hyperythra*
896.	White-browed Scimitar Babbler	*Pomatorhinus schisticeps*

SHRIKE-BABBLERS AND ALLIES

897.	Black-eared Shrike-babbler	*Pteruthius melanotis*
898.	Black-headed Shrike-babbler	*Pteruthius rufiventer*

899.	Blyth's Shrike-babbler	*Pteruthius aeralatus*
900.	Clicking Shrike-babbler	*Pteruthius intermedius*
901.	Green Shrike-babbler	*Pteruthius xanthochlorus*
902.	Himalayan Shrike-babbler	*Pteruthius ripleyi*
903.	White-bellied Erpornis	*Erpornis zantholeuca*

SHRIKES

904.	Bay-backed Shrike	*Lanius vittatus*
905.	Brown Shrike	*Lanius cristatus*
906.	Burmese Shrike	*Lanius collurioides*
907.	Great Grey Shrike	*Lanius excubitor*
908.	Grey-backed Shrike	*Lanius tephronotus*
909.	Isabelline Shrike	*Lanius isabellinus*
910.	Lesser Grey Shrike	*Lanius minor*
911.	Long-tailed Shrike	*Lanius schach*
912.	Masked Shrike	*Lanius nubicus*
913.	Red-backed Shrike	*Lanius collurio*
914.	Red-tailed Shrike	*Lanius phoenicuroides*
915.	Woodchat Shrike	*Lanius senator*

SKUAS

916.	Arctic Skua	*Stercorarius parasiticus*
917.	Brown Skua	*Stercorarius antarcticus*
918.	Long-tailed Skua	*Stercorarius longicaudus*
919.	Pomarine Skua	*Stercorarius pomarinus*
920.	South Polar Skua	*Stercorarius maccormicki*

SMALLBABBLERS, FULVETTAS AND ALLIES

921.	Abbott's Babbler	*Malacocincla abbotti*
922.	Buff-breasted Babbler	*Pellorneum tickelli*
923.	Eyebrowed Wren Babbler	*Napothera epilepidota*
924.	Indian Grassbird	*Graminicola bengalensis*

925.	Long-billed Wren Babbler	*Napothera malacoptila*
926.	Puff-throated Babbler	*Pellorneum ruficeps*
927.	Rufous-diroated Fulvetta	*Schoeniparus rufogularis*
928.	Rufous-winged Fulvetta	*Schoeniparus castaneceps*
929.	Rusty-capped Fulvetta	*Schoeniparus dubius*
930.	Spot-uiroated Babbler	*Pellorneum albiventre*
931.	Streaked Wren Babbler	*Gypsophila brevicaudata*
932.	White-hooded Babbler	*Gampsorhynchus rufulus*
933.	Yellow-throated Fulvetta	*Schoeniparus cinereus*

SOUTHERN STORM-PETRELS

934.	Black-bellied Storm-petrel	*Fregetta tropica*
935.	White-faced Storm-petrel	*Pelagodroma marina*
936.	Wilson's Storm-petrel	*Oceanites oceanicus*

SPARROWS AND SNOWFINCHES

937.	Black-winged Snowfinch	*Montifringilla adamsi*
938.	Blanford's Snowfinch	*Pyrgilauda blanfordi*
939.	Eurasian Tree Sparrow	*Passer montanus*
940.	House Sparrow	*Passer domesticus*
941.	Rock Sparrow	*Petronia petronia*
942.	Rufous-necked Snowfinch	*Pyrgilauda ruficollis*
943.	Russet Sparrow	*Passer cinnamomeus*
944.	Sind Sparrow	*Passer pyrrhonotus*
945.	Spanish Sparrow	*Passer hispaniolensis*
946.	White-rumped Snowfinch	*Onychostruthus taczanowskii*
947.	Yellow-throated Sparrow	*Gymnoris xanthocollis*

STARLINGS AND MYNAS

948.	Asian Glossy Starling	*Aplonis panayensis*
949.	Asian Pied Starling	*Gracupica contra*

950.	Bank Myna	*Acridotheres ginginianus*
951.	Brahminy Starling	*Sturnia pagodarum*
952.	Chestnut-cheeked Starling	*Agropsar philippensis*
953.	Chestnut-tailed Starling	*Sturnia malabarica*
954.	Collared Myna	*Acridotheres albocinctus*
955.	Common Myna	*Acridotheres tristis*
956.	Common Starling	*Sturnus vulgaris*
957.	Daurian Starling	*Agropsar sturninus*
958.	Golden-crested Myna	*Ampeliceps coronatus*
959.	Great Myna	*Acridotheres grandis*
960.	Jungle Myna	*Acridotheres fuscus*
961.	Malabar Starling	*Sturnia blythii*
962.	Red-billed Starling	*Spodiopsar sericeus*
963.	Rosy Starling	*Pastor roseus*
964.	Spot-winged Starling	*Saroglossa spilopterus*
965.	White-cheeked Starling	*Spodiopsar cineraceus*
966.	White-headed Starling	*Sturnia erythropygia*

STILTS AND AVOCETS

967.	*Black-winged Stilt	*Himantopus himantopus*
968.	Pied Avocet	*Recurvirostra avosetta*

STORKS

969.	Asian Openbill	*Anastomus oscitans*
970.	Black Stork	*Ciconia nigra*
971.	Black-necked Stork	*Ephippiorhynchus asiaticus*
972.	Painted Stork	*Mycteria leucocephala*
973.	Woolly-necked Stork	*Ciconia episcopus*

SUNBIRDS

974.	Black-throated Sunbird	*Aethopyga saturata*

975.	Crimson Sunbird	*Aethopyga siparaja*
976.	Crimson-backed Sunbird	*Leptocoma minima*
977.	Fire-tailed Sunbird	*Aethopyga ignicauda*
978.	Green-tailed Sunbird	*Aethopyga nipalensis*
979.	Little Spiderhunter	*Arachnothera longirostra*
980.	Loten's Sunbird	*Cinnyris lotenius*
981.	Mrs Gould's Sunbird	*Aethopyga gouldiae*
982.	Olive-backed Sunbird	*Cinnyris jugularis*
983.	Purple Sunbird	*Cinnyris asiaticus*
984.	Purple-rumped Sunbird	*Leptocoma zeylonica*
985.	Ruby-cheeked Sunbird	*Chalcoparia singalensis*
986.	Streaked Spiderhunter	*Arachnothera magna*
987.	Van Hasselt's Sunbird	*Leptocoma brasiliana*
988.	Vigors's Sunbird	*Aethopyga vigorsii*

SWALLOWS AND MARTINS

989.	Asian House Martin	*Delichon dasypus*
990.	Barn Swallow	*Hirundo rustica*
991.	Dusky Crag Martin	*Ptyonoprogne concolor*
992.	Eurasian Crag Martin	*Ptyonoprogne rupestris*
993.	Grey-throated Martin	*Riparia chinensis*
994.	Hill Swallow	*Hirundo domicola*
995.	Nepal House Martin	*Delichon nipalense*
996.	Northern House Martin	*Delichon urbicum*
997.	Pacific Swallow	*Hirundo tahitica*
998.	Pale Martin	*Riparia diluta*
999.	Red-rumped Swallow	*Cecropis daurica*
1000.	Sand Martin	*Riparia riparia*

1001. Streak-throated Swallow — *Petrochelidon fluvicola*
1002. Striated Swallow — *Cecropis striolata*
1003. Wire-tailed Swallow — *Hirundo smithii*

SWIFTS

1004. Alpine Swift — *Tachymarptis melba*
1005. Asian Palm Swift — *Cypsiurus balasiensis*
1006. Blyth's Swift — *Apus leuconyx*
1007. Brown-backed Needletail — *Hirundapus giganteus*
1008. Common Swift — *Apus apus*
1009. Himalayan Swiftlet — *Aerodramus brevirostris*
1010. Indian House Swift — *Apus affinis*
1011. Nepal House Swift — *Apus nipalensis*
1012. Pacific Swift — *Apus pacificus*
1013. Plume-toed Swiftlet — *Collocalia affinis*
1014. Silver-backed Needletail — *Hirundapus cochinchinensis*
1015. White-rumped Spinetail — *Zoonavena sylvatica*
1016. White-throated Needletail — *Hirundapus caudacutus*

SYLVIA WARBLERS AND ALLIES

1017. Asian Desert Warbler — *Curruca nana*
1018. Barred Warbler — *Curruca nisoria*
1019. Common Whitethroat — *Curruca communis*
1020. Eastern Orphean Warbler — *Curruca crassirostris*
1021. Garden Warbler — *Sylvia borin*
1022. Lesser Whitethroat — *Curruca curruca*

THICK-KNEES

1023. Beach Thick-knee — *Esacus magnirostris*

1024. Great Thick-knee — *Esacus recurvirostris*

1025. Indian Thick-knee — *Burhinus indicus*

THRUSHES AND ALLEES

1026. Alpine Thrush — *Zoothera mollissima*

1027. Black-breasted Thrush — *Turdus dissimilis*

1028. Black-throated Thrush — *Turdus atrogularis*

1029. Chestnut Thrush — *Turdus rubrocanus*

1030. Chinese Thrush — *Otocichla mupinensis*

1031. Dark-sided Thrush — *Zoothera marginata*

1032. Dusky Thrush — *Turdus eunomus*

1033. Eyebrowed Thrush — *Turdus obscurus*

1034. Fieldfare — *Turdus pilaris*

1035. Grandala — *Grandala coelicolor*

1036. Green Cochoa — *Cochoa viridis*

1037. Grey-sided Thrush — *Turdus feae*

1038. Grey-winged Blackbird — *Turdus boulboul*

1039. Himalayan Forest Thrush — *Zoothera salimalii*

1040. Indian Blackbird — *Turdus simillimus*

1041. Japanese Thrush — *Turdus cordis*

1042. Kessler's Thrush — *Turdus kessleri*

1043. Long-billed Thrush — *Zoothera monticola*

1044. Long-tailed Thrush — *Zoothera dixoni*

1045. Mistle Thrush — *Turdus viscivorus*

1046. Naumann's Thrush — *Turdus naumanni*

1047. Orange-headed Thrush — *Geokichla citrina*

1048.	Pied Thrush	*Geokichla wardii*
1049.	Purple Cochoa	*Cochoa purpurea*
1050.	Red-throated Thrush	*Turdus ruficollis*
1051.	Scaly Thrush	*Zoothera dauma*
1052.	Siberian Thrush	*Geokichla sibirica*
1053.	Song Thrush	*Turdus philomelos*
1054.	Tibetan Blackbird	*Turdus maximus*
1055.	Tickell's Thrush	*Turdus unicolor*
1056.	White-collared Blackbird	*Turdus albocinctus*

TITS

1057.	Azure Tit	*Cyanistes cyanus*
1058.	Cinereous Tit	*Parus cinereus*
1059.	Coal Tit	*Periparus ater*
1060.	Fire-capped Tit	*Cephalopyrus flammiceps*
1061.	Green-backed Tit	*Parus monticolus*
1062.	Grey-crested Tit	*Lophophanes dichrous*
1063.	Ground Tit	*Pseudopodoces humilis*
1064.	Himalayan Black-lored Tit	*Machlolophus xanthogenys*
1065.	Indian Black-lored Tit	*Machlolophus aplonotus*
1066.	Rufous-naped Tit	*Periparus. rufonuchalis*
1067.	Rufous-vented Tit	*Periparus rubidiventris*
1068.	Sultan Tit	*Melanochlora sultanea*
1069.	Yellow-browed Tit	*Sylviparus modestus*
1070.	Yellow-cheeked Tit	*Machlolophus spilonotus*

TREE-CREEPERS AND ALLIES

1071.	Bar-tailed Treecreeper	*Certhia himalayana*
1072.	Hodgson's Treecreeper	*Certhia hodgsoni*
1073.	Hume's Treecreeper	*Certhia manipurensis*

1074. Indian Spotted Creeper   *Salpornis spilonota*

1075. Rusty-flanked Treecreeper   *Certhia nipalensis*

1076. Sikkim Treecreeper   *Certhia discolor*

TROGONS

1077. Malabar Trogon   *Harpactes fasciatus*

1078. Red-headed Trogon   *Harpactes erythrocephalus*

TROPICBIRDS

1079. Red-billed Tropicbird   *Phaethon aethereus*

1080. Red-tailed Tropicbird   *Phaethon rubricauda*

1081. White-tailed Tropicbird   *Phaethon lepturus*

WALLCREEPER

1082. Wallcreeper   *Tichodroma muraria*

WAXWINGS

1083. Bohemian Waxwing   *Bombycilla garrulus*

WEAVERS

1084. Baya Weaver   *Ploceus philippinus*

1085. Black-breasted Weaver   *Ploceus benghalensis*

1086. Streaked Weaver   *Ploceus manyar*

WHISTLERS

1087. Mangrove Whistler   *Pachycephala cinereal*

WHITE-EYES, YUHINAS AND ALLIES

1088. Black-chinned Yuhina — *Yuhina nigrimenta*
1089. Chestnut-flanked White-eye — *Zosterops erythropleurus*
1090. Indian White-eye — *Zosterops palpebrosus*
1091. Rufous-vented Yuhina — *Yuhina occipitalis*
1092. Striated Yuhina — *Staphida castaniceps*
1093. Stripe-throated Yuhina — *Yuhina gularis*
1094. Whiskered Yuhina — *Yuhina flavicollis*
1095. White-naped Yuhina — *Yuhina bakeri*

WOODPECKERS AND ALLIES

1096. Bay Woodpecker — *Blythipicus pyrrhotis*
1097. Black-rumped Flameback — *Dinopium benghalense*
1098. Brown-capped Pygmy Woodpecker — *Yungipicus nanus*
1099. Brown-fronted Woodpecker — *Dendrocoptes auriceps*
1100. Common Flameback — *Dinopium javanense*
1101. Crimson-breasted Woodpecker — *Dryobates cathpharius*
1102. Darjeeling Woodpecker — *Dendrocopos darjellensis*
1103. Eurasian Wryneck — *Jynx torquilla*
1104. Freckle-breasted Woodpecker — *Dendrocopos analis*
1105. Fulvous-breasted Woodpecker — *Dendrocopos macei*
1106. Great Spotted Woodpecker — *Dendrocopos major*
1107. Greater Flameback — *Chrysocolaptes guttacristatus*
1108. Greater Yellownape — *Chrysophlegma flavinucha*
1109. Grey-capped Pygmy Woodpecker — *Yungipicus canicapillus*
1110. Grey-headed Woodpecker — *Picus canus*
1111. Himalayan Flameback — *Dinopium shorii*

1112.	Himalayan Woodpecker	*Dendrocopos himalayensis*
1113.	Lesser Yellownape	*Picus chlorolophus*
1114.	Pale-headed Woodpecker	*Gecinulus grantia*
1115.	Rufous Woodpecker	*Micropternus brachyurus*
1116.	Rufous-bellied Woodpecker	*Dendrocopos hyperythrus*
1117.	Scaly-bellied Woodpecker	*Picus squamatus*
1118.	Sind Woodpecker	*Dendrocopos assimilis*
1119.	Speckled Piculet	*Picumnus innominatus*
1120.	Streak-throated Woodpecker	*Picus xanthopygaeus*
1121.	Stripe-breasted Woodpecker	*Dendrocopos atratus*
1122.	White-bellied Woodpecker	*Dryocopus javensis*
1123.	White-browed Piculet	*Sasia ochracea*
1124.	White-naped Woodpecker	*Chrysocolaptes festivus*

WOODSHRIKES AND ALLIES

1125.	Bar-winged Flycatcher-shrike	*Hemipus picatus*
1126.	Common Woodshrike	*Tephrodornis pondicerianus*
1127.	Large Woodshrike	*Tephrodornis virgatus*
1128.	Malabar Woodshrike	*Tephrodornis sylvicola*

WOODSWALLOWS

1129.	Ashy Woodswallow	*Artamus fuscus*
1130.	White-breasted Woodswallow	*Artamus leucorynchus*

WREN BABBLERS

1131.	Nepal Wren Babbler	*Pnoepyga immaculata*
1132.	Pygmy Wren Babbler	*Pnoepyga pusilla*

1133. Scaly-breasted Wren Babbler   *Pnoepyga albiventer*

WRENS

1134. Eurasian Wren   *Troglodytes troglodytes*

PART C : REPTILES

Sl. No.	Common Name	Scientific Name

GECKOS

1.	Banded Bent-toed Gecko	*Cyrtodactylus fasciolatus*
2.	Clouded Indian Gecko	*Cyrtodactylus nebulosus*
3.	Collegal Ground Gecko	*Cyrtodactylus collegalensis*
4.	Deccan banded gecko	*Cyrtodactylus albofasciatus*
5.	Deccan Ground Gecko	*Cyrtodactylus deccanensis*
6.	Varad Giri's Ground Gecko	*Cyrtodactylus varadgirii*

TURTLES

7.	Asian leaf turtle	*Cyclemys gemeli*
8.	Brown roofed Turtle	*Pangshura smithii*
9.	Indian Black Turtle	*Melanochelys trijuga*

LIZARDS

10.	Asian Glass Lizard	*Dopasia gracilis*
11.	Anamalai spiny lizard	*Salea anamallayana*
12.	Horsfield's spiny lizard	*Salea horsfieldii*
13.	Southern flying lizard	*Draco dussumieri*

BOAS

14.	All species of the Family	*Boidae* exceptfor those listed in Schedule I

SNAKES

15.	Blind Snakes	All species of the Family *Typhlopidae*

16.	Colubrid Snakes	All species of the Family *Colubridae* except those listed in Schedule I
17.	Elapid Snakes	All species of the Family *Elapidae* except for those listed in Schedule I
18.	Sand snakes	All species of Family *Psammophiidae*
19.	Shield-tailed Snakes	All species of the Family *Uropeltidae*
20.	Sunbeam Snake	All species of the Family *Xenopeltidae*
21.	Thread Snakes	All species of the Family *Leptotyphlopidae*
22.	Vipers	All species of the Family *Viperidae* except for those listed in Schedule I

PART D : AMPHIBIANS

Sl. No.	Common Name	Scientific Name
	TOADS	
1.	Kemp's Tree Toad	*Bufoides kempi*
2.	Khasi Hills Toad	*Bufoides meghalayanus*
3.	Malabar Tree Toad	*Pedostibes tuberculosus*
	FROGS	
4.	Aloysi Pond Frog	*Phrynoderma aloysii*
5.	Annandale's Frog/Assam Hills Frog	*Clinotarsus alticola*
6.	Bompu Litter Frog	*Leptobrachium bompu*
7.	Chin Woodfrog	*Sylvirana lacrima*
8.	Cope's Frog	*Hydrophylax leptoglossa*
9.	Crab-eating Frog/Mangrove Frog	*Fejervarya moodiei*
10.	Ghosh's Frog/Manipur Frog	*Euphlyctis ghoshi*
11.	Giant Gliding Frog	*Zhangixalus smaragdinus*

12.	Himalayan Cascade Frog	*Amolops himalayanus*
13.	Indian Bullfrog	*Hoplobatrachus tigerinus*
14.	Indian Pond Frog	*Phrynoderma hexadactylum*
15.	Indian Skittering Frog	*Euphlyctis cyanophlyctis*
16.	Indoburman Cascade Frog	*Amolops indoburmanensis*
17.	Jerdon's White-lipped Horned Frog	*Megophrys major*
18.	Kalasgram Skittering Frog	*Euphlyctis kalasgramensis*
19.	Karaavali Pond Frog	*Phrynoderma karaavali*
20.	Khare's Gliding Frog	*Pterorana khare*
21.	Kerala Pond Frog	*Phrynoderma kerala*
22.	Liebig's Frog/Sikkim Paa Frog	*Nanorana liebigii*
23.	Littoral Bullfrog	*Hoplobatrachus litoralis*
24.	Mawphlang Hill Stream Frog	*Odorrana mawphlangensis*
25.	Mokokchung Frog	*Nanorana mokokchungensis*
26.	Orissa Frog	*Fejervarya orissaensis*
27.	Perching Frog/Six-Lined Tree Frog/Terai tree frog	*Polypedates teraiensis*
28.	Senchal Cascade Frog	*Amolops senchalensis*
29.	Sikkim Ombrana	*Ombrana sikimensis*
30.	Terai Wart Frog	*Minervarya teraiensis*
31.	Twin-spotted Tree Frog	*Rhacophorus bipunctatus*
32.	Yellow-spotted White-lipped Horned Frog *Megophrys flavipunctata*	

PART E : FISHES

No.	Common Names	Scientific Name

RAYS

1.	Sicklefin Devil Ray	*Mobula tarapacana*
2.	Mottled Eagle Ray	*Aetomylaeus maculatus*
3.	Ocellate Eagle Ray	*Aetomylaeus milvus*

4. Ornate Eagle Ray   *Aetomylaeus vespertilio*

SHARKS

5. Great Hammerhead   *Sphyrna mokarran*
6. Oceanic Whitetip Shark   *Carcharhinus longimanus*
7. Smooth Hammerhead   *Sphyrna zygaena*
8. Winghead Shark   *Eusphyra blochii*

SNAKEHEADS

9. Barca snakehead   *Channa barca*
10. Gollum snakehead   *Aenigmachanna Gollum*

PART F : MOLLUSCA

No.	Common Name	Scientific Name
	CONCHES	
1.	Chiragra Spider Conch	*Harpago arthriticus*
2.	Harpago Spider Conch	*Harpago chiragra*
3.	Milleped Spider Conch	*Lambis millepeda*
4.	Orange Spider Conch	*Lambis crocata*
5.	Scorpio Spider Conch	*Lambis scorpius*
6.	Sibald's Conch	*Dolomena plicata sibbaldii*
7.	Trapezium Horse Conch	*Pleuroploca trapezium*
8.	Truncate Spider Conch	*Lambis truncata*
	COWRIES	
9.	Limacina Cowrie	*Staphylaea limacina*
10.	Map Cowrie	*Leporicypraea mappa*
11.	Mole Cowrie	*Talparia talpa*

OYSTERS

12. Windowpane Oyster   *Placuna placenta*

TOP SHELLS

13. Commercial Top Shell *Tectus niloticus*

TURBANS

14. Green Turban *Turbo marmoratus*

VOLUTES

15. Vaxillate Volute/Gold Banded Volute *Harpulina arausiaca*

PART G: ARTHROPODS (OTHER THAN INSECTS)

No.	Common Name	Scientific Name

CRABS

1. Indo-Pacific Horseshoe Crab *Tachypleus gigas*
2. Mangrove Horseshoe Crab *Carcinoscorpius rotundicauda*

SPIDERS

3. Anantagiri Parachute Spider *Poecilotheria tigrinawesseli*
4. Bengal Ornamental/Chota Nagpur Parachute Spider *Poecilotheria miranda*
5. Indian Ornamental Spider/Regal Parachute Spider *Poecilotheria regalis*
6. Mysore Ornamental Spider/Striated Parachute Spider *Poecilotheria striata*
7. Peacock Tarantula/Gooty Ornamental tarantula *Poecilotheria metallica*
8. Rameswaram Ornamental Tarantula /Rameshwaram Parachute Spider *Poecilotheria anumavilasumica*
9. Red Slate Ornamental Tarantula *Poecilotheria rufilata*
10. Salem Ornamental Tarantula *Poecilotheria Formosa*

PART H: BUTTERFLIES (LEPIDOPTERA)

No.	Common Name	Scientific Name
	FAMILY	**HESPERIIDAE**
1.	Indian Ace	*Halpe homolea*
2.	Orange-tailed Awlet	*Badamia sena*
	FAMILY LYCAENIDAE	
3.	Albocerulean	*Udara albocaerulea*
4.	Assam Pierrot	*Tarucus waterstradti*
5.	Banded Royal	*Eliotiana jalindra*
6.	Barred Lineblue	*Prosotas aluta*
7.	Bhutya Lineblue	*Prosotas bhutea*
8.	Black Cupid	*Tongeia kala*
9.	Black-branded Royal	*Tajuria culta*
10.	Blue Darkie	*Allotinus subviolaceus*
11.	Blue Gem	*Poritia erycinoides*
12.	Blue Quaker	*Pithecops fulgens*
13.	Blue Tit	*Chliaria kina*
14.	Branded Royal	*Tajuria melastigma*
15.	Branded Yamfly	*Yasoda tripunctata*
16.	Broad Spark	*Sinthusa chandrana*
17.	Brown Tit	*Hypolycaena theclodies nicobarica*
18.	Cerulean Hairstreak	*Neozephyrus suroia*
19.	Chestnut-and-black Royal	*Tajuria yajna*
20.	Chinese Royal	*Tajuria luculenta*
21.	Chocolate Royal	*Remelana jangala*
22.	Chumbi Green Underwing	*Patricius younghusbandi*
23.	Common Gem	*Poritia hewitsord*
24.	Common Tinsel	*Catapoecilma major*

25.	Dark Blue Royal	*Pratapa icetas mishmia*
26.	Dark Mottle	*Logania distanti*
27.	Dark Tinsel	*Acupicta delicatum*
28.	de Niceville's Dull Oakblue	*Amblypodia agrata*
29.	Dull Green Hairstreak	*Esakiozephyrus icana*
30.	Dusky Bushblue	*Arhopala paraganesa*
31.	Dusky Meadow Blue	*Alpherakya devanica*
32.	Elwes' Silverline	*Spindasis elwesi*
33.	Falcate Oakblue	*Mahathala ameria*
34.	Felder's Lineblue	*Catopyrops ancyra*
35.	Frosted Cerulean	*Jamides kankena*
36.	Glazed Oakblue	*Arhopala paralea*
37.	Great Spotted Blue	*Phengaris atroguttata*
38.	Green Flash	*Artipe eryx*
39.	Green Sapphire	*Helipphorus androcles*
40.	Hampson's Hedge Blue	*Acytolepis lilacea*
41.	Hedge Cupid	*Bothrinia chenneili*
42.	Hewitson's Dull Oakblue	*Arhopala oenea*
43.	Indigo Flash	*Rapala varuna*
44.	Jakama Hair streak	*Shirozuozephyrus jakamensis*
45.	Kabru Green Hairstreak	*Chrysozephyrus kabrua*
46.	Khaki Silverline	*Spindasis rukmini*
47.	Kirbari Hairstreak	*Shirozuozephyrus kirbariensis*
48.	Large Fourlineblue	*Nacaduba pactolus*
49.	Lilac Oakblue	*Arhopala camdeo*
50.	Lilac Oakblue	*Arhopala camdeo*
51.	Lilac Silverline	*Apharitis lilacinus*
52.	Lister's Hairstreak	*Pamela dudgeonii*
53.	Long-banded Silverline	*Spindasis lohita*

54.	Malayan	*Magisba malaya*
55.	Many-tailed Oakblue	*Thaduka multicaudata*
56.	Metallic Cerulean	*Jamides alecto*
57.	Metallic Hedge Blue	*Callenya melaena*
58.	Moore's Cupid	*Shijimia moorei*
59.	Naga Saphire	*Heliophorus kohimensis*
60.	Narrow Spark	*Sinthusa nasaka*
61.	Nilgiri Tit	*Hypolycaena nilgirica*
62.	Pale Bushblue	*Arhopala aberrans*
63.	Pale Fourlineblue	*Nacaduba hermus*
64.	Pale Grand Imperial	*Neocheritra fabronia*
65.	Pale Spark	*Sinthusa virgo*
66.	Pallid Oakblue	*Amblypodia alesia*
67.	Pallid Royal	*Tajuria albiplaga*
68.	Peacock Royal	*Tajuria cippus*
69.	Plain Plushblue	*Flos apidanus*
70.	Plane	*Bindahara phocides*
71.	Pointed Ciliate Blue	*Anthene lycaenina*
72.	Pointed Lineblue	*Ionolyce helicon*
73.	Pointed Pierrot	*Niphanda cymbia*
74.	Powdered Green Hairstreak	*Chrysozephyrus zoa*
75.	Red Imperial	*Suasa lisides*
76.	Refulgent Flash	*Rapala refulgens*
77.	Royal Cerulean	*Jamides caeruleus*
78.	Scarce Shot Silverline	*Spindasis elima*
79.	Scarce Silverstreak Blue	*Iraota rochana*
80.	Scarce Slate Flash	*Rapala scintilla*
81.	Shot Flash	*Rapala buxaria*
82.	Silver Hairstreak	*Inomataozephyrus syla*

83.	Silver Royal	*Ancema blanka*
84.	Silver grey Silverline	*Spindasis nipalicus*
85.	Silver-Streaked Acacia Blue	*Zinaspa todara*
86.	Small Green Underwing	*Albulina metallica*
87.	Spotless Oakblue	*Arhopala fulla*
88.	Spotted Pierrot	*Tarucus callinara*
89.	Straight Pierrot	*Caleta roxus*
90.	Straightline Royal	*Tajuria diaeus*
91.	Straightwing Blue	*Orthomiella pontis*
92.	Sylhet Oakblue	*Arhopala silhetensis*
93.	Tailless Bushblue	*Amblypodia ganesa*
94.	Tailless Lineblue	*Prosotas dubiosa*
95.	Tailless Metallic Green Hairstreak	*Shirozuozephyrus khasia*
96.	Tailless Phishblue	*Flos areste*
97.	Tamil Oakblue	*Arhopala bazaloides*
98.	Truncate Imperial	*Cheritrella truncipennis*
99.	Tytler's Green Hairstreak	*Chrysozephyrus vittatus*
100.	Tytler's Lascar	*Pantoporia bieti paona*
101.	Tytler's Rosy Oakblue	*Arhopala allata suffusa*
102.	Una	*Una usta*
103.	Uncertain Royal	*Tajuria ister*
104.	Violet Onyx	*Horaga onyx*
105.	Violet Onyx	*Horaga albimacula*
106.	White Cerulean	*Jamides pura*
107.	White Royal	*Pratapa deva*
108.	White Royal	*Tajuria illurgioides*
109.	White Royal	*Tajuria illurgis*
110.	White-spotted Hairstreak	*Shizuyaozephyrus ziha*
111.	White-tipped Lineblue	*Prosotas noreia*

| 112. | Witch | *Araotes lapithis* |
| 113. | Wonderful Hairstreak | *Thermozephyrus ataxus zulla* |

FAMILY NYMPHALIDAE

114.	Autumn Leaf	*Doleschallia bisaltide*
115.	Bamboo Treebrown	*Lethe europa*
116.	Banded Marquis	*Euthalia teuta*
117.	Black Rajah	*Charaxes solon*
118.	Blackvein Sergeant	*Athyma ranga*
119.	Blue Duchess	*Euthalia duda*
120.	Blue Forester	*Lethe scanda*
121.	Blue Oakleaf	*Kallima horsfteldi*
122.	Blue-tailed Jester	*Symbrenthia niphanda*
123.	Branded Evening Brown	*Cyllogenes suradeva*
124.	Broad-banded Sailer	*Neptis sankara*
125.	Broadstick Sailer	*Neptis narayana*
126.	Bronze Duke	*Euthalia nara*
127.	Brown Argus	*Ypthima hyagriva*
128.	Brown Forester	*Lethe serbonis*
129.	Brown Prince	*Rohana parvata*
130.	Chestnut-streaked Sailer	*Neptis jumbah*
131.	China Nawab	*Polyura narcaeus*
132.	Chinese Bushbrown	*Mycalesis gotama*
133.	Chinese Yellow Sailer	*Neptis cydippe kirbariensis*
134.	Clear Sailer	*Neptis clinia*
135.	Clipper	*Parthenos sylvia*
136.	Comma	*Polygonia c-album*
137.	Commodore	*Auzakia danava*
138.	Common Archduke	*Lexias pardalis jadeitina*
139.	Common Baron	*Euthalia aconthea*

140.	Common Beak	*Libythea lepita*
141.	Common Forester	*Lethe insana*
142.	Common Nawab	*Polyura athamas*
143.	Courtesan	*Euripus nyctelius*
144.	Creamy Sailer	*Neptis soma*
145.	Danaid Eggfly	*Hypolimnas misippus*
146.	Dark Archduke	*Lexias dirtea*
147.	Dark Baron	*Euthalia merta*
148.	Dark Forester	*Lethe brisanda*
149.	Dark Forester	*Lethe goalpara*
150.	De Niceville's Bushbrown	*Mycalesis misenus*
151.	Desert Fourring	*Ypthima bolanica*
152.	Dot-dash Sergeant	*Athyma kanwa*
153.	Dusky Labyrinth	*Neope yama*
154.	Eastern Fivering	*Ypthima similis*
155.	False Comma	*Polygonia l-album*
156.	Freak	*Calinaga buddha*
157.	French Duke	*Euthalia franciae*
158.	Grand Duchess	*Euthalia patala*
159.	Great Archduke	*Lexias cyanipardus*
160.	Great Evening Brown	*Melanitis zitenius*
161.	Great Sergeant	*Athyma larymna*
162.	Great Yellow Sailer	*Neptis radha*
163.	Grey Baron	*Euthalia anosia*
164.	Grey Commodore	*Bhagadatta austenia*
165.	Grey Count	*Cynitia lepidea*
166.	Highbrown Silverspot	*Argynnis jainadeva*
167.	Jewelled Nawab	*Polyura delphis*
168.	Jezabel Palmfly	*Elymnias vasudeva*

169.	Large Tawny Wall	*Raphicera satricus*
170.	Lavender Count	*Cynitia cocytus*
171.	Lepcha Bushbrown	*Mycalesis lepcha*
172.	Long-branded Blue Crow	*Euploea algea*
173.	Malabar Tree Nymph	*Idea malabarica*
174.	Manipur Goldenfork	*Lethe kabrua*
175.	Manipur Woodbrown	*Lethe kanjupkula*
176.	Many-tufted Bushbrown	*Mycaleisis mystes*
177.	Marbled Map	*Cyrestis codes*
178.	Moeller's Silverfork	*Lethe moelteri*
179.	Mongol	*Araschnia prorsoides dohertyi*
180.	Moore's Bushbrown	*Mycalesis heri*
181.	Mountain Silverspot	*Issoria altissima*
182.	Naga Treebrown	*Lethe naga*
183.	Painted Courtesan	*Euripus consimilis*
184.	Pale Forester	*Lethe latiaris*
185.	Pale Green Sailer	*Neptis zaida*
186.	Pale Hockeystick Sailer	*Neptis manasa manasa*
187.	Pallid Argus	*Cailerebia scanda*
188.	Panther	*Neurosigma siva*
189.	Pasha	*Herona marathus*
190.	Plain Bushbrown	*Mycalesis tnalsarida*
191.	Plain Tbxeering	*Ypthima lycus*
192.	Queen of Spain Fritillary	*Issoria lathonia*
193.	Red Lacewing	*Cethosia biblis*
194.	Red-spot Duke	*Euthalia evelina*
195.	Ringed Argus	*Cailerebia annada*
196.	Scarce Blue Oakleaf	*Kallima knyvetti*
197.	Scarce Evening Brown	*Cyllogenes janetae*

198.	Scarce Mountain Argus	*Erebia kalinda kalinda*
199.	Scarce Red Forester	*Lethe distans*
200.	Scarce Tawny Rajah	*Charaxes aristogiton*
201.	Scarce Wall	*Lasiommata maerula*
202.	Scarce Woodbrown	*Lethe siderea*
203.	Sergeant Emperor	*Mimathyma chevana*
204.	Shandur Rockbrown	*Chazara heydenreichi*
205.	Short-banded Sailer	*Phaedyma columella*
206.	Silverstreak	*Argynnis clara*
207.	Siren	*Hestina persimilis*
208.	Small Goldenfork	*Lethe atkinsoni*
209.	Small Leopard	*Phalanta alcippe*
210.	Small Silverfork	*Lethe jalaurida*
211.	Small Woodbrown	*Lethe nicetella*
212.	Sordid Emperor	*Chitona sordida*
213.	Spotted Blue Crow	*Euploea midamus*
214.	Spotted Mystic	*Lethe tristigmata*
215.	Spotted Palmfly	*Elymnias malelas*
216.	Spotted Sailer	*Neptis magadh khasiana*
217.	Stately Nawab	*Polyura dolon*
218.	Striped Ringlet	*Ragadia crisilda*
219.	Studded Sergeant	*Pantoporia asura*
220.	Tailed Red Forester	*Lethe sinorix*
221.	Tamil Catseye	*Zipotis saitis*
222.	Tamil Lacewing	*Cethosia nietneri*
223.	Tawny Rajah	*Charaxes bernardus*
224.	Tibetan Jewel Blue	*Phengaris eversmanni*
225.	Tibetan Satyr	*Oeneis buddha*
226.	Travancore Evening Brown	*Parantirrhoea marshalli*

227.	Treble Silverstripe	*Lethe baladeva*
228.	Unbroken Sergeant	*Athyma pravara*
229.	Variegated Fivering	*Ypthima methora*
230.	Variegated Rajah	*Charaxes kahruba*
231.	Variegated Sailer	*Neptis armandia*
232.	Veined Labyrinth	*Lethe pulaha*
233.	Watson's Bushbrown	*Mycalesis adamsoni*
234.	Wavy Maplet	*Chersonesia intermedia*
235.	White Commodore	*Parasarpa dudu*
236.	White Oakleaf	*Kallima albofasciata*
237.	White Owl	*Neorina patria*
238.	Whitebar Bushbrown	*Mycalesis anoxias*
239.	White-edged Bushbrown	*Mycalesis mestra*
240.	White-edged Woodbrown	*Lethe visrava*
241.	White-ringed Meadowbrown	*Hyponephele davendra*
242.	Wizard	*Rhinopalpa polynice*
243.	Wood-Mason's Bushbrown	*Mycalesis suaveolens*
244.	Yellow Argus	*Paralasa mani*
245.	Yellow Kaiser	*Penthema lisarda*
246.	Yellow Owl	*Neorina hilda*
247.	Yellow Rajah	*Charaxes marmax*
248.	Yellowjack Sailer	*Lasippa viraja nar*
	FAMILY	**PAPILIONIDAE**
249:	Andaman Mormon	*Papilio mayo*
250.	Blue-striped Mime	*Papilio slateri*
251.	Brown Gorgon	*Meandrusa lachinus*
252.	Chain Swordtail	*Graphium aristeus*
253.	Chinese Windmill	*Byasa plutonius*

254.	Common Banded Peacock	*Papilio crino*
255.	Common Bluebottle	*Graphium sarpedon*
256.	Common Mime	*Chilasa clytia*
257.	Common Red Apollo	*Parnassius epaphus*
258.	Common Yellow Swallowtail	*Papilio machaon*
259.	Crimson Rose	*Pachliopta hector*
260.	Fourbar Swordtail	*Graphium agetes*
261.	Glassy Bluebottle	*Graphium cloanthus*
262.	Golden Birdwing	*Troides aeacus aeacus*
263.	Great Blue Mime	*Papilio paradoxa*
264.	Great Jay	*Graphium eurypylus*
265.	Green Dragontail	*Lamproptera meges virescens*
266.	Keeled Apollo	*Parassius jacquemonti*
267.	Lesser Mime	*Papilio epycides*
268.	Malabar Banded Peacock	*Papilio buddha*
269.	Regal Apollo	*Parnassius charltonius*
270.	Rose Windmill	*Byasa latreillei*
271.	Scarce Jay	*Graphium albociliatis*
272.	Southern Birdwing	*Troides minos*
273.	Spotted Jay	*Graphium arycles*
274.	Spotted Zebra	*Graphium megarus*
275.	Tailed Redbreast	*Papilio bootes*

FAMILY PIERIDAE

276.	Bhutan Blackvein	*Aporia harrietae*
277.	Blue Nawab	*Appias wardii*
278.	Broadwing Jezabel	*Delias lativitta*
279.	Chocolate Albatross	*Appias lyncida*
280.	Common Albatross	*Appias albina*
281.	Dusky Blackvein	*Aporia nabellica*

282.	Fiery Clouded Yellow	*Colias eogene*
283.	Kashmir White	*Pier is deota*
284.	Ladak Clouded Yellow	*Colias ladakensis*
285.	Lesser Bath White	*Pontia chloridice*
286.	Lesser Gull	*Cepora nadina*
287.	One-spot Grass Yellow	*Eurema andersoni*
288.	Orange Clouded Yellow	*Colias stoliczkana*
289.	Pale Wanderer	*Pareronia avatar*
290.	Plain Puffin	*Appias indra*
291.	Plain Sulphur	*Dercas lycorias*

FAMILY RIODINIDAE

292.	Lesser Punch	*Dodona dipoea*
293.	Orange Punch	*Dodona egeon*
294.	Straight Plum Judy	*Abisara kausambi*
295.	Striped Punch	*Dodona adonira*
296.		

PART I: PORIFERA

No.	Common Name	Scientific name
1.	Sponges	All species of the Class *Calcarea*]

SCHEDULE III

(*See* Chapter III-A and Sections 50, 51, 54 and 57) SPECIFIED PLANTS

Sl. No.	Scientific Name	Common Name
1	*Strobilanthes kunthianus*	Neel kurinji
2	*Coptis teeta*	Gold threat, Mishmi teeta
3	*Coscinium fenestration*	Tree turmeric
4	*Taxus wallichiana*	Common yew
5	*Vanda coerulea*	Blue vanda
6	*Nepenthes khasiana*	Pitcher plant
7	*Renanthera imschootiana*	Red vanda
8	*Cycas* spp.	
9	*Ceropegias* spp.	
10	*Aenhenrya rotundifolia*	
11	*Odontochilus grandiflorus*	
12	*Odontochiluste trapterus*	
13	*Rhomboda pulchra*	
14	*Vrydagzynea viridiflora*	
15	*Zeuxine andamanica*	
16	*Ipsea malabarica*	Daffodil orchid
17	*Habenaria barnesii*	
18	*Podophyllum hexandrum*	Indian podohyllum
19	*Dolomiaea costus*	Kuth]

subject to the provisions of the Convention in accordance with Article I, paragraph (

SCHEDULE IV

(*See* Chapter VB and Sections 39, 50, 51, 54, 57) Interpretation

1. Species included in these Appendices are referred to:

(a) by the name of the species; or

(b) as being all of the species included in a higher taxon or
   2. The abbreviation "spp." is used to denote all species of a higher taxon. designated part thereof.

3. Other references to taxa higher than species are for the purposes of information or classification only. The common names included after the scientific names of families are for reference only. They are intended to indicate the species within the family concerned that are included in the Appendices. In most cases this is not all of the species within the family.

4. The following abbreviations are used for plant taxa below the level of species: (*a*) "ssp." is used to denote subspecies; and

(*b*) "var(s)." is used to denote variety (varieties).

5. As none of the species or higher taxa of FLORA included in Appendix I is annotated to the effect that its hybrids shall be treated in accordance with the provisions of Article III of the Convention, this means that artificially propagated hybrids produced from one or more of these species or taxa may be traded with a certificate of artificial propagation, and that seeds and pollen (including pollinia), cut flowers, seedling or tissue cultures obtained *in vitro*, in solid or liquid media, transported in sterile containers of these hybrids are not subject to the provisions of the Convention.

6. The names of the countries in parentheses placed against the names of species in Appendix III are those of the Parties submitting these species for inclusion in this Appendix.

7. When a species is included in one of the Appendices, the whole, live or dead, animal or plant is included. In addition, for animal species listed in Appendix III and plant species listed in Appendix II or III, all parts and derivatives of the species are also included in the same Appendix unless the species is annotated to indicate that only specific parts and derivatives are included. The symbol # followed by a number placed against the name of a species or higher taxon included in Appendix II or III refers to a footnote that indicates the parts or derivatives of animals or plants that are designated as

'specimens' *b*), subparagraph (*ii*) or (*iii*). Numbers not preceded by a # symbol placed against the name of a species or higher taxon refer to a footnote that indicates specific conditions or restrictions that are applicable to trade of such species or higher taxon under the Convention.

8. The terms and expressions below, used in annotations in these Appendices, are defined as follows:

Extract

Any substance obtained directly from plant material by physical or chemical means regardless of the manufacturing process. An extract may be solid (e.g. crystals, resin, fine or coarse particles), semi-solid (e.g. gums, waxes) or liquid (e.g. solutions, tinctures, oil and essential oils).

Finished musical instruments

A musical instrument (as referenced by the Harmonized System of the World Customs Organization, Chapter 92; musical instruments, parts and accessories of such articles) that is ready to play or needs only the installation of parts to make it playable. This term includes antique instruments (as defined by the Harmonized System codes 97.05 and 97.06; Works of art, collectors' pieces and antiques).

Finished musical instrument accessories

A musical instrument accessory (as referenced by the Harmonized System of the World Customs Organization, Chapter 92; musical instruments, parts and accessories of such articles) that is separate from the musical instrument, and is specifically designed or shaped to be used explicitly in association with an instrument, and that requires no further modification to be used.

Finished musical instrument parts

A part (as referenced by the Harmonized System of the World Customs Organization, Chapter 92; musical instruments, parts and accessories of such articles) of a musical instrument that is ready to install and is specifically designed and shaped to be used explicitly in association with the instrument to make it playable.

Finished products packaged and ready for retail trade

Products, shipped singly or in bulk, requiring no further processing, packaged, labelled for final use or the retail trade in a state fit for being sold to or used by the general public.

Powder

A dry, solid substance in the form of fine or coarse particles.

Shipment

Cargo transported under the terms of a single bill of lading or air waybill, irrespective of the quantity or number of containers, packages, or pieces worn, carried or included in personal baggage.

Ten (10) kg per shipment

For the term "10 kg per shipment", the 10 kg limit should be interpreted as referring to the

weight of the individual portions of each item in the shipment made of wood of the species concerned. In other words, the 10 kg limit is to be assessed against the weight of the individual portions of wood of Dalbergia/Guibourtia species contained in each item of the shipment, rather than against the total weight of the shipment.

Transformed wood

Defined by Harmonized System code 44.09 : Wood (including strips, friezes for parquet flooring, not assembled), continuously shaped (tongued, grooved, v-jointed, beaded or the like) along any edges, ends or faces, whether or not planed, sanded or end-jointed.

Woodchips

Wood that has been reduced to small pieces.]

Changes in Wild Life (Protection) Amendment Act, 2022

Prohibition of hunting of wild animals. Protection and management of wildlife areas and the animals, birds and plants in these areas. Establishing new protected areas such as National Parks and wildlife Sanctuaries. Control of illegal wildlife trade.

1. Changes in the Preamble

Instead of words "protection of wild animals, birds and plants", the words "conservation, protection and management of wild life" were substituted in the preamble.

2. Reduction of number of Schedules

- The Bill reduces the number of schedules from 6 to 4.
- Schedule I- Animal species that will enjoy the highest level of protection including those which are critically endangered.
- Schedule II- Animal species that will be subject to a lesser degree of protection.
- Schedule III- Protected plant species.
- Schedule IV- Specimens listed in the Appendices under CITES (scheduled specimens)

3. Implementation of CITES

Addition of Chapter VB provides regulation of International Wildlife Trade as per provisions laid by CITES. The Central Government shall form a Managing Authority and a Scientific Authority to regulate import and export of specimens of species.

4. Management of Wildlife Sanctuaries

Under section 33B, the Bill provides power to State Governments to form an Advisory Committee Consisting of Chief Wildlife Warden, members of legislature, wildlife NGOs and Panchayati Raj to manage wildlife sanctuaries. This committee along with Gram sabha shall formulate management plans for wildlife sanctuaries and conservation reserves. This is the first step to transfer the decision making process towards being people centric.

5. Criteria to declare animals "vermin"

The Principal Act (under schedule V) and the Amendment both use the term 'vermin' to describe species which can be hunted under certain conditions, to keep their numbers in check. eg.mice, rats, crows.

6. References to Forests Rights Act, 2006 (FRA)

According to clause 13, 15, and 17 which seek to amend section 33, 35 and 38 of the Principal Act, the Management of sanctuaries should be done according to the provisions of the FRA Act wherever applicable.

The amendment Bill empowers the Gram sabha and other local village institutions to collectively protect the forests, wild animals and bio diversity and take action against any activity posing threat to wildlife.

7. Permission to carry out subsistence fishing in and around Protected Areas.

Under section 29 and 33, the Bill allows low intensity, small-scale fishing in rivers and other water bodies in and around protected areas. This lifts the blanket ban which prohibits all types of fishing activity in and around Protected Areas, which had caused many people to lose their livelihood.

8. Invasive Species

The Amendment to section 62A, of the Principal Act, recognizes the threat to eco-systems from invasive alien species and also provides for the establishment of a scientific Authority (as per CITES) to advise on matters related to trade of such species. It also grants power to the Central Government to regulate or prohibit import, trade, possession or proliferation of such species.

9. Use of protected Areas

Under the Amendment of section 29, the Bill relaxes the norms on grazing of cattle and use of drinking water by the local communities living inside the protected areas until they are settled elsewhere.

10. Trade Live Elephants

The Amendment proposes a new sub-section (4) under section 43. "Provided that, the transfer or transport of a captive elephant for a religious or any other purpose by a person having a valid certificate of ownership shall be subject to such terms and conditions as may be prescribed by the Central Government". This amendment can lead to legalization of elephant trade in India. This is potentially problematic given the horrific plight of India's captive elephants.

11. Ownership of captive animals and trophies

Under section 42A, any person possessing a captive animal or a trophy can voluntarily surrender it to the Government without expecting any compensation for the same. Such live animals will be taken under care of rescue centres if they are not suitable to be released in the wild.

12. Prohibition of renewal of license of firearms

Under amendment of section 34, No renewal of any licence under the arms Act, 1959, shall be granted to any person residing within ten kilometres of a sanctuary except under the intimation to the Chief Wildlife Warden or the authorised officer.

13. Enhanced Penalties

The Bill also enhances the penalties prescribed for violation of provisions of the Act. For 'General Violations', the maximum fine has been increased from rupees.25,000 to rupees one lakh. In the case of specially protected animals, the minimum fine of rupees 10,000 has been increased to rupees 25,000.

14. Change in definition of 'Zoos'

Zoos will hereby serve as the areas for ex-situ conservation, rescue centres and breeding centres in addition to their purpose being that of exhibition of animals.

Challenges and criticisms of the WPA Amendment Act, 2022

- There are many loop holes in this Amendment. Certain clauses and sections which were amended are not clearly defining the purpose for the amendment. Certain important topics like human-wildlife conflict, exploitation of animals on religious grounds, the illegal wildlife trade and conservation of endangered species are ignored in the Amendment Bill.

- Certain topics such as Conservation of Marine bio diversity are not covered in this Bill.

- The most important reason for introducing the Bill, being the need to provide legislative backing to commitments made by India over the past many years to the CITES.

- The new schedule IV added in the WLPA enlists all the species found in CITES appendices I, II and III and regulates their trade as prescribed via chapter VB. Under this Chapter, any person having a registration certificate can legally posses, transfer and carry out captive breeding of schedule iv species.

- An unexpected exemption came in the form of an amendment under section 43, which deals with trade of 'live' elephants. While the Principal Act prohibited any form of commercial sale of wild animal, its parts or trophies, the amendment sought exemption to carry out trade and transport of live elephants for religious use after permission from Central and State Government. Elephants being scheduled I species, under the Principal Act elephants can only be owned when inherited. This major loophole cannot only lead to smuggling of captive elephants, but also illegal capture of wildlife elephants.

- India has a coastline of 7000 km and a vast range of marine bio diversity. The island groups are fragile eco systems harbouring many endemic species. All marine resources are protected under the coastal Regulation Zone (CRZ) of 1991 which extends its protection to the coral reefs also. However not all coral reefs are protected under this Act. Tourism industry, construction, mining and quarrying activities pose threat to not only the coral reefs but the entire marine species are consumed as food in India and their trade may soon be rendered illegal.

- Lack of taxonomical accuracy while enrolling the species in their respective schedules. Many endangered species are not listed in schedules I and II and some are omitted completely.

- Several migratory birds which are listed in CITES appendices but not specified currently in schedule I-IV, in the Principal Act, are winter visitors to India. These species are hunted widely by the local gangs, however neither there birds are notified, no are they referred to in the Amendment Bill.

- The Bill has amended section 6 which will allow the State boards of wildlife to establish a standing committee for exercising, powers thereby reducing the State's hold over its wildlife.

- The illicit wildlife trade includes trafficking in animal parts such as ivory, rhino horns, tiger bones and genitals, leopard pelts and paws and bear paws and shark fins for use in traditional African and Asian medicines. Certain parts are also traded for making clothing, rugs and wall hangings.

- The Wildlife experts have raised concern over the importance given to zoos and also questioned the mere existence if such areas which are used to display animals for re- creation purposes.

Legislative Interventions for the Protection of Animals: Important Laws

The Animal Welfare Board of India is a statutory advisory body on Animal Welfare Laws and promotes animal welfare in the country. Established in 1962 under section 4 of The Prevention of Cruelty to Animals Act, 1960 (No. 59 of 1960), the Animal Welfare Board of India was started under the stewardship of Late Smt. Rukmini Devi Arundale, well known dancer and humanitarian. From ensuring that animal welfare laws in the country are diligently followed, to provide grants to Animal Welfare Organizations and advising the Government of India on animal welfare issues, the Board has been the face of the animal welfare movement in the country for the last 60 years. Through its services, Board ensures that animal welfare laws in the country are diligently followed, provides grants to Animal Welfare Organizations and advises the Government of India on animal welfare issues. The Board consists of 28 members including 6 members of Parliament (2 members of Parliament from Rajya Sabha and 4 Members of Parliament from Lok Sabha). The term of office of members is for a period of 3 years.

- **Prevention of Cruelty to Animals Act, (1960)**

It was passed by the Indian Parliament in 1960 to amend the laws about the prevention of cruelty to animals and to prevent the infliction of needless pain or suffering on animals. This Act provides for punishment for causing unnecessary cruelty and suffering to animals. This Act discusses different forms of cruelty, exceptions and killing of a suffering animal, in case any cruelty has been committed against it, so as to relieve it from further suffering. The act enshrines the provisions relating to the exhibition of the performing animals and offences committed against the performing animals. The Animal Welfare Board of India, was established in 1962 under section 4 of the Act. This Board established by the Indian Government by the legal requirements. The Board undertakes the following functions,

1. Advising the Central Government regarding amendments and rules to prevent unnecessary pain while transporting animals, performing experiments on animals, or storing animals in captivity.

2. Encouragement of financial assistance, rescue homes, and animal shelters for old animals.

3. Advising the Government on medical care and regulations for animal hospitals.

4. Imparting education and awareness on humane treatment of animals.

5. Advising the Central Government regarding general matters of animal welfare.

Animal slaughter in public is prohibited by the Prevention of Cruelty Act of 1960. Because of this, the Act mandates that any state in India select a slaughterhouse for any slaughter that takes place inside municipal corporation boundaries. The number of slaughterhouses and animals sacrificed in a given area should be proportional to that area's population.

Chickens cannot be slaughtered anywhere other than a slaughterhouse, according to Rule 3 of the Prevention of Cruelty to Animals, (Slaughterhouse) Rules, 2001. The killing of sick or pregnant animals is prohibited.

According to section 11(1) (h) of the Prevention of Cruelty to Animals Act, 1960, it is considered cruelty to an animal if the owner of the animals fails to provide it with enough food, water, or shelter.

An individual who neglects an animal by depriving it of necessary food, water, shelter, and exercise or by keeping it chained or imprisoned for an excessive amount of time may be subject to a fine, up to three months in jail, or both.

- **Cow Slaughter and Cattle Preservation Act, 1964**

Prohibition of Slaughter of Cattle – Notwithstanding anything contained or any law, custom or usage to the contrary, no person shall slaughter or offer or cause to be offered for slaughter or otherwise intentionally kill or offer or cause to be offered for killing any cattle.

Cattle Slaughter in India, especially cow slaughter is controversial because of cattle's status as endeared and respected living beings to adherents of Dharmic religions like Hinduism, Buddhism, Sikhism and Jainism. Also, many Zorastrians/Parsis living in India stepped eating beef out of respect, as it is sacred for the people of Dharmic religions. Cattle Slaughter also been opposed by various Indian religions because of ethical principle of Ahimsa (non-violence) and belief in the unity of all life. Legislation against Cattle Slaughter is in place throughout most of the states and territories in India.

The Karnataka Prevention of Cow Slaughter and Cattle Preservation Act, 1964

Statements of objects and reasons

I

Act of 35 of 1964 – The laws regulating preservation of animals in force in State of Mysore are, the Mysore Prevention of Cow Slaughter Act, 1948, in force in Mysore Area and The Bombay Animal Preservation Act, 1954, in force in the Bombay Area. Under Section 2 of Mysore Act, "cow" is defined to it includes bull, bullock, buffalo and calf and Section 3 of the Act imposes a ban on the Slaughter of Cows except when certified by a qualified veterinarian to be affected with rabis. In view of the decision of the Supreme Court in Mohammed Hanif Qureshi and others V State of Bihar (1958) and the decision of the Mysore High Court in Qureshi & others V The State of Mysore, it is considered necessary to have a uniform law for the whole state in conformity with those decisions.

Hence this bill

(Published in the Karnataka Gazette (Extraordinary), Part IV-2A dated 20th November 1963 as No.144 at page.9.

II

Amending Act of 24 of 1966 -Section 16 of the Mysore Prevention of Cow Slaughter and Cattle Preservation Act, 1964, lays down that the Act shall not apply to any cow or animal operated upon for vaccine lymph, serum or for any experimental or research purpose or any cow or animal, slaughter of which is certified by a veterinary officer or be necessary in the interest of the public health or which is suffering from any disease which is certified by a veterinary officer as being contagious and dangerous to other animals. The Government of India have started that regulations for the army contain provisions for the destruction of Army Cattle when they have been certified by a veterinary officer as suffering from an incurable disease or injury. They have requested that in order to enable destruction of such animals suitable provision may be made in the Mysore Act.

Hence this Bill.

(Published in the Karnataka Gazete (Extraordinary) Part IV-2A, dated 21st July 1966 as No.122 at page. 3.)

III

Amending Act 26 of 1975- Under clause (c) of section 16 of the Act, a cow or animal belonging to the central Government in the Ministry of Defence, Slaughter of which is certificate by a veterinary officer of the Indian Army to be necessary on the ground that it is suffering from incurable disease or injury is exempt from the provisions of the Act. It is considered that similar exemption should also be made applicable in the case of slaughter of a cow or animal certified by a veterinary officer authorised by State Government as one suffering from an incurable disease or injury.

Karnataka Prevention of Cow Slaughter and Cattle Prevention Act,1964,- An Act to provide for the prevention of slaughter of cows, calves of cows and calves of she buffaloes and for the preservation of other cattle in the State. Karnataka Prevention of Slaughter and Preservation of Cattle Act, 2010, the Ordinance prohibits.

(i) The Slaughter of cows, bulls and bullocks of all ages and buffaloes upto the age of 13 years and

(ii) Sale, purchase and disposal of these animals for slaughter. It also restricts intra state and inter-state transport of these animals for slaughter.

Those who found guilty can be imprisoned for not less than 3 years and upto 7 years conviction with fines of not less than 50,000 rupees upto 10 lakh. The underlying presumption is that the cow is sacred and sacrosanct and killing it is automatically considered illegal.

The Prevention of Cruelty to Animals (Tamil Nadu Amendment) Act, 2017- an act to amend the Prevention of Cruelty to Animals Act, 1960, so as to preserve the cultural heritage of the State of Tamil Nadu and to ensure the survival and well being of the native breed of bulls. Recently, in 2023 Supreme Court upheld the amendments made by Tamil Nadu, Karnataka and Maharashtra to the Prevention of Cruelty to Animals Act, 1960, to allow the traditional bull-taming sport of Jallikattu, Kambala (Karnataka) and bullock-cart racing.

Jallikattu Amendment Act

A five judge constitution bench headed by Justice K M Joseph, since retired, had delivered a unanimous verdict on May 18th 2023, upholding the validity of amendment Acts of Tamil Nadu, Maharashtra and Karnataka which allowed "Jallikattu", bullock-cart races and buffalo racing sport "kambala'. The sport was banned by Supreme Court in a decision citing cruelty to animals based on law suit filed by the animal rights groups People for the Ethical Treatment of Animals (PETA) which asserted that it violates the Prevention of Cruelty to Animals Act (PCA) 1960. Cow Slaughter Amendment Act, the ordinance was promulgated on 5th January 2021. It replaces the Karnataka Prevention of Cow Slaughter and Cattle Preservation Act, 1964.

On 26thOctober 2005, the Supreme Court landmark judgement upheld the constitutional validity of Anti-Cow Slaughter Law enacted by various State

Governments of India. 20 out of 28 States in India had various laws regulating the Act of Slaughtered Cow, Prohibiting the Slaughter of sale of cow, Government ordered banning Cow Slaughter on 30th August 1976. The First state banned Cow Slaughter in India is Tamil Nadu in 1976. On 26th October 2005, the Supreme Court landmark judgement, in State of Gujarat V Mirzapur Moti Kureshi Kasab Jamat &Ors. (2005), as per meat export policy in India, the export of beef is prohibited. Bone in meat, carcass, half carcass of Buffalo is also prohibited and is not permitted to be exported. Only boneless meats of buffalo, goat, sheep and birds are permitted for export. The "Preservation, protection and improvement of stock and prevention of animal diseases, veterinary training and practice" is Entry is the State List of the 7th Schedule of the Constitution, meaning that State Legislatures have exclusive powers to legislate the Prevention of Slaughter and Preservation of Cattle. State permit the slaughter of cattle with restrictions like a "fit-for-slaughter" certificate which may be issued depending on factors like age and sex of cattle continued economic viability etc.

"Jallikattu" is a Tamil word, which comes from the term "Callikattu" where "Calli" means coins and "kattu" means a package. Jallikattu refers to silver or gold coins tied on the bull's horns. People in the earlier time, used to fight to get at the money placed around the bulls horns, which depicted as an act of bravery. Later, it became a sport conducted for entertainment and was called "eruthu kattu", in which a fast moving bull was corralled with ropes around its neck. Started as a simple act of bravery, later assumed different forms and shapes like Jallikattu (in the present form) bull, race etc., which is based on the concept of fight. Jallikattu includes Manjuvirattu, Oorumadu, Vadamadu, Erudhu, Vadam, Vadi and all such events involve taming of bulls.

In Animal Welfare Board of India V A. Nagaraja & Ors (2014), during the course of Investigation, one bull died and many were injured. Bulls are forced to participate and were deliberately fainted, formented, mutilated, stabbed, beaten, chased and denied even their most basic needs, including food, water and sanitation. The findings of this investigation clearly show that bulls, are used in Jallikattu are subjected to extreme cruelty and unmitigated suffering.

In Animal Welfare Board V Union of India, 2017, in this case upheld that the practice of Jallikattu as per the 2017 Tamil Nadu Amendment to the Prevention of Cruelty to animals Act, 1960. The Supreme Court held that the State Amendment (Prevention of Cruelty to Animals Tamil Nadu Amendment) Act of 2017 and Prevention of Cruelty to Animals (Conduct of Jallikattu) Rules of 2017 did not violate the constitution and the Supreme Court 2014 ruling banning Jallikattu. The case, involves a challenge to the

Tamil Nadu amendment allowing Jallikattu, based on the argument that it goes against the central law prohibiting the cruelty to animals.

Andhra Pradesh Prohibition of Cow slaughter and Animal Preservation Act,1977, Section 5 of Prohibition of slaughter of cow or calf of she-buffaloe – Notwithstanding anything in any other law for the time being in force or any custom, or usage to the contrary, no person shall slaughter or cause to be slaughtered, or offer or cause to be offered for slaughter or otherwise intentionally kill or offer or cause to be offered for killing, any cow or calf, whether male or female, of a she-buffaloe. Section 10 is Penalty for the violation, whoever shall convicted with imprisonment for a term which may extend to six months, or with fine which may extend to one thousand rupees or both.

Cockfighting is prohibited under sections 11(1) (m) (ii) and (n) of the Prevention of Cruelty Act, 1960. Cockfighting in India takes place in January coinciding with Makara Sankranthi in January every year. This Practice is widespread in coastal districts of Andra Pradesh including Krishna, Guntur, East Godavari, and West Godavari districts and Tamil Nadu, despite being illegal in India. In Narahari Jagadish Kumar V state of Andhra Pradesh (2016) is to declare that the inaction of the respondents, is not taking steps to implement the provisions of the Prevention of Cruelty to Animal Act, 1960, and Andhra Pradesh Gaming Act,1974, against anti-social elements organizing cock fights with betting, selling illicit liquor, gambling, and subjecting animals and birds to cruelty during sankranthi festival, in the west Godavari District of Andhra Pradesh as being arbitrary illegal and against the provisions of the 1960 act and 1974 Act. Fights between birds and roosters are said to been arranged in Ancient India as a mode of entertaintment. It is recorded that outcome of Battle of Palnadu (1178-1182) was decided by a rooster fight, following which cockfight gained foothold in Andhra Pradesh.

Telangana Prohibition of Cow Slaughter and Animal Prevention Act, 1977, must be followed and the collector of each district serves as the Board's chairperson who is responsible for making sure that no animals were killed in public areas without permission.

Main Features of legislations enacted by the State/Union Territories on Cow Slaughter

Andhra Pradesh – The Andhra Pradesh Prohibition of Cow Slaughter and Animal Preservation Act, 1977, Definitions, "Cow"- includes heifer or a calf, whether male or femaleof a cow. "Calf"-age not defined. Slaughter of cow prohibited. Slaughter of bull, bullock allowed on 'fit- for- slaughter' certificate, to be given only if the animal is not economical or is not likely to become economical for the purpose of breeding or draught/agricultural operations. Imprisonment up to maximum of 6 months or fine of up to Rs. 1,000 or both.–cognisable.

Assam – Consumption and transportation of cattle. Sufficient legal provisions to regulate the Slaughter, consumption and transportation of cattle by repealing The Assam Cattle Preservation Act, 1950. Cow slaughter banned except on issue of 'fit-for-slaughter' certificate at designated places, to be given if cattle is over 14 years of age or has become permanently, it become permanently incapacitated for work or breeding due to injury, deformity or any incurable disease. Imprisonment up to maximum of 6 months or fine of up to Rs. 1,000 or both.- cognisable. Definitions- "cattle" means bulls, bullocks, cows, calves, male and female buffaloes and buffalo calves. "calf" not defined.

Bihar – Bihar Preservation And Improvement of Animals Act, 1955. This Act prohibits the slaughter of Cows, Calves, Bulls and bullocks in the State of Bihar with the exception of bulls, bullocks and she buffalos which may be slaughtered based on certain conditions such as permanent incapability that has not been caused deliberately. Bulls, bullocks older than 15 years allowed. Incapaciated for work or breeding due to njury, deformity or any incurable disease. Violators had to face six months imprisonment or rupees 1000 fine or both. Cognisable. Definitions- "Bull"- uncastrated male of above 3 years. "Bullock" castrated male of above 3 years. "Calf" male or female below 3 years. "Cow" female above 3 years. Export of cows, calves, bulls and bullocks from Bihar is not allowed for any purpose.

Chattisgarh – Chattisgarh Agricultural Cattle Preservation Act, 2004, Schedule I, Section 2(b) Agricultural Cattle means cows of all ages, calves of cows and of she buffaloes, bulls, bullocks, male and female buffaloes. Slaughter of cow, buffalo, bull, bullock, calf and possession of their meat banned transport, export to other states for slaughter also banned; attracts same punishment of 7 years imprisonment and fined upto 50,000 rupees.

Daman & Diu, Goa – The Goa, Daman & Diu Prevention of Cow Slaughter Act, 1978 – Definitions "Cow" includes cow, heifer or calf. Age of calf not defined. Total ban on slaughter of cow except when cow is suffering pain or contagious disease or for medical research. Prohibition of sale of beef or beef products in any form. Imprisonment upto 2 years or fine up to Rs. 1,000 or both. Both cognisable and non-bailable. Applicable to bulls, bullocks, male calves and buffaloes of all ages. All the animals can be slaughtered on 'fit- for- slaughter' certificate which is not given if the animal is likely to become economical for draught, breeding or milk (for she/buffaloes) purposes. Prohibition of sale of beef obtained in contravention of above provisions, except beef imported from other States. Imprisonment upto maximum 6 months or fine upto Rs. 1,000 or both - Cognisable.

Delhi – Delhi Agricultural Cattle preservation Act,1994, An Act to provide or the preservation of animals suitable for milch, draught, breeding or agricultural purposes. This Act provides for preservation of agricultural cattle in the State of Delhi. Section 4 prohibits any person from slaughtering any agricultural cattle including cows, calves of cows, bulls and bullocks. Slaughter of "agricultural cattle"- cow, calf, bull, bullock and "possession of (their) flesh" even if they are killed outside Delhi banned. Buffalo meat or carabeef is allowed. Imprisonment should not be less than 5 years and fine upto Rs. 10,000, provided that normally imprisonment should not less than 6 months and fine not less than Rs. 1,000. Burden of proof is on the accused. Both cognisable and non-bailable.

Gujarat – The Gujarat animal Preservation Act, 1954, The Act specific to the western Indian state of Gujarat, prohibits the slaughter of cattle. A person transporting cattle from one region or the state to another is deemed to be transporting them for slaughter unless they are able to prove otherwise. Slaughter of cow, calf, bull and bullock; transport, sale of their meat banned. Punishment imprisonment for a term of 7 years or 50,000 rupees fine. Buffalo meat or cara meat is allowed. The Bombay Animal Preservation Act, 1954 (applied to Gujarath), applicable to bulls, bullocks, cows, calves and male/female buffalo calves. Slaughter of cow, calf, bull or bullock totally prohibited. Slaughter of buffaloes permitted on certain conditions. Imprisonment upto maximum of 6 months or fine of upto Rs. 1,000 or both. – Cognisable.

Haryana –the Haryana Gauvansh Sanrakshan and Gausamvardhan Act, 2015, any usage or custom to the contrary, no person shall slaughter or cause to be slaughtered or offer or cause to be offered for slaughter any cow in any place in the State: Provided that killing of a cow in an accident or self defence shall not be considered as slaughter under the Act. To stop cow slaughter and smuggling and ensure welfare of cattle in the state. Under clauses of the Act, cow trafficking, slaughtering and possessing or consuming beef were prohibited. Rigorous imprisonment upto 5 years or fine upto Rs. 5,000 or both.

Himachal Pradesh – The Himachal Pradesh prohibition of Cow Slaughter Act, 1979, An Act to prohibit the slaughter of cow and its progeny in Himachal. Slaughter of all bovines punishable with imprisonment for a term of 5 years. Killing is allowed in the interest of research, or if animal has contagious disease. The Punjab Prohibition of Cow Slaughter Act, 1955 (applicable to the State of Himachal Pradesh).

Jammu and Kashmir – The Ranbir Penal Code, 1932, voluntary slaughter of any bovine animal such as ox, bull, cow or calf shall be punished with imprisonment of either description which may extend to 10 years and shall also be liable to fine. Fine may extend to five times the price of the animals slaughtered as determined by the court. Possession of flesh of killed or slaughtered animals is also an offence punishable with imprisonment upto 1 year and fine upto Rs. 500. The Jammu & Kashmir Ranbir Penal Code, 1989, prohibits the slaughter of bovines (oxes, bulls, cows and calves). Persons may not keep in their possession the flesh of slaughtered bovines. The provisions criminalize the sale and possession of the untanned hide, meat or flesh of gonds or possesses the carcass of a gond. The Jammu & Kashmir Bovine Breeding Act, 2018, Jammu &Kashmir Bovine Breeding Rule, 2019, the Jammu and Kahmir administration had issued an order to ban illegal slaughter of bovine animals, reportedly full ban.

Karnataka – The Karnataka Prevention of Cow Slaughter and Cattle Preservation Act, 1964. Definitions- Animal means bull, bullock and all buffaloes. Cow includes calf of a cow, male or female. Slaughter of cow, calf of a cow or calf of a she-buffalo totally prohibited. Slaughter of bulls, bullocks and adult buffaloes permitted on fit- for- slaughter certificate provided cattle is over 12 years of age or is permanently incapacitated for breeding, draught or milk due to injury, deformity or any other cause. Transport for slaughter to a place outside a state not permitted. Sale purchase or disposal of cow or calf for slaughter not permitted. Imprisonment upto maximum of 6 months or fine of upto Rs. 1,000 or both. – Cognisable.

Kerala – No State legislation- only Panchayat Act/Rules. Kerala Panchayat (Slaughter Houses and Meat Stalls) Rules, 1964, Panchayat laws provide for prohibition of slaughter of useful animals in Panchayat (non-municipal) areas in the State. Under the Kerala Panchayat (Slaughter Houses and Meat Stalls) Rules, 1964, no certificate shall be granted under Rule 8 in respect of a bull, bullock, cow calf, he-buffalo or she-buffalo or buffalo calf unless the animal is over 10 years of age and is unfit for work or breeding or the animal has become permanently incapacitated for work or breeding due to injury or deformity. In 1976, the Kerala Government issued an executive order banning the slaughter of useful animals in the Municipal areas as well.

Madhya Pradesh – The Madhya Pradesh Agricultural Cattle Preservation Act, 1959. Definitions- Agricultural cattle means cows of all ages, calves of cows, bull, bullocks and all buffaloes. Slaughter of cow, calf of cow, bull, bullock and buffalo calf prohibited. However, bulls and bullocks are being slaughtered in the light of Supreme Court Judgement, provided the cattle is over 15 years or has become unfit for work or breeding. Transport or export for slaughter not permitted. Export for any purpose to another State where cow slaughter is not banned by law is not permitted. Sale, purchase, disposal of cow and its progency and possession of flesh of cattle is prohibited. Imprisonment upto 3 years fine of Rs.5,000. Normally imprisonment shall not be less than 6 months and fine not less than Rs. 1,000. Burden of Proof is on the accused. – Cognisable.

Maharashtra- The Maharashtra Animal Preservation Act, 1976. Definitions, 'cow' includes a heifer or male or female calf of a cow. Slaughter of cow totally prohibited. Slaughter of bulls, bullocks and buffaloes allowed on fit-for-slaughter certificate, if it is not likely to become economical for draught, breeding or milk (in the case of she-buffaloes) purposes. Imprisonment upto maximum of 6 months and fine of upto Rs.1,000. Burden of proof is on the accused- Cognisable.

Manipur- Proclamation by Maharaja-Darbar Resolution of 1936, "According to Hindu religion the killing of cow is a sinful act. It is also against Manipur Custom. I cannot allowed such things to be committed in my State. So if any one is seen killing a cow in the State he should be prosecuted".

Meghalaya- No Legislation.

Nagaland- No Legislation.

Odisha – The Orissa Prevention of Cow Slaughter Act, 1960. Definition "Cow" includes heifer or calf. Slaughter of cow totally prohibited. Cow Slaughter, old bulls, bullocks, can be killed fit-for- slaughter certificate, if cattle is over 14 years of age or has become permanently unfit for breeding, draught (cow if it suffers from contagious disease). 2 years imprisonment or 1,000 rupees fine or both. – Cognisable.

Pondicherry- The Pondicherry Prevention of Cow Slaughter Act, 1968. Definition Cow' includes heifer or calf. Slaughter of cow totally prohibited. Slaughter of bull or bullock permitted on 'fit-for-slaughter' certificate provided it is over age of 15 years or has become permanently unfit for breeding or draught. Prohibition on sale, transport of beef. Imprisonment upto maximum of 2 years or fine upto Rs.1,000 or both. Cognisable and non-bailable.

Punjab- Punjab Prohibition of Cow Slaughter Act 1955, 15 of 1956, Notwithstanding anything contained in any cow slaughter. Other law for the time being in force or any usage of custom of the contrary, no person shall slaughter or cause to be slaughtered or after or cause to be offered for slaughter any cow in any place in Punjab. "Beef" does not include imported beef; "cow" includes, bull, bullocks, oxen, heifer and halves. Slaughter allowed for export, of the government allows. Imprisonment upto maximum of 2 years or fne upto Rs. 1,000 or both. Burden of proof is on the accused. Cognisable and non-bailable.

Rajasthan- The Rajasthan Bovine Animal (Prohibition of Slaughter and Regulation of Temporary Migration or Export) Act, 1955. Definitions,

'Bovine' means and includes cow, calf, heifer, bull or bullocks. 'Bull' means uncastrated male above 3 years. 'Bullock' means castrated male above 3 years. 'Calf' means castrated or uncastrated male of 3 years and below. 'Cow' means female above 3 years;'Heifer' is female of 3 years or below. Slaughter

of all bovine animals prohibited. Possession sale, transport of beef and beef products is prohibited. Export of bovine animal for slaughter is prohibited. Custody of seized animals to be given to any recognised voluntary animal welfare agency failing which to any Goshala, Gosadan or a suitable person who volunteers to maintain the animal. Rigorous imprisonment of not less than 1 year and upto maximum of 2 years and fine upto Rs. 10,000. Burden of proof is on the accused.

Tamil Nadu- The Tamil Nadu Animal Preservation Act, 1958, Definition, 'Animal' means bulls, bullocks, cows, calves; also buffaloes of all ages. All animals can be slaughtered on 'fit-for-slaughter' certificate. Certificate given if animal is over 10 years of age and is unfit for work and breeding or has become permanently incapacitated for work and breeding due to injury deformity or any incurable disease. Imprisonment of upto 3 years or fine upto Rs. 1,000 or both. Slaughter of cows and heifers (cow) is banned in all slaughter houses in Tamil Nadu. The Government orders banning cow slaughter dated 30th August 1976.

Uttar Pradesh – Uttar Pradesh Prevention of Cow Slaughter Act, 1955, Except as herein excepted and notwithstanding anything contained in any other law for the time being in force, no person shall sell or transport or, offer for sale or transport or cause to be sold or transported beef or beef-products in any form except for such medicinal purposes as may be prescribed. In U P Cabinet Cow Slaughter Prevention (Amendment) Ordinance, 2020, has provision to punish accused under the law with maximumrigorous imprisonment of 10 years and a fine upto 5 lakh. The aim of the law is to protect and prevent cow Slaughter.

West Bengal- The West Bengal Animal Slaughter Act, 1950. Definition, 'Scheduled Animals' – bulls, bullocks, cows, calves and buffaloes of all types/ages. Slaughter of all animals permitted on 'fit-for-slaughter' certificate. Certificate given if animal is over 14 years of age and unfit for work or breeding or has become permanently incapacitated for work and breeding due to age, injury, deformity, or any incurable disease. Imprisonment upto maximum of 6 months or fine upto Rs. 1,000 or both.- Cognisable.

February 14 as Cow Hug Day, had come from Animal Welfare Board in India which called Cows "the backbone of Indian culture and rural economy, keeping in mind the importance of the mother cow and making life happy and full of positive energy. This approach aims to promote the spiritual and mental well-being of all the citizens of India".

- **The Rajasthan Camel (Prohibition of Slaughter & Regulation of Temporary Migration or Export) Act, 2015.**

According to the law, no person shall posses, sell or transport for sale or cause to be sold or transported camel meat or camel meat products in any form. Whoever intentionally causes grievious injuries to a camel shall, on conviction, be punished with rigorous imprisonment for a term which shall not be less than one year but may extends to three years or with fine which may extends to 7000 rupees.

Camel is called as the 'ship of Desert', because it is the only means of transport found in deserts. Camel was declared as the State Animal of Rajasthan in 2014. Rajasthan Government came with the 2015 Act, to prohibit temporary migration of camels out of Rajasthan and stop its slaughter. This affects Camel rearing in the State was reduced, thus there was a decline in their population. Camel Slaughter was banned in India, inorder to save the camel, the Government of Rajasthan enacted Camel (Prohibition of Slaughter and Regulation of Temporary Migration or Export) Bill 2015, providing severe punishment for selling camels for slaughter for taking them outside the state for castrating them and even for using the nose peg.

In Scouts & Guides For Animals and Birds V Union Of India & Ors. reported on 2nd September 2022, PIL was filed in Delhi High Court, against alleged illegal transportation of camel to the national Capital from their natural habitat in Rajasthan, for demonstration in Republic Day Parade. The petition has been filed by an organisation namely Scouts & Guides for Animals & Birds, alleging that impugned actions not only violative of statutory prescription. It is made clear that the respondents make sure strict compliance of the amendment to (Prevention of Cruelty to Animals), The Transport of Animals Rules, 2020 while transporting the camels in future also for the purpose of their participation in Republic Parade, or any other purpose also. The PIL stands disposed.

- **Wild Life Protection Act, 1972**

The Act provides for the protection of the country's wild animals, birds and plants species, in order to ensure environmental and ecological security. Hunting of certain wild species, including Indian Elephants, Indian Lions, snow Leopards, Tigers, Great Indian bustards, etc., is prohibited by section 9 of the Wildlife Protection Act of 1972. The Act empowers the Government to declare areas as any one of the following protected areas: National Parks, Wildlife sanctuaries. The Act focuses on the preservation of habitats and the preservation of wildlife exploitation.

- **Cosmetics Rules, 2020**

The Ministry of Health and Family Welfare adopted the revised Cosmetics Rules, 2020 as a consequence of suggestions provided by PETA India. The prescribed rules established a distinct and modernized regulatory framework for the development, production, distribution, and importation of cosmetic items. The regulations also included clauses assuring that the importing of cosmetics subjected to animal testing is strictly prohibited. India became the first nation in Asia to outlaw both animal testing of cosmetics and the components used in them as well as the importing of the tested goods. An important aspect of the established regulations is that any suffering of animals cannot be justified by the possible advantages of novel cosmetics.

- **Constitutional Protection for Animal Rights.**

The constitution of India is the supreme law of India which lays down the fundamental political code, Rights and Duties of citizens, Directive Principles of State Policy, procedures, structures and powers of governmental institutions. In the context of animal rights, the Supreme court has brought some animal rights under the ambit of the right to the Right to Life through an expansive reading in the case of Animal Welfare Board of India V A. nagaraja & ors. (the Jallikattu case) 2014, the Supreme Court ruled infavour of Animal Welfare Board and upheld enforcement of the ban on Jallikattu. It further held that article 51 A (g) of the Constitution is the "Magna Carta of Animal Rights" and made several observations to safeguard the "life" of animals under Article 21. With regard to Article 21, the Supreme Court notably held, Every species has a Rght to Life and Security subject to the law of the land, which includes depriving its life, out of human necessity. Article 21 of the Constitution, while safeguarding the rights of humans, protects life and the word "life" has been given an expanded definition and any disturbance from the basic environment which includes all forms of life, including animal life, which are necessary for human life, fall within the meaning of Article 21 of the constitution. So far as animals are concerned, in our view "life" means something more than mere survival or existence or instrumental value for human beings, but to lead a life with some intrinsic worth, honour and dignity. Article 51 A (g) places a duty on the citizens of India to protect and improve the natural environment and have compassion for all living creatures. In Animal Welfare Board of India's case, the Supreme Court held that compassion for all living creatures includes concern for their suffering and well-being. In this case Supreme Court regarded 51 A (g) along with the duty to develop scientific temperament under 51 A (h) as the Magna Carta of Animal Rights Jurispudence in India.

Article 48 A lays down for the directive principle for protection and improvement of environment and safeguarding of forests and wild life. Article 48 A was added by the 42nd Amendment, 1976 and places an obligation on the state to protect the environment and wildlife, while not judicially enforceable under the ambit of the Right to Life under Article 21. In M. C. Mehta V Union of India (2002) the Supreme Court heard a PIL in the matter of air pollution in Delhi. The Court made the following observation regarding Article 48A and public health: Articles 39, 47 and 48A by themselves and collectively cast a duty on the State to secure the health of the people, improve public health and protect and improve the environment. The State shall endeavour to protect and improve the environment and to safeguard the forest and wildlife of the country. Article 48 lay down that, the State shall endeavour to organise agriculture and animal husbandry on modern and scientific lines and shall, in particular, take steps for preserving and improving the breeds and prohibiting the slaughter of cows and calves and other milk and draught cattle. Cattle slaughter especially, is a deeply contentious issue in India because of the sacred value held by cows to sects of Hindus, Jains, Zorastrians and Buddhist. In the case of Abdul Hakim Qureshi V State of Bihar (1961) Supreme Court heard a petition regarding the constitutionality of cow slaughter ban laws in Bihar.

In State of Gujarat V Mirzapur Moti Kureshi Kassab Jamat & ors.(2005), the Supreme Court held that the intention of the Parliament in enacting Article 51A was for it to be read with Articles 48 and 48 A, ensuring that the spirit of all provisions are honoured.

The State and Concurrent list has been assigned the following items about animal rights. The States are given the authority to "preserve, maintain and improve stock and prevent animal diseases and enforce veterinary training and practice" according to State list item 14. The concurrent list contains legislation that both the centre and the states may pass,

o   "Prevention of animal cruelty" which is mentioned in item 17.

o   "Protection of wild animals and birds" which is mentioned as item 17B.

- **(Indian Penal Code (IPC), 1860) replaced by Bharatiya Nyaya Sanhita (BNS) Bill 2023 provisions for Animal Protection**

o   **Section 428 IPC-** Mischief by killing or maiming animal of the value of ten rupees- Whoever commits mischief by killing, poisoning, maiming or rendering useless any animal or animals of the value ten rupees or upwards, shall be punished with imprisonment of either description for a term which may extend to two years, or with fine, or with both.

- **Section 429 IPC-** Mischief by killing or maiming cattle, etc., of any value or any animal of the value of fifty rupees.- Whoever commits mischief by killing, poisoning, maiming or rendering useless, any elephant, camel, horse, mule, buffalo, bull, cow or ox, whatever may be the value thereof, or any other animal of the value of fifty rupees or upwards, shall be punished with imprisonment of either description for a term which may extend to five years or fine or with both.

- **Clause 323, Bharatiya Nyaya Sanhitha (BNS) Bill 2023** , Whoever commits mischief by killing, poisoning, maiming or rendering useless any animal shall be punished with imprisonment of either description for a term which may extend to five years, or with fine, or with both.

- Implication of revision of this section criminalises killing, poisoning, maiming or rendering useless any animal, thus possibly criminalising the killing of animals for any reason. The IPC's logic was to criminalise the killing of animals which were of value to someone, possibly covering domesticated animals killed by a third person without the consent of the owner of the animal. Clause 323 of BNS, 2023, by removing the value of the animal, appears to criminalise the killing of any animal, domesticated or otherwise. In light other legislations such as Prevention of Cruelty Act, 1960, the Wildlife Protection Act, 1972 etc., this section should have ideally been repealed.

Important Wildlife Conservations

Wildlife Conservation is an activity in which humans make conscious efforts to protect plants and other animal species and their habitats. Wildlife Conservation is very important because wildlife and wilderness play an important role in maintaining the ecological balance and contribute to human quality of life. Wildlife Conservation can be defined as preventing wildlife from uneven killing and poaching. It is also involves the practice of making people aware by telling them about the importance of wildlife. The goal of Wildlife Conservation is to support the survival of wildlife and educate others about sustainable practices and also to protect animals and plants. The purpose of conservation, the protection, preservation, management or restoration of natural environment and the ecological communities that inhabit them.

There are four types of Conservations;

- Environmental Conservation
- Animal Conservation
- Marine Conservation
- Human Conservation
- Environmental Conservation

The global problem of the present day is the environmental pollution. The environmental pollution is a serious threat to the existence and survival of humans and the entire wildlife. Unpolluted air to breathe, uncontaminated water to drink, nutritious food to eat and hygienic condition to live are unavoidable essentials for survival of human race. According to section 2(a) of the Environmental (Protection) Act, 1986, "environment includes water, air and land and the inter-relationship, which exists among and between water, air and land and human beings, other living creatures, plants, micro organism and property". Environmental pollution causes either natural forces such as cyclone, flood, earthquake etc., or through artificial causes such as population growth, industrialisation etc.,

In M C Mehta V Union of India (1987), the Supreme Court held that the right to life under Article 21 of the Constitution includes Right to live in a pollution free environment.

Environment pollution divided into;

(1) Water pollution- industries and factories manufacture useful goods also responsible for creating harmful waste products called "effluents". Use of pesticides and chemical fertilizers causes pollution to water. The presence of pollutants in water especially toxic substances either in the sea, tanks, ponds or wells have affected life on earth badly.

(2) Air pollution- The industrialisation, motor traffic, construction works, housing fuels, incineration (burning of wastes like rubber, plastic products etc. in open place) natural causes such as earthquake, cyclone etc., causes air pollution.

(3) Land or Soil pollution- The household refuse, commercial rubbish, industrial wastes, garbage, trash, automobile, tyres, cans, waste paper, etc., most dangerous pollutant is the plastic components such as plastic bags, plastic papers, plastic wrappers, other plastic products, these materials remain undecayed for a long time in the soil, dumping solid wastes into oceans will affect marine eco-system as well as territorial eco-system. Chemical fertilizers and pesticides, both are poisonous and harmful to human beings and animals.

(4) Noise or Sound pollution- Industries, stone quarries, loudspeakers, automobiles, aircrafts, trains, construction works, Radio, Television etc., are the main sources of noise pollution.

(5) Food Pollution- Food pollution begins when chemicals are used for plant growth. Food also gets polluted processing, storage, transportation and retailing.

(6) Radio-active Pollution – This pollution caused by blast of atoms, elements like radium, uranium, etc., emits invisible effects known as radiations. Nuclear power plants and testing of atom bombs are the main sources of radio active pollution. Atomic pollution is a slow and silent killer.

The environmental Conservations includes;

    (1) Conservation of soil and land

    (2) Water and energy Conservation

    (3) Bio diversity and Environment Conservation

    (4) Conservation of other natural resources

    (5) Energy conservations.

The aims to protect environmental conservations are the preservation of generation of resources of the future. A minimal amount of depletion of the resources, examples of conservation in ecology, national parks, marine parks, zoos, frozen zoos, botanical garden, seed banks. The role of environment conservation by preserving natural eco systems, reducing pollution, adopting sustainable practices and promoting awareness. Each individual action can contribute to the collective effort of safeguarding the planet, resources and diversity. The major scope of the environmental conservation are (1) control of environmental pollution and natural resource utilisation and development (2) addressing issues related to global warming and climate change.

Conservation is generally held to include the management of human use of natural resources for current public benefit and sustainable social, economic utilization. There are Two types of Conservation;

(1)   In situ - Conservation of habitats, species and eco systems where they naturally occur.

(2)   Ex situ – The conservation of elements of bio diversity out of the context of their natural habitats is referred to as ex-situ conservation.

The term flora relates to all plant life and the term fauna represents all animal life. The flora and fauna in India are diverse with a variety of plants and animal varieties. The popular fauna of India includes 500 different varieties of mammals, 2000 species of birds, 30,000 types of insects and several varieties of fish, amphibians and reptiles. The reason for the rich heritage of flora and fauna in India, is due to varied climatic conditions in India, presence of many rivers. India has varied physiological features like plateau, deserts, coastal areas, islands and mountains. The highest bio diversity in India is found in the western ghats, a mountain range that runs along the western coast of the country. This region home to a wide variety of plant and animal species. Many of which are found nowhere else in the world. The Andaman and Nicobar Islands are the region with maximum biodiversity. The state which has the least bio diversity is Rajasthan because a large percentage of total area is desert. India is a host to 4 bio diversity hotspots- the Western ghats, the Himalayas, the Indo-Burma region and the Sundaland region. Bio diversity hotspots area those regions of the world that are rich in species which are endemic to that region only. Flora and Fauna are important role for human existence. The flora liberates oxygen that is consumed by the fauna for respiratory activities. Fauna releases carbondioxide, the flora consumes for photosynthesis.

In State of Bihar V Murad Ali Khan Farukh Salauddin &...(1988), offences against respondent under section 51 of WPA,1972. The policy and object of the wildlife laws have a long history and are the result of an increasing awareness of the compelling need to restore the serious ecological imbalances introduced by the depredating inflicted on nature by man. The State to which the ecological imbalances and the consequent environmental damage have reached is so alarming that unless immediate, determined and effective steps were taken the damage might become irreversible. The preservation of the fauna and flora, some species of which are getting extinct at an alarming rate has been a great and urgent necessity for the survival of humanity and these laws reflect a last-ditch battle for the restoration. The tragedy of the predicament of the civilised man is that "Every source from which man has increased his power on earth has been used to diminish the prospects of his successors". The criminal case initiated on the complaint proceed with in accordance with law.

The Judiciary has consistently emphasized the protection of endangered species. Landmark cases such as M C Mehta V Kamal Nath (1997), there was massive encroached of land and of Beas River by Span Motel Pvt. Ltd. The Supreme Court ordered the closure of a polluting factory in Delhi that was harming the habitat of the Critically Endangered Black Buck Antelope. This case is considered to be a landmark case in Indian Environmental law due to the fact that Public Trust Doctrine and the Polluter Pays Principle were applied.

In Narmada Bachao Andolan V Union of India (2000), Supreme Court examined the importance of water in relation to Article 21 of the Indian Constitution. In this case, a critical over the water of the Narmada River emerged among the States of Rajashan, Madhya Pradesh and Gujarat. The dispute centred around the control, usage and allocation of the river waters.

- **Animal conservation**

Animal conservation is the act of protecting eco systems and environment to protect the animals that live there. The conservation of wildlife is necessary for prevention of drought, new deserts, fires as well as flood. The conservation ensures that the upcoming generations of human and wildlife will be surrounded by nature thereby loving it and understanding the significance of wildlife. Wildlife Conservation Projects aim to preserve and use natural resources in a sustainable manner. This is done to ensure that future generations can benefit from these resources. Wildlife is an essential element of nature, so it must be protected. Conservation Programmes are designed to bridge the gap between evolutionary theory and environmental realities. This assists in forecasting how wildlife will respond to current and future environmental changes. It was designed to ensure their survival because global warming, farming, population increase, pollution and hunting pose significant threats to them. The Government of India has initiated many wildlife conservation like Project Snow Leopard, Project Tiger, Project Rhino Vision, Project Hangul, etc.

(1)   **Project Snow Leopard, 2009**

The Snow Leopard also known as the 'ounce', is a felid in the genus Panthera native to the mountain ranges of Central and South Asia. The Snow Leopard (also known as the ghost of the mountains), acts as an indicator of the health of the mountain eco system in which they live, due to their position as the top predator in the food web. Project Snow Leopard (PSL), was launched in 2009 to promote an inclusive and participatory approach to conserving snow leopards and their habitat. Snow Leopard can be found in the Himalayan region as well as in States such as Jammu & Kashmir, Uttarakhand, Arunachal Pradesh, Sikkhim and Himachal Pradesh. India is a unique country to have good presence of 5 big cats, including the Snow Leopard. The other 4 are Lion, Tiger, common Leopard and Clouded Leopard. The Indian Government issued the "First National Protocol on Snow Leopard Population Assessment" in 2019. This entails using technology such as camera traps and scientific surveys. The IUCN World Conservation Union's Red List of Endangered Species classifies the snow leopard as vulnerable. It is also included in Appendix 1 of the Conservation on International Trade in Endangered Species (CITES). The Wildlife Act, 1972 includes in schedule I. It is also included in the Convention on Migratory Species (CMS) giving the species the highest conservation status both globally and in India. This program was created as part of the Global Snow Leopard and Ecosystem Protection Programm's global protocol. The Protected Areas are,

(a) The sacred Himalayan Landscape

(b) Kibber wildlife Sanctuary

(c) Great Himalayan National Park

(d) Hemis National Park

(e) Dibang Wildlife Sanctuary

(f) Pin Valley National Park.

Hemis National park is the biggest National Park in India and also has a good presence of Snow Leopard. The main threat of Snow Leopard is threatened because of the loss of natural prey species, retaliatory killing due to conflict with humans and illegal trade of its fur and bones. The Government of India has identified the Snow Leopard as a flagship species for the high-altitude Himalayas. India is also a party to the Global Snow Leopard & Eco System Protection (GSLEP) Programme since 2013. Himal San Rakshak- is a community volunteer programme, to protect Snow Leopards, launched in October 2020. In 2019, First National Protocol was also launched on Snow Leopard Population Assessment which has been very useful for monitoring populations. Global Environment Facility (GEF), United Nations Development Programme (UNDP) funded the project on the conservation of high altitude bio-diversity and reducing the dependency of local communities on the natural ecosystem. The Snow Leopard is listed in 22 critically endangered programe of the Ministry of

Environment Forest and Climate Change. The Snow Leopard Conservation breeding programme is undertaken at Padmaja Naidu Himalayan Zoological Park, Darjeeling, West Bengal. Globally, in 2013, the Bishkek Declaration set a goal of protecting at least 20 snow leopard landscapes with viable snow leopard populations by 2020. It led to the formation of the Global Snow Leopard and Eco system Protection Programme (GSLEP) programme since 2013. The GSLEP is a high- level inter- governmental alliance of all the 12 snow leopard range countries. It majorly focuses on the need for awareness and understanding the value of snow leopard to the eco system. Every year October 23rd is observed as International Snow Leopard Day since 2014. The day commemorates the anniversary of the Bishkek Declaration and celebrates this endangered cat and raises awareness for its conservation and protection. Project Snow Leopard is an Indian initiative launched by MoEF & CC for strengthening wildlife conservation in the Himalayan high attitudes. It aims to promote a knowledge based and conservation frame work that fully involves the local communities, this project Snow Leopard is designed for all biologically important habitats within the snow leopard's range, irrespective of their ownership eg: protected areas, common land etc.

(2) Project Tiger, 1973

The Tiger (panther tigris) is the largest living cat species and a member of the genus Panthera. It belongs to the family Felidae. The Tiger is considered to be the largest living felid species. The Tiger is listed as Endangered on the IUCN Red list. India hosts the largest tiger population. Major reasons for tiger population decline are habitat destruction, habitat fragmentation and poaching for fur and body parts. Tigers are also victims of human-wildlife conflict, due to encroachment in areas with a high human population density. Tiger population in India have been targeted by poachers since the 1990s and were extirpated in two tiger reserves in 2005 and 2009. Seizure data from India during 2001-2021 indicates that tiger skins were the most often traded by the body parts, followed by claws, bones and teeth trafficking routes mainly passed through the states of Maharashtra, Karnataka, Tamil Nadu and Assam. Demand for tiger body parts for use in traditional chinese medicine has also been cited as a major threat to tiger population. Local people killing tigers in retaliation for attacking and preying on livestock is a threat to tiger species. Tiger hunt is an established sport under Mughal Empire in the sixteenth century. The National Tiger Conservation Authority (NTCA), was established in India in December 2005, following a recommendation of the Tiger Task Force. The Prime Minister of India established it to recognise the management of Project Tiger and many Tiger Reserves in India. A programme for protection called (Tiger Protection Programme) 'Project Tiger' was started in 1973, by the Government of India in co-operation with WWF. In June

2010, a detailed survey by the Wildlife Institute of India (WII) which used accurate camera traps for counting tigers rather than the more traditional method of counting footprints, reported that previous estimates of tiger numbers in India may be highly optimistic.

The population of Indian Tiger was rapidly dropping at the end of the twentieth century. As a result, a nationwide Tiger was conducted in 1972 to estimate the Tiger population large-scale development operations like as dams, mines, railway projects and the construction of enterprises, resulted in deforestation and increased habitat loss. Project Tiger was established in the Palamau Tiger Reserve, Jim Corbett National Park, Uttarakhand, in 1973. This is a Ministry of Environment & Forest sponsored initiative. It is primarily governed by the WPA, 1972. The National Tiger Conservation Authority, which was founded in December 2005, oversees the project. The Project's goal is to save tigers from extinction by ensuring that the animal has a viable population in its native habitat. The Project began with 9 Reserves in 1973-74 and has now expanded to 50 Reserves. The initiative has had tremendous success in restoring the habitat and population of tigers in the protected areas. It is critical that a legislative authority with sufficient legal backing be established for proper project implementation. The National Board for wildlife suggested the formation of a Task Force to investigate problems encountered during the execution of Tiger Conservation Projects across the country. The Tiger Task Force was formed as a result of this. The TTF proposed the formation of the National Tiger Conservation Authority (NTCA). July 29th International Tiger Day celebrating every year.

A healthy eco system supplies people and nature with food, fresh water and health. Protecting wild Tigers and their habitat can be benefit numerous species. Safeguards have been provided for ensuring the agricultural, livelihood, developmental and other interests of the people living inside a forest or in and around a Tiger Reserve. The core as well as buffer areas have been explicitly explained to avoid ambiguity. In S P Chockalingam V Principal Chief Conservator of Forest and Chief Wildlife Warden (2022), petitioner which passess through Satyamangalam Tiger Reserve, for a direction to the respondents to impose complete ban on vehicles and ban on commercial vehicles on road between Bannari and Karappalam in NH 918. The purpose of declaring Eco-sensitive Zones around National Parks and Sanctuaries is to create some kind of "shock absorber' for the Protected Areas. They would also act as a transition zone from areas of high protection to areas involving lesser protection. As decided by the National Board for wildlife, the activities in the Eco-sensitive zones would be a regulatory nature, rather than prohibitive nature, unless and otherwise so required.

(3) Project Elephant, 1992

Elephant belongs to the family Elephantidae. The Elephants are extremely social animals. The elephants are the only natives of Africa and Asia, they have cultural and symbolic significance around the world. India is often referred as the " Elephant Country", Due to large population of wild elephants. Elephants are considered sacred in Hinduism and associated with Buddha and Indian deity Ganesh, to symbolize power, wisdom, strength, protection of home, fertility and good luck.

Project Elephant is a Central Government sponsored scheme launched in February 1992. The population of these animals was about 15,000 when the project was started and has increased since then. Through the Project Elephant scheme, the Government helps in the protection and management of elephant's to the States having wild elephants in a free ranging population. Karnataka State has the highest elephant population in India. WHO declared Elephant Reserves in India, a country wide data base management system for the management for the protection and conservation of elephants. Elephant Reserves was initiated by Project Elephant Division, MoFF & CC, Government of India. WWF –World Wildlife Fund supports human-elephant conflict, migration, bio-diversity conservation and awareness to local communities in elephant habitats, in the Eastern Himalayas, the North Bank Landscape and Kaziranga Karbi-Anaglong Landscape and in the Nilgiris Eastern Ghats Landscape in the South India. Government of India in 2020 declared Elephant as the National Heritage animal of the country on the recommendations of the standing committee of the National Board for wildlife. This ensures sufficient protection to elephants was provided, before their numbers fall to panic levels like Tigers.

Hathi Gaon (Elephant Village) is a small village that was set up by the Government in 2010 to give proper shelter and water facilities to all the families and their elephants that served tourists in and around Amer fort during the day. It is world's third and India's first elephant village. The Ministry of Environment and Forest in partnership with Wildlife Trust of India has launched a campaign Haathi Mera Saathi. The aim of the campaign was to increase public awareness and develop friendships between elephants and the local population. The campaign for the welfare of the elephants, to conserve and protect the elephants in India. This campaign was launched in Delhi on 24th May 2011 at the Elephant-8 Ministerial Meetings. The countries are participated in this meetings are, Kenya, Srilanka, Botswana, Republic of Congo, Tanzania, Indonesia, Thailand and India. The increased tension due to rampant retaliatory killing of elephants and human-elephant conflict prompted the Government to set up the Elephant Task Force. The aim to the task force is to bring pragmatic solutions for the conservation of elephants in the long-term.

The Kerala Elephant Owners Federation, comprising people who own and rent elephants for festivals and other occasions in the State, approached the Union Minister For Environment and Forest on 18th January 2024, with a request to relax regulations concerning the ownership and inter-state transfer of elephants. As per media reports on 16th March 2024, the Ministry of Environment, Forest and Climate change notified the Captive Elephant (Transfer or Transport) Rules, 2024 with the purpose of easing the Transfer and movement of captive elephants. The modified rules stipulate that Chief Wildlife Warden can transfer elephants between states, if the existing owner cannot provide adequate case for the animal or if the animal will be better maintained under the changed circumstances. The CWW can order the relaxation of the elephant to ensure better maintenance. While the new set of rules has significantly benefited elephant owners, animal rights and activists are concerned that the new provisions could be misused to facilitate easy sale and transfer of elephants, despite the legal prohibition against it under the WPA, 1972. As per the Act, Elephants are classified as a schedule I species and thus afforded the highest protection in the country. Capturing or tracking elephants is not permissible, regardless of whether they are in the wild, or in captivity section 12 of the WPA, 1972, stipulates that relocation can be permitted only for particular reasons, such as teaching and scientific research. The transportation of the captive elephants, has been allowed due to their historical significance in forest management timber transportation, their status as assets of former royal families and their traditional roles in temple for religious ceremonies.

The protection of elephant is particularly crucial because it has been classified as a national heritage of the country. Elephant Corridors are short swaths of forested terrain that serve as a link between bigger Elephant habitats. The Corridors are divided into 2 categories (1) high ecological priority (2) medium ecological priority. The classification is based on the frequency with which elephants move, the size of the population, the area of habitats connected and the presence of other routes nearby. The corridors are also related for conservation fearibility.

Ivory traders & Manufactures Association V Union of India (1997), the case is based on the trading of ivory which is illegal. Basically, the meaning of ivory is teeth of Elephant. It is used for making the amendments and other articles. And we know that it is banned because the trading of ivory is illegal. The animal gets harm due to this. It is found tusks of elephant. The State has the power to completely prohibit a trade or business which has an adverse impact on the preservation of species of wildlife which are on the verge of extinction both because it is inherently dangerous practice to destroy such animals in terms of ecology and also because of the Directive Principles contained in Article 48 A of the Constitution.

V. K. Venkitachalam V State of Kerala (2010), Supreme Court warned owners of captive elephants in Kerala, including temples of severe consequences if the animal was found abused or harassed in an order on August 18th, the Court said the owners would be subject to criminal prosecution for cruelty against elephants.

V. K. Venkitachalam V State of Kerala (2015), to direct the Chief Wildlife Warden shall see to it that all the captive elephants existing In the State of Kerala are counted and in the absence of obtainment of requisite certificate under section 42 of WPA, 1972, and the declaration made under section 40, appropriate action shall be initiated against the owners. It is stated that all necessary actions are being taken to implement the provisions of Wildlife (Protection) Act, 1972 and also Kerala Captive Elephants (Management and Maintenance) Rules, 2012.

S. Muralidharan V Principal Chief Conservator of Forest (2019), It may be pointed out that it shall be the obligation of the owner and the mahout to take care of the elephants whenever found sick, injured, unduly stressed or otherwise. A medical check-up has to be arranged for the elephant once in a year and for that, the owner has to inform the Chief Wildlife Warden, as also its examination by a Veterinary Doctor in order to eradicate any distress or the ailment being suffered by the elephant.

(4) Project Rhino Vision 2020 (launched in 2005)

The word 'Rhinoceros' came from the Greek words 'Rhino' means 'nose' and 'ceros' means 'horn'. The number of horns that a rhino has varies from other species. The Indian rhinocerors also known as greater one-horned rhinocerors, or Indian rhino for short, is a rhinocerors species native to the Indian sub continent. It is listed as vulnerable on the IUCN Red list. Indian rhino species are inherently at risk because over 70% of its population occurs at a single site, kaziranga National Park, as diseases, civil disorder, poaching or habitat loss would have a devastating impact on the Indian rhinos may be prone to inbreeding depression. Hunting as a sport in the late 19th and early 20th centuries, one of the reason for the decline of Indian rhinos, after conservation measures were put in place from the beginning of the 20th century, when legal hunting is ended.

Project Rhino was launched in India in 2005 to protect one-horned rhinos. Assam declared a new special Rhino Protection Force it was formed on 1st July 2019, to tackle the menace of poaching in the National Park. In Assam, rhinos were found in only 3 protected areas. Kaziranga National Park, Orang National Park, Pobitora Wildlife Sanctuary. Kaziranga is the largest National Park, this park which hosts two-third of the world's rhinos, is a

UNESCOs world heritage site. Assam Government will observe September 22nd as Rhino Day, to generate public awareness on protection of the one-horned Rhinos.

Project Rhino launched in 2005, was an ambitious initiative to achieve a wild population of at least 3,000 larger one horned rhinos scattered throughout 7 protected areas in the Indian State Assam in 2020. Kaziranga, Pobitora, Orang, Manas, Larkhowa, Burachapori Wildlife Sanctuary, Dibru Saikhowa Wildlife Sanctuaries are 7 Protected Areas. Bengal Rhinoceros Preservation Act, 1932 this Act prohibits the killing or capturing of wild rhinoceros and also prohibits the possessing, selling or buying of any parts of the rhinoceros.

Indian Rhino Vision 2020, the programme will contribute to the mixing of genes from rhinos from Kaziranga National Park and Pobitora Wildlife Sanctuary, which will set up a healthy, breeding population of rhinos for the future of the species. Project Rhino launched in 2005, the Indian Rhino Vision 2020 set out an ambitious goal to achieve a population at least 3000 greater one-horned rhinos across 7 Protected Areas in Assam by the year 2020. In a Partnership with the Assam Forest Department and other Organisations like WWF Indian Rhino Vision 2020 (IRV 2020) in 2005. These programmes vision was to increase the total rhinos in Assam about 3,000 by the year 2020. World Animal Protection is working to prevent poaching of Rhinos by raising awareness on the nature of Rhino horn Trade and the medicine. Both Governmental and non-Governmental agencies are working to safe guard the habitat of rhinos in Assam and West Bengal as well as in Nepal.

(5) **Project Hangul, 1970**

The Jammu & Kashmir Government in collaboration with the International Union for Conservation of Nature (IUCN) and World Wildlife Fund (WWF), developed a programme in the 1970s to protect and conserve the Kashmir Red Stag and its habitat. This initiative was dubbed Project Hangul. Hangul is widely known as Kashmir Red Stag. The population of this species had increased to 340 by 1980. As per IUCN Red list, Hangul categorized Critically Endangered Species. In recent past, the Government in UT of J&K has taken several steps to take a stock of the population of endangered animals. Further, there have been encouraging signs of their movement to the adjoining forest regions of the Dachigam National Park, primarily considered one of the existing protected area habitats of the species.

Hangul is a sub species of the elk native to India. Earlier, the Kashmir Stag was categorised as a sub species of European Red Deer. Later, Hangul, was categorised as the sub species of elk after the Mitochondrial DNA Genetic

Study revealed that it belongs to the Asian family of elk. The Hangul was once widely distributed in the mountains of Kashmir Himalaya, the Chenab valley in Jammu and parts of the only viable population is in the Greater Dachigam land scape North East of Sringar, centred in Dachingam National Park and adjoining Protected areas. Hangul lives in groups in the riverine forests, high valley's and mountains in Kashmir and the Northern Chamba district of Himachal Pradesh. Hangul is found in conservation reserves of Bren Nishat, including Cheshmashahi Forest Reserve, Khrew Khanagund Shikargh and Overa Wildlife Sanctuary. The Hangul is the only surviving species of the Asiatic members of the Red Deer family. The society of Hangul is matriarchal. Since, 1950s it is considered as one of the rarest species of mammals in the Indian sub continent. Hangul inhabits deciduous woodland, upland moors and open mountainous areas, natural grass lands, pastures and meadows.

The main threat for Hangul is Poaching, by both civilian and military personnel, was identified as the main cause of the decline of the Hangul in the past and present. Lack of patrolling to prevent the wildlife crimes. Difficulty in implementing protection activities adequately due to security issues in parts of the Dachigam National Park. Competition for grazing grounds with livestock and the associated risk of disease transmission are also potential threats to Hangul. An imbalance in the male-female ratios has been documented although a population viability analysis suggests that the population has the potential to recover if stringent protection and other conservation measures are implemented. The fragmentation of habitat has hampered the genetic flow across its different population. It has also been responsible for the Hangul population becoming locally scarce and event extinct.

The Hangul's range needs to be expanded by ensuring the sub alpine and alpine meadows of Upper Dachigam and other formerly. A 'mega preserve' of Greater Dachigam has been proposed to strengthen the protection in the Buffer zone by upgrading conservation reserves. Conservation breeding has to be given high priority to safeguarding the Hangul. Reintroducing the Hangul in its earlier local habitats and putting in place mechanisms and adequate conservation measures. Earlier habitats such as Overa Wildlife Sanctuary and Shikargah conservation Reserve, which once held a large number of Hangul, are almost free of human interference and are crucial for this purpose. Wildlife Conservation Fund launched Hangul Conservation Project (HCP) which will try to resolve the various issues which are related to the threatened Hangul species in Kashmir, particularly in the Dachigam National Park. South Korea celebrated Hangul Day on 9th October. Manipur University celebrated its annual Hangul day from 9th to 10th October 2023, at court hall, Manipur University sponsored by the Academy of Korean Studies (AKS) from South Korea.

(6) **Crocodile Conservation Project, 1975**

This project was introduced in 1976. The chief objective of the project was to protect the nation's 3 different crocodile species are Fresh water crocodile, Gharial and the Salt water crocodile. To ensure that the breeding of species remain captive. The Crocodile Project began with the goal of increasing the population to the point where sightings of five to six crocodiles per kilometer length of water were possible. The Gharial and Salt Water Crocodile Conservation Programme was first implemented in Odisha in early 1975, subsequently the Mugger Conservation Programme, the estimated number of Salt water crocodiles increased from 96 in 1976 to 1,640 in 2012.

Crocodiles are among the largest reptiles in the world, but very small in size. Crocodiles mostly lives in water, but they can also be found in dry land. Crocodiles are cold-blooded reptiles with scaly skin. Crocodile skin is primarily used in the production of hangbags and other luxury items such as shoes, belts, wallet, upholstery and furniture. The Salt Water Crocodiles are found in Andaman Nicobar Islands and the North Eastern coast. A significant population can be found in and around the Bhitarkanika Wildlife Sanctuary in Odisha. The Sundarbans also have smaller populations. The hide of salt water crocodile is considered very valuable. Many people will pay large amount of money to have crocodilian products and salt water crocodile leather products are the most prized farms are run for this specific purpose. Funding and technical support for the project were provided by UNDP/ FAO through the Government of India. The primary objective of the crocodile Project was to attempted to compensate for natural losses caused by death and predation. 17th June celebrated as Crocodile Day in India.

(7) **The Manipur Brow-Antlered Deer Project, 1981**

This project was started in Manipur in 1981, to conserve the brow-antlered deer (cerevus eldi eldi) which is on the verge of extinction. Brow-Antlered Deer is also known as Sangai. Sangai is called the Dancing Deer. Sangai is a medium-sized deer, with uniquely distinctive antlers with extremely long brow tine, which form the main beam. The forward protruding beam appears to come out from the eye brow. This signifies its name brow-antlered deer. It is listed as Endangered Species in Schedule I of the WPA, 1972, and IUCN Red list. Sangai is the State animal of Manipur. As this festival is being celebrated to promote Manipur as a world class tourism destination, it show cases the States contributions to art and culture, handloom handicrafts, fine arts, indigenous sports, as well as natural environment. The Sangai, endemic to Manipur, is found only at the Keibul Lamjas National Park (KLNP), the world's only floating National park. Sangai faces threat from steadily degenerating habitat of phumdi as a result of continuous inundation and flooding caused due to artificial reservoir. Water quality of the reservoir is degrading due to pollution and stoppage of nutrient supply. There is also invasion of non- native plants like paragrass.

(8) Project Himalayan Musk Deer, 1981

The white-bellied Musk Deer or Himalayan Musk Deer (Moschur leucogaster) is a musk deer species occurring in the Himalayas of the Nepal, Bhutan, India, Pakistan and China. It is listed as endangered on the IUCN Red list because of over exploitation resulting in a probable serious population is in constant decline, primarily due to excessive poaching for illegal trade of its lucrative musk pod. Himalayan musk deer project was launched in 1981 to save the endangered musk deer which is facing extinction. Captive breeding has yielded good results. The main threat is poaching, as the musk deer glands used for traditional medicines. This is illegal trade not only poses a direct threat to the species but also disrupts the delicate balance of the eco system in which the Himalayan Black Deer inhabits.

(9) Lesser Cats Project, 1976

This Project aims to secure population and habitats of wild cats subject to habitat encroachment, human-wildlife conflict, poaching and illegal trade in priority landscapes of northern, north-eastern and western India. The project was launched in 1976, with the assistance of WWF in India for conservation of 4 species of lesser cats, eg; Felis Bengalensis Kerr, Felis Marmorta Martin, Felis Lemruinki Vigors Horsfield and Felis Viverrina Bennet, found in Sikkim and Northern part of West Bengal.

(10) The Gir Lion Sanctuary Project,1972 re launched in 2020

The lion (panthera leo) is a large cat of the genus Panthera, native to Africa and India. It belongs to the family Felidae. The lions inhabits grasslands, savannah and shrublands. Lion is one of the widely recognised animal symbols in human culture, extensively depicted in sculpture and paintings on the national flags, in literature and films. Lions have been kept in menageries since the time of the Roman Empire and have been a key species sought for exhibition in zoological gardens across the world since the late 18th century. Lion is the most social all wild felid species living in groups of related individuals with their offspring, such group is called a 'pride'.

Asiatic lion is also known as Persian lion or Indian lion is a member of panthera leo. The Asiatic lion is one of the 5 pantherine cat native to India, the others are, the Bengal tiger, Indian leopard, Snow leopard, and the clouded leopard. Owing its small population and restricted area of occupancy the International Union for Conservation of Nature (IUCN) has listed the Asiatic lion as an endangered species. Gir National Park of Gujarat is known as the remaining Asiatic lions in the world. Asiatic lions are protected under WPA, 1972, listed under CITES Appendix I and are designated as Endangered by the IUCN Red list. Asiatic lion were once distributed up to the state of West Bengal in east and Rewa in M P in Central India. The Asiatic lion faces threat of poaching and habitat fragmentation, and the major roads and railway track pass through Gir protected Areas.

This project by the Government of India to protect the remaining population of the Asiatic lion through relocation to other parts of the country via re introduction. The Maharaja of Gwalior carried out a Conservation Project of his own. Lord Curzon in 1905, introduced African lions cubs in the wild near sheopur. In 1956, Indian Wildlife Board proposed that chakia forest in U P designated a second home 2 lionesses and one lion were transported, Gir and after that they were placed in Sakkarbaug zoo in Junagadh for a time, they were relocated to Chandra Prabha Sanctuary near Varanasi in 1957, these lions thrived initially population died out.

The Wildlife Institute of India (WII) in 1990 suggested the creation of a second wild population in order to protect the primary population of the Asiatic Lion species in Gir National Park. It was decided that the Kuno Wildlife Sanctuary was the most suitable habitat for the re introduction of Asiatic Lion. World Lion Day celebrated every year 10th August to raise awareness about the conservation of lions and their habitats.

The animals should not be named after reserved figures like Gods, mythological heroes, freedom fighters or nobel laureater. The Jalpaiguri circuit bench of Calcutta High Court verbally suggested that the West Bengal Government to change the name of lioness 'sita' and lion 'Akbar' of siliguri zoo. The court also granted the petitioners the liberty to amend their pleadings in the form of a PIL instead of writ petition. The Vishwa Hindu Parishad, had filed a writ petition. High Court claiming the naming the lioness after Goddess Sita and the Lion after Mughal emperor Akbar at the North Bengal wild animals park in Siliguri was "irrational", "illogical" and "tantamount to blasphemy". Justice, Saugata Bhattacharya urged the State Government to consider giving 2 big cats some other names to ensure that the "controversy is put to rest" (reported on 23 February 2024). Bengal plans to rename lions as per court affidavit Kolkata. "Akbar" may become "Suraj", "Sita" may be named "Tanaya". State Government has proposed to Central Zoo Authority (CZA) new names for the 2 lions that came from Tripura (reported on 18th April 2024).

The International Union for Conservation of Nature (IUCN), which categorised the Asiatic lion as "endangered" in 2008, has reclassified it as "vulnerable", indicating a positive shift in its conservation status. IUCN's first global report underlines a significant difference between African and Indian lions in the risk of decline the iconic predators face-the likelihood of a 33% decline in lion population in Africa is 19 times higher than in India, primarily due to rampant poaching there. Gujarat is the only abode of Asiatic lions in the world and by the IUCN report, Saurashtra is much safer. The lion population in Africa is estimated to have a 41% probability of declining by one third (33%) within three lion generations (past, present, future), while the risk is estimated to be at just 2% in Saurashtra, India. All the majestic cats found 3 regions came to be classified as Panthera leo leo, earlier the Asiatic Lions were classified Panthera Leo Persica. According to IUCN estimates, there are 23,000 lions in the wild today including 74 in Gujarat. According to IUCN, rising incidents of poaching have been reported from Botswana, Namibia, Tanzania, Zim-babwe, Cameroon and Zambia. In Gujarat, lions are conserved more compared to their counter parts in Africa. The incidence of man-animal conflict is much higher in that part of the world.

(11)   Sea Turtle Project, 1999

The Sea Turtle Project began in 1999 at the Indian Institute of wildlife, Dehradun with the collaboration of UNDP (United Nations Development Programe) and India's Ministry of Environment, Forest and Climate Change, aim to conserve endangered marine turtles, especially Olive Ridley Turtles. The project is being implemented in 10 coastal states of the country with special emphasis in the State of Orissa. Sea Turtles are large, air breathing reptiles that live in tropical and sub tropical seas all over the world. Almost all sea turtle species are now endangered. Out of seven, 3 species remaining critically endangered. Every winter, a significant proportion of the world's Olive Ridley Turtle population migrates to Indian coastal waters to nest, primarily along the eastern coast. This project is being carried out in ten coastal states of the country with a particular emphasis on the state of Orissa. This project establishes guidelines for development activities in the area, with the goal of securing turtle breeding areas and protecting them from other types of disruptions. One of the significant achievements has been the demonstration of the use of satellite Telemetry to locate the migratory route of Olive Ridley Turtles in the sea, as well as sensistising fishermen and the State Government to the use of Turtle Exclusion Devices (TED) in fishing trawlers to reduce turtle morality in fishing nets. Olive Ridley Turtles are the world's smallest and numerous sea turtles. Pollution and waste in the seas, Human consumption, plastic Garbage, Trawlers or grill nets, Government of Odisha initiated the Sea Turtle Conservation scheme in Bhitarkanika Sanctuary in 1975. In 2002, an organization called Sahyadri Nisarg Mitra launched the Turtle Conservation Scheme, which releases some new born turtles every year by hoisting the konkan turtle festival. 23rd May celebrated as World Turtle Day.

(12) Ganges Dolphin Project, 2021

In an effort to conserve Dolphins and their habitat, Tamil Nadu Government has issued orders to implement Project Dolphin under the Union Governments integrated Development of wildlife habitat scheme. Project Dolphin activities will include strengthening of patrolling and surveillance, improving habitat through restoration of coastal eco systems, removing ghost nets and encouraging involvement of locals with incentives. India's first Dolphin research centre located near the Ganga river in Patna, Bihar, the NDRC aim to be a hub for comprehensive research on various aspects of Gangetic dolphins including behaviour, survival skills and causes of morality. Bihar is the home to around half of the estimated 3000 Gangetic dolphins in India. After demands were made for a Project to save dolphins in India, Project Dolphin was launched as an India Government initiative to conserve both riverine and oceanic dolphin species 2021. The Ganges river dolphin is important because it is a reliable indicator of the health of the entire river eco system. Dolphins play an important role in keeping their environment inbalance. The Mission Dolphin Project is to end dolphin exploitation and slaughter as Dolphins are captured, harassed, slaughtered and sold into captivity around the world all in the name of profit. The Gulf of Mannar extends from Rameswaram to Kanniyakumari and has a chain of 21 un inhabited islands stretching along 140 km. of the coast. The aim of Project dolphin involves a status monitoring of the species and their potential threats in order to develop and implement a conservation action plan for protecting dolphins and the aquatic habitat. The project will provide financial support for conservation and anti-poaching activities.

Protected Areas

Protected areas are the corner stone of bio diversity conservation, they maintain key habitats, provide refugia, allow for species, migration and movement and ensure the maintenance of natural process across the landscape. The challenges of protected areas include logging, poaching of protected animals, mining, hunting, encroachment by human settlements and agriculture. The protected areas are includes National Parks, Wildlife Sanctuaries, Biosphere Reserves, Reserved and Communal Forests, Private Protected Areas and conservation areas.

There are 5 types of protected areas defined in the Wildlife Protection Act, 1972. They are;

1. Sanctuary- Sanctuary is a place of refuge where injured, abandoned and abused wildlife is allowed to live in peace in their natural environment without any human intervention.

2. National Park- National Parks are the areas that set by the Government to conserve the natural environment.

3. Conservation Reserves- The State Government may declare an area as conservation reserves after consulting with local communities.

4. Community Reserves- The State Government may declare any private or community land as a community reserve after consultation with the local community or an individual who has volunteered to conserve the wildlife.

5. Tiger Reserves – These areas are reserved for the protection and conservation of tigers in India. They are declared on the recommendations of the National Tiger Conservation Authority.

Courts have recognised the significance of preserving ecosystems and habitats crucial for wildlife survival. In T N Godavarman Thirumulpad V Union of India (2006), the Supreme Court declared all forested areas, irrespective of their classification as deemed forests, strengthening protection measures for wildlife habitats.

In Re: T N Godavarman Thirumulpad V Union of India (2010), we would be called upon to clarify the position as to whether mining activities would be permissible beyond the distance of one kilometre from the boundary of the protected area, irrespective of the fact that such an area falls under the Eco- Sensitive Zone (ESZ), notified by the Ministry of Environment Forest and Climate Change (MoEF) The order dated 3rd June 2022, direct that mining within the National Park and wildlife Sanctuaries shall not be permissible.

State of Maharastra V Gajanan D Jambhulkar (2002), when any vehicle is seized on the allegation that it was used for committing the offence under the WPA, 1972 the same should not normally be returned to the party seeking its release till the culmination of the criminal proceedings in respect of the material so collected the prima facie discloses involvement the vehicle in respect of commission of the offence under the WPA, 1972.

State of Maharastra V Salman Khan (2016), For the incident of hunting, which is alleged to have taken place on 2 /09/ 1998, and pertains to FIR No. 162/98 accused Salman Khan has been convicted for the offence under section 51 of the Wildlife Protection Act, 1972 and sentenced to undergo 1 years simple imprisonment along with fine of rupees 5000/-.

PILs have been instrumental in addressing issues such as illegal wildlife trade, encroachments in protected areas and the conservation of specific species. Cases like, People for Animals V Union of India (2013), Animal Welfare Board of India V A K Jain (2003) and Centre for Environmental Law V Union of India (2002) have paved the way for positive changes in wildlife conservation policies.The illicit wildlife trade includes trafficking in animal parts such as ivory rhino horns, tiger bones and genitals, leopard pelts, paws, bear paws, shark fins, for the use of traditional African and Asian medicines. Certain parts are also traded for making clothing, rugs and wall hanging. Wildlife experts have raised concern over the importance given to zoos and also questioned the mere existence of such areas which are used to display animals recreation purposes. It has been more than 50 years ever since the Wildlife Protection Act, came into existence, signifying an end to rampant poaching, decimating illegal wildlife trade and providing protection to abundant wildlife of the country.

- **Wildlife Corridors**

Wildlife Corridors are connected with protected areas. In 2017, the Wildlife Trust of india (WTI) identified 101 elephant corridors. In 2023, the number of elephant corridors identified by centre came up to 150. Wildlife corridors frequently by other species are yet to be identified by the Government of India. A wildlife corridor, habitat corridor or green corridor is an area of habitat connecting wildlife populations separated by human activities or structures (such as development, roads, or land cleaning) allowing the movement of individuals between populations that may help prevent negative effects of in breeding and reduced genetic diversity that can occurs within isolated populations corridors also help facilitate the re-establishment of populations that have been reduced or eliminated due to random events (such as fires or disease) and may moderate some of the worst effects of habitat fragmentation, through urbanization that splits up habitat areas, causing animals to close both their natural habitat and the ability to move between regions to access resources. Corridors can be dominated by edge effects, can increase risk of parasitism and disease and can facilitate dispersal of invasive species. Corridors can be unsuccessful if they do meet the movement or habitat requirements for the largest species.

- **Marine Conservation**

In order to conserve Marine Species, Government of India has notified 130 Marine Protected Areas across the Coastal States and the Islands, in addition to 106 coastal and marine sites have been identified and prioritized as Important Coastal and Marine Bio Diversity Areas (ICMBA) to take care of marine species conservation, ocean society of India. The motto of OSI is to inspire working professionals, researchers, students and to empower the community to conserve and sustainably use the oceans and its resources. Marine Conservation is also known as Ocean Conservation is the protection, preservation of eco systems in oceans and seas through planned management in order to prevent the over-exploitation of these marine resources. WPA, 1972 provides legal protection to many marine animals.

There are total of 31 major marine protected areas in India covering coastal areas that have been notified under WPA, 1972.

Coral Reef Recovery Project- Mithapur launched in 2008, this project seek to develop and implement appropriate strategies for the conservation of the Mithapur Reef, situated 12km south of the Gulf of Kutch in Gujarat. The Marine National Park in Gulf of Kutch is the largest Marine National Park in India and India's first Marine Wildlife Sanctuary and the first Marine National Park were created here in the Gulf of Kutch in 1980 and 1982, respectively. The Sanctuary covers 458 sq.km, of which the park covers 163 sq km. It is an archipelago of 42 tropical islands along the northern coast of Jamnagar district and the southern coast of kutch. The smallest Marine National Park is the South Button Island National Park is the smallest in India. This National Park is located on the Andaman and Nicobar Island off the sea coast of India, the protected island has a total area of about 2 sq miles.

There are total six marine National Parks in India namely: Mahatma Gandhi Marine National Park, Malvan Marine Sanctuary, Sindhudurg district in Konkan region of Maharastra, Gahirmatha Marine Sanctuary, Gulf of Mannar National Park, Rani Jhansi Marine National Park, all these sites are precious for Marine life of India. One and only floating National Park Keuibul Lamjo National Park is the world's only Floating National Park. It is located on the floating Loktak Lake of Manipur. It is a wetland eco system known for patches and rings of bio mass called phumdis.

Marine areas protected by the Environment (protection) Act, 1986, Coastal Regulation Zone Notification, 1991, and National Bio Diversity Act, 2002 have been enacted in India for conservation of coastal and marine environment, along with the WPA, 1972. The WPA 1972, provides legal protection to many marine animals. There are total of 31 major marine protected areas in India covering coastal areas that have been notified under WPA, 1972. Marine Protected Areas declared by National, Regional, State and local authorities. India's bio diversity protection programe have been highly successful with six hundred protected areas across 161,221sq.km.

The functions of Marine conservation aim to maintain or restore genetic population, species, habitat, community and eco system diversity on all scales. The marine Conservation is important because ocean affects us all in positive ways no matter on the coast line in the desert. It provides climate regulation, food, Jobs, livelihoods and economic progress. The objectives of Marine protected areas are to conserve bio diversity, protect endangered species and sustain fisheries. Marine protected Areas (MPA) are established with the primary aim of conserving the bio diversity of Marine eco system. Marine conservation is important it provide climate regulation, food jobs, livelihood, and economic progress. Over fishing is the threatening food security for hundreds of millions of people and destroying ocean eco systems world wide. 08th June World Oceans Day celebrated every year.

- **Human Conservation**

In many instances, human conservation refers to the actions taken by humans to conserve natural resources or environmental effects on human health. The human conservation is important because, it is to protect wildlife and promote big diversity, protecting wildlife and preserving it for future generations also. For human conserve we had to follow three "R"s.-Reduce, Reuse, Recycle to conserve natural resources and landfill space.

Plants and animals are the back bone of life on the earth, it is important to conserve them and save from getting extinct, maintaining their right population that help in enriching the bio diversity or the richness of flora and fauna worldwide. Flora is the plants and fauna are animals. The definition of flora and fauna includes any plants or animals considered as a group individual species will influence and have interdependent relationships with other species. These connections form the basis of an eco system.

Conservation of Plants Project

Plant Conservation is a broad group of activities which aims to prevent plant from becoming extinct. It includes the direct conservation of wild population, collection of plants with gardens, education programmes, invasive species, species control, restoration work, research programmes etc. Around 1300 to 1500 plant species are considered to be endangered in India. The top most endangered plant species in the world are, the western underground Orchid, Wood's Cycad, Pennantia Baylisiana, Cabbage Tree Palm, Rafflesia Arnoldii, Encephalartos Woodii, Rothschild's slipper Orchid, Kokia Cookeri, Hibiscadelphus Woodii and Franklinia Alatamaha. Some of the endangered plant species in India are Milkwort (rare, Gujarat), Bird foot (rare, Gujarat), Assam Catkin Yew (threatened, Arunachal Pradesh), Ebony (threatened, Karnataka), Umbrella tree (rare, Karnataka), Spider wort (rare and endangered, Madhya Pradesh) Malabar Lily (threatened, Tamil Nadu).

The Medicinal Plants Cultivation Project was started in 2019 with support from NABARD. It is being implemented in 4 tribal villages of Sholayur Panchayath of Attappady block, (kerala) benefitting 100 tribal farmers. This Project is supported by NABARD under the Farm Sector Promotion Fund (FSPF). In many cases medicinal plants have been mis-identified. For these reasons, any country's programme to use and conserve medicinal plants should include a stock-taking to identify its medicinal plants, outline, distributions and assess their scarcity or abundance. Medicinal plant conservation areas are being maintained by the department with the help of local people. Under this programme works such as maintenance of MPCA , chain link fence or cattle proof trenching, protection measures, soil working, weeding planting of medicinal plant species, publishing of books or other publicity materials are taken up. The legal frame work for the conservation of medicinal plants in India is governed by the Biological Diversity Act (2002). This Act emphasizes the conservation and sustainable use of biological resources, including medicinal plants and the fair and equitable sharing of benefits arising from their use. The main aim of plant conservation is to conserve the necessary ecological activities and life supporting systems, to conserve species diversity and range of genetic material. According to the Botanical Survey of India, India is the home to more than 8000 species of medicinal plants. The country has a rich history of traditional healing systems, many of which list the use of these plants. Ex-Situ conservation of medicinal plants species is a complementary action to conserve the genetic diversity of medicinal plants species, thereby reducing pressure on wild habitats and augmenting raw material availability. The traditional method of plant conservations include domestication, beliefs in sacred forests, beliefs in sacredness of trees, respect for cultural forests, protection of at burial rites, selective harvesting, secrecy, use of energy- saving traditional stoves, and collection of deadwood for firewood. Valley of flowers National Park was established in 1982 to protect the floral wealth of the region and contribute to conservation of flowering plants in India.

Conservation of rare flora aims to conserve plants with dwindling population and becoming rare by each passing day by establishing cultivation reserves for them such as Rare and Threatened Plant Parks. Conservation of bio diversity is protection, upliftment and scientific management of biodiversity so as to maintain it at its threshold level and derive sustainable benefits for the present and future generation. Slogal of conservation of flora and fauna, Chipko Movement (hugging movement) is a Forest Conservation Movement in India. Opposed to commercial logging and the Government's policies on deforestation, protesters in the 1970s engaged in tree hugging, wrapping their arms around trees so that they could not fell. "Join hands and save the wildlife earth without wildlife is the life without beautiful things. Help the animals to thrive before they become extinct. Never support animal abuse or abusers". 28th July World Nature Conservation Day Celebrated.

Animals that helps people and the eco system

Birds

The first law for the protection of wildlife was passed in 1887 by the British Indian Government. This Act was known as the Wild Birds Protection Act, 1887, this made it illegal to possess and sell wild birds which were either killed or captured. A second law was enacted in 1912 called the Wild Birds and Animals Protection Act, this Act was Amended in 1935 when the Wild Birds and Animals Protection (Amendment) Act 1935 was passed. Bird Preservation Act, 1912, An Act to make better provision for the protection and preservation of certain wild birds and animals, to make better provisions for the protection and preservation of certain wild birds and animals. The Wildlife (Protection) Act,1972 was enacted by the Parliament in order to conserve animals, birds, plants connected there within 1972. The 42nd Amendment Act, 1976, Forests and Protection of Wild Animals and birds was transferred from State to Concurrent list. Wildlife Protection Amendment Bill, 2021, emphasizing the implementation of Convention on International Trade of Endangered Species (CITES) and protection of endangered species. Killing Birds are covered under Wildlife Protection Act, 1972 making it illegal to catch, keep, kill, buy/sell birds or damage their nests. Trade in Foreign birds is restricted by CITES. The Government of India has banned certain animals, including the Rose Ringed Parakeet, Red Munia, Jungle Maina, African Grey Parrot, Blue- throated Macaw, Yellow-Crested Cockatoo. National Bird Day, which has American origin celebrated annually on 5th January, to raise awareness about the value of the Birds in the eco system. Birds play a crucial role in a healthy eco system. They play a vital role in controlling pets, act as pollinators and maintaining island ecology. Birds are important to humans in many ways, such as serving as a source of food and providing fertilizer in agricultural settings. Pollination by birds is an important element in influencing the genetic structure of tree populations. Many of these ecosystems functions vary by latitude and by season. In return, forests provide food, nesting sites, and in some cases, thermal refugia for birds. The Government of India leads a new era for bird conservation in Central Asia. Today at the Conventions of Migratory Species (CMS CoP 14), Governments along the Central Asian Flyway have committed to secure the passage of migratory birds in 30 countries from Siberia all the way to the Maldives. Indian Bird Conservation Network (IBCN), it aims at conserving actions through sound research. It is open to all who believe that conservation of birds can contribute to the conservation of all bio diversity and in return, beneficial in the spiritual and material well-being of human life.

Bird Conservation in India under WPA, 1972, rare and endangered species of Birds including migratory birds, are included in schedule I, WPA 1972 thereby according to the highest degree of protection stringent punishments provided WPA, for violation of the provisions of the Act. Important habitats of birds, including migratory birds have been notified as Protected Areas under the WPA for better conservation and protection of birds and their habitat. Financial and technical assistance is provided to the State Governments and Union Territories for the protection and management of protected areas. Wildlife Crime Control Bureau has been established for the control of illegal trade in wildlife and its parts and products. The World Migratory Bird Day celebrated on the second Saturday in May and second Saturday in October – is an annual global campaign dedicated to raise awareness of migratory birds and the need for International Co-operation to conserve them.

Ramsar Treaty 1971- Ramsar is a city in Iran. In 1971, International Treaty for Conservation and Sustainable use of wetlands was signed at Ramsar. The Convention mission is "conservation and wise use of all wetlands through local and national actions and International co-operation, as a contribution towards achieving sustainable development through out of the world". (1) India signed Ramsar Treaty in February 1982 (2) currently, India has 27 Ramsar sites (3) The area conveted in India of these wetlands is approximately 11,120 sq.km. Indian Bird Natural History Society, Bird Life International, Royal Society for Protection of Birds, Salim Ali Centre for Ornithology and History, Indian Institute of Public Administration, Wildlife Institute of India and other NGO's on the ground. It aims at conservation actions through sound research. This project had major advocacy, education and scientific components and it supports the existing conversation initiatives such as the bio diversity conservation prioritisation Project and IIPA Review Protected Areas. 4 important Bird areas have been identified in India.

Bird Sensitivity Mapping Tool (2019), The Union Environment Ministry has approved a 3 year study called the 'Bird Sensitivity Mapping Tool' to chart the pathways of migratory bird under the Central Asian Fly way (CAF) across India. Fly ways are used by groups of birds or species during their annual cycle to travel to breeding areas stopovers and wintering zones. Globally, 9 migratory fly ways have been identified under the Convention of Migratory Species (CMS). CAF is one of them covering migratory bird routes across 30 countries with maximum routes passing through India. Apart from mapping and safeguarding bird pathways, the study will help policy development for proposed Infrastructure projects and civil aviation bird alert issues, from the Ministry of Environment, Forests and Climate Change (MoEFCC). The first and foremost strategy fora birds NGO revolves around habitat conservation and restoration. India has unique eco systems from wetlands and forests to grasslands each provides a habitat from a variety of bird species. The Government of India leads a new era of bird conservation in central asia. A ten year old plan proposed by the Indian Government – the " visionary of perspective plan (2020-2030) for the conservation of avian diversity, their eco systems, habitats and landscapes in the country"hopes to advance action on the conservation of birds and their habitats in India. The National Action Plan for Conservation of Migratory Birds, aims to reduce the population decline of migratory birds and secure their habitats. The short term goal is to stop the decline by 2027. India Bird Conservation Network (IBCN), is open to all who believe that conservation of birds can contribute to the conservation of all biodiversity and in return, beneficial in the spiritual and material well-being of human life. Bharatpur Bird Sanctuary also known as Keoladeo National Park, is the largest bird sanctuary in India. It hosts thousands of birds with almost 400 species. It is located in Bharatpur, Rajasthan. Vedanthangal Bird Sanctuary in Tamil Nadu is the smallest Bird Sanctuaries in India and situated in Kancheepuram district of Tamil Nadu. This bird sanctuary of Tamil Nadu is believed to house around 4000 birds out of which around 26 species are rare. In Madhya Karnataka Ranganathittu bird sanctuary is famous Forest Bird Sanctuary.

Peacock

peacock is India's National Bird since 1963 and protected under schedeule I of WPA 1972. 15th November celebrated as World Peacock Day. Every year 25th March Celebrated National Peacock Day. The glorious fanned tail display of the peacock an ancient Indian symbol of mysticism and beauty, fortunately remains common view across the country. They are hunted for feathers, fat, meat. The transport, transfer and trade in the peacock tail feathers are exempted, the incidents of high morality in some areas denote poaching. The killing a peacock is strict prohibited and as per section 51(1-A) WPA, 1972, attracts imprisonment which may extend to 7 years and also a fine which shall not be less than 10,000/-.

Dr. T. Patanjali Sastry, President V Chairman A.P. Pollution (2001), the respondents are duty to bound to ensure free flow of water in Kolleru lake upto Plus 7 contour which is normal monsoon level and the inlets into Kolleru lake so as to preserve the lake. The pollution levels in the lake going up because of discharge of untreated sewage from 7 Municipalities mixed with agriculture run off and aquaculture discharge and the Pollution Board and Government have not taken any effective measures to contain the pollution. A management plan was prepared for restricting the encroachments, pollution and disturbances of habitat and for improvement of "flora" and "fauna". As far back in 1958 Indian Board of Wildlife recommended to declare the Kolleru lake as a bird sanctuary. From the admitted facts in the present case, it is clear that the pollution level in Kolleru lake is alarming.

People For Animals V Md. Mohazzid (2015), the Delhi High Court ruled that the rights of captured birds sold in the markets had been violated and that they deserve sympathy in 2014. Birds have fundamental rights including the right to live with dignity and they cannot be subjected to cruelty by any one human beings have no right to keep them in small cages for the purpose of their business or otherwise.

Abdulkadar V State (2011), Birds cannot be kept in small cages. The aforesaid act is prima facie against the provision of Prevention of Atrocities on Animal Act,1960.

Dogs

Dog is a domesticated descendant of the wolf. Also called the domestic dogs, it is originated from extinct gray wolves and the gray wolf is the dog's closest living relative. The dog was the first species to be domesticated by humans. It belongs to the family Canidae. Their main role is to remove the sick or diseased and dead creatures from the environment remains and clean. They have great smelling power. Dogs are domesticated they are the companions of humans.

Animal Birth Control (Dog) Rules, 2001, passed under the Prevention of Cruelty to Animals Act, forbid the throwing or driving of stray dogs from one region to another, as well as sterilisation and vaccination as methods of stabilizing/ reducing stray dogs population and removing the risk of rabies. Even killing of stray dogs was outlawed by Supreme Court of India in certain of its decisions.The Stray Dog Management Rules of 2001, the canines must be sterilised, given their shots and the brought back to the same location. The city can't taken away pets that have received their shots and been spayed or neutered. This created in 2004, by Colleen Paige, a pet and family lifestyle expert and animal advocate who chose to celebrate the day on 2nd August as National Dog Day- to honour all dogs, no matter shapes, sizes, age and breeds and encourage adoption to all those who have yet to find a home and a family forever. The Environment (Protection) Act, 1986 and Wildlife (Protection) Act 1972, at various places protects the stray dogs against any kind of cruelty. The Supreme Court of India in 2009 gave a stay order against removal culling or disclosing of a dog anywhere in India in M R Ajayan V State of Kerala (2009).

In Tamil Nadu state 141 people died of Rabies in six years (2018- 2023). "if a pet owner does not procure a licence, then the corporation gives notice to get it in seven days. No penaly is imposed on not having licence", according to the corporation officials. But section 10 of the Tami Nadu Animals and Birds in Urban Areas (Control and Regulation) Act, 1997 asks the Governments to seize unlicensed animals and birds. The maximum penalty is three year imprisonment and 5000 rupees fine, or both. The Union

Government 8 years ago for breeding on a commercial basis across the country. In flats, pedigree (breed) were asked to register themselves with the State Animal Husbandary Department has not received many registrations till date. The absence of monitoring of selective breeding of pedigree canines is also one of the reasons for these breeds attacking children and people. A notification issued by the Director General of Foreign Trade (DGFT) of that time said that, " the import of dogs would only be allowed for defence and police forces, research and development organisations for conducting research, and people getting pet dogs into India with a valid pet book and other relevant documents." To keep track of commercial breeders and the number of pedigree pups, the Union Government advised pedigree breeders to register with state animal husbandry department. The pet licences issued by Greater Chennai Corporation until May 15th 2024 GCC has issued 1,232 pet licences has issued, 2,837 applications are being considered, 4,270 applications are rejected, a local body has estimated 27,000 pet dogs in the city) contain the corporation logo, photo of the pet concerned apart from serial number, name and other details of the owner and the pet, along with the vaccination due date, age, breed and colour. The soft copy also has electronic signatures of officials, including veterinarians and revenue department staff, but it can be easily tampered with. Experts suggests micro chipping, to get data easily from RFID (radio-frequency identification) chip. If pets go missing or owners abandon them, we can track them. The veterinarians and Governments can get access to the data base to treat and observe disease trends. The Experts says the civic body's in efficiency has ensured that scientific methods such as ABC (Animal Birth Control) don't offer a solution. First is the lack of veterinary surgeons, and second, poorly maintained ABC centres. ABC Rules 2023 make it mandatory for each centre to have at least one veterinarian who has conducted at least 2,000 ABC surgeries. There is no post-operative care for sterilised animals.

Legislation and Public Health Laws Related to Rabies Control-

Prevention and Control of Infection and Contagious Diseases in Animals Act, 2009, any person who believe that an animal is infected by rabies, a schedule disease, should report it to the village officer who in turn will report it to the nearest available vetenarian.

The Epidemic Diseases Act, 1897, prevention of spread of dangerous epidemic diseases.

Prevention of Animal Cruelty Act, 1960 and Animal Birth Control (dog) Rules, 2023, prescribes humane methods to manage street dog population ensuring rabies eradication and mitigate man-dog conflicts. In Animal Welfare Board of India V People for Elimination of Stray Troubles (2023), the issue of attacks by stray dogs has always been an issue in the State of

Kerala. The Court appointed a committee to entertain the complaints with regard to the injuries sustainable by the persons from dog bites, nature and gravity of the injury, availability medicines and the treatment administered to them, the failure of treatment and its cure and in care of unfortunate death, the particulars of the deceased, the reasons behind the same.

Under Bharatiya Nyaya Sahanhita (BNS), has hiked the punishment for one's pet animal attacking someone. BNS aimed at (replacing IPC), if your pet animal attacks a human, you can be fined upto 5,000 rupees along with imprisonment upto six months. Negligent conduct with respect to animal section 291 of BNS states, "whoever knowingly or negligently omits to take such measures with any animal in his possession as is sufficient to guard against any probable danger of grievous hurt from such animal, shall be punished with imprisonment of either description for a term which may extends to six months or with fine which may extend to 5000 rupees or with both.

23 dangerous dog breeds banned by the Government in India on 18th March 2024- Addressing the increasing number of dog attack cases lately the Central Government wrote to the State Governments asking them to ban the import sale and breeding of certain dog breeds which are considered dangerous in India. The idea to ban these dog breeds are not only dangerous but their attacks could also be a reasons for human deaths. According to a report by ET, the department of Animal Husbandry and Dairying sent a letter to all States, wherein local bodies were urged to refrain from giving licences or permits to people for the sale or breeding of these "banned" dogs and they were urged to get their pets sterilised to prevent from breeding. The banned dog breeds are;

(1) Pitbull Terrier

(2) Tosa Inu

(3) American Staffordshire Terrier

(4) Fila Brasileiro

(5) Dogo Argentino

(6) American Bulldog

(7) Boesboel

(8) Kangal

(9) Central Asian Shephered Dog

(10) Caucasian shepherd dog

(11) South Russian Shephered Dog

(12) Tornjak, Sarplaninac

(13) Japanese Tosa & Akita

(14) Martiffs

(15) Rottweiler

(16) Terriers

(17) Rhodesian Ridgeback

(18) Wolf Dogs

(19) Canario

(20) Akbash

(21) Moscow Guard

(22) Cane Corso

(23) Bandog

Bees

Bees are part of the bio diversity on which we all depend for our survival. They provide high quality food-honey, royal jelly and pollen and other products such as bees wax propolis and honey bee venom. By pollinating trees, bushes and herbaceous plants, the bees are important for the food production of all the other animals and birds in the forest eco system dependent on it for food berries, seeds and fruits, bees and tree belong together. The honey bees and stingless bees have originally developed in forest biotopes. Bees have cultural and environmental importance as pollinators and producers of honey and medicinal products. The movement of pollen between plants are necessary for plants to fertilize and reproduce. Both farmed and wild bees control the growth and quality of vegetation – when they thrive, so do crops. Bees are protected by the WPA, 1972 mindlessly killing the bees with toxic chemicals is not an option. Sweet Revolution in India also known as Honey Mission or Mithi Kranti is launched to increase the promotion of the development of scientific bee keeping and production of honey and related products to double the farmers income. India has approved a new Central Sector Scheme entitled "National Bee Keeping and Honey Mission (NBHM)" for 2 years for overall promotion and development of scientific bee keeping in mission mode to achieve the goal of "Sweet Revolution" in the country by giving specific focus on women, input support for promotion and production, setting up of Integrated Bee Keeping Development Centres (IBDC) other Infrastructure digitilization / online Registration etc. In Ayurveda, honey is used for both Internal and external applications. It is mainly used for the treatment of eye diseases, cough, thirst, phlegm, hiccups, blood in vomit, leprosy, diabetes, obesity, asthma, diarrhea and healing wounds. India's first honey village is at Manghar. Under the ambit of Project Honey Bee", the Koi and village Industries commission has decided to launch the village of Honey scheme in Maharastra's Managhar Village.

Pangolin

Indian Pangolins, also called thick-tailed pangolin and scaly ant eaters, are the mammals of the order Pholidota. It belongs to the family Manidae. Pangolins are the most trafficked mammal in the world, with demand primarily in Asia and in growing amounts in Africa, for their meat and scales. There is also demand in United States for Pangolin products particularly for their loather to be used in boots, bags and belts. Eight Species of Pangolins are found on Asia and Africa. They range from Vulnerable to Critically Endangered,

The 4 Species live in Africa: Black-Bellied Pangolin (phataginus tetradactyla), White-Bellied Pangolin (phataginus tricuspis), Giant Ground Panagolin (smutsia gigantea) and Temminck's Ground Pangolin (Smutsia temminckii)

The 4 Species found in Asia : Indian Pangolin (manis crassicaudjata), Philippine Pangolin (manis culionensis), Sunda Pangolin (manis javanica) and the Chinese Pangolin (mani's pentadactyla).

Pangolins play a vital role in maintaining a healthy eco system through their unique ecological functions. As insectivores, Pangolins help central populations of ants and termites, which can have significant impacts on vegetation and soil health. Pangolins are known as the guardians of the forest because they protect forests from termite destruction, maintaining a balanced eco system. Pangolins are high demand in China and Vietnam. Their meat is considered a delicacy and Pangolin scales are used in traditional medicines, Pangolin scales and bones were the most prevalent prescribe body parts and indicated the highest cultural significance, it is the source of food and medicine, scales are used as an aphrodisiac or made into rings or charms. Pangolin blood used for various healing properties such as treatment of skin disease and improved breathing. Both Indian and Chinese Pangolins are protected under Part I schedule I of WPA, 1972. 3rd Saturday of February World Panogolin Day celebrated every year.

In Devaji V The State of Madhya Pradesh (2015), the applicant and co-accused would get wild animal Pangolins killed in mass scale by local inhabitants of Buffer Zone. Pench Tiger Reserve Area of Seoni district by giving them money and get from them their skins which they and other co-accused would sell in black market and smuggle them into other countries, where as the hunting of Pangolins are prohibited as per schedule I of the WPA,1972, for they come in the category of endangered species.

Goat

Goat or domestic goat is a species of domesticated goat- antelope that is mostly kept as livestock. It was domesticated from the wild goat of South West Asia and Eastern Europe. The Goat is a member of the family Bovidae. Goats are among the earliest animals domesticated by humans. They are used for milk, meat, fur and skins, goat cheese across the world. 21st August is considered as Goat day.

Is a wild goat is a scheduled animal in Wildlife Protection Act, based on the data provided WPA, 1972, defines, a "scheduled animal" as an animal specified in schedule I or part II of the schedule II in Rekhchand V State of Madhya Pradesh (1998).

Horse

The horse (Equus Ferus Caballus) is a domesticated animal, belongs to the family Equidae. The relationship between horse and humans are unique. The horse is a partner and friend. It has ploughed fields and brought in the harvest hauled goods and conveyed passengers, variety of sport competitions, re-creational pursuits as well as activities like, police, agriculture, entertainment and warfare. Horse is protected under section 2, Schedule 2 of the WPA, 1972. The Horse Protection Act (HPA) was passed in 1970 to prohibit the showing, sale, auction, exhibition or transport of sored horses. 13th December is celebrated as National Horse Day, it honours the significant contributions of Horse.

Sharks

Sharks keep food food webs in balance and encourage bio-diversity to flourish by feeding on those species a chance to also grow in number. Good eco-system need bio-diversity and in turn, sharks are an important element of healthy bio-diversity. 160 shark species reported in India, only 26 sharks rays have been given the highest protection status under the Amended Wildlife (Protection) Act, 1972 by listing them in Schedule I and II. 14th July World Shark Day celebrated every year.

Giraffe

Giraffes are vital to keeping eco systems in balance. They eat the browse that others cannot reach, which promotes growth of forage and other smaller browsers to make use of. It belongs to the family of Giraffidae. Giraffe brought to India 150 years from Africa may be critically endangered species. About 150 years ago, British colonialist brought batches of what they thought were a single species of the Northern Giraffe to India, from their other colonial possession in Africa. A recent genealogical study of largest captive herd in India at the Alipore Zoological Garden in Kolkata has confirmed "critically endangered". Giraffes as a species are not considered endangered. Some Giraffe sub-species out of eight, two are the reticulated Giraffe and Masai Giraffe are classified as endangered. Another two, the Kordofan and the Nubian Giraffe, are critically endangered. Mysuru Zoo is reckoned to be one of the leading Indian zoos to have successfully bred Giraffes in captivity. A person cannot own a Giraffe in India. Giraffe is not a commodity to be owned. Giraffes are wild animals and they like to be wild. World Giraffe Day is 21st June. Giraffe comes under schedule I of the WPA 1972.

Whales

Whales are unique, beautiful, mysterious nature, from friendships, play, sing, co-operate with one another. Despite living in water, whales breath air, like humans, they are warm-blooded mammals. A thick layer of fat called blubber insulates them from cold ocean waters. Whales play a significant role in capturing carbon dioxide from the atmosphere, each great whale sequesters an estimated 33 tons of carbon dioxide on average, they are playing an important role to fight against climate change. Six out of 13 great whale species are classified as endangered or vulnerable even after decades of protection. WWF is working as an exiting new initiatives to promote the conservation of whales and around the world. Over a thousands of whales are killed every year because some people want to make money from selling their meat and body parts, their oil, blubber and cartilage are used in pharmaceuticals and health supplements. Whales provide the vital nutrients the sustain phytoplankton at the surface of the water because the algae is unable to draw it from the ocean floor. Nitrogen, Iron and phosphorus found food chain. 3rd Sunday in February every year celebrated Whales Day.

Rats

Rats are occasionally kept as pets and still for fancy, but majority of domestic rats are obtained from laboratory animal breeders for use in bio medical research, testing and education. Rats are the second most commonly used animal in bio medical activities. Rats are important economically pharmaceutical and scientific testing, mouse traps, rat poison, exterminators, pet trade as in pets and in feeders for the other animals also makes real or personal property damages, crops, etc. Rats eat food wastes, agicultural products from farm and other things. They are Important in the predatory eco system as owls, falcons, hawks, other predatory animals feed on them. 4th April Rats Day celebrated every year.

Animals as legal persons

The Punjab and Haryana High Court declared that animals and birds have legal rights just as humans. It further declared citizens as the "guardians of [the] animal kingdom" with the duty to ensure this welfare and protection. According to the formalist view, legal personality is an artificial construct that is not restricted to humans. It cannot be justified after this provision that if the fact, the animals biologically fall into the species of humans so, they can be prevented from being classed as legal persons. In India, there are no special provisions regarding the legal status of animals in the country like other European Countries. But there is some provision for the protection of animals or animal welfare in the form of Directive Principles of State Policy in the Indian Constitution itself and there are some case laws regarding the Protection from the Cruelty to Animals. The whole animal kingdom, including avian and aquatic species, has been found by the Punjab and Haryana High Court to be legal entities with a separate persona and the attendant rights, obligations and liabilities of a living person in the case of Karnail Singh & Others V State of Haryana (2019), on 31st May 2019, Honourable High Court of Punjab and Haryana held, "All the animals have honour and dignity. Every specie(s) has an inherent right to live and is required to be protected by law. The rights and privacy of animals are to be respected and protected from unlawful attacks. The corporations, hindu idols, holy scriptures, rivers have been declared legal entities and thus, in order to protect and promote greater welfare of animals including avian and aquatic animals are required to be conferred with the status of legal entity/legal person. The animals should be healthy, comfortable, well nourished, safe, able to express innate behaviour without pain, fear and distress. They are entitled to justice. The animals cannot be treated as objects or property." All citizens of the State of Haryana were declared persons in loco parentis (in place of a parent), which will enable them to act on 31st May 2019, the High Court of Punjab and Haryana, in this case Karnail as guardians for all non human animals within the State of Haryana.

PETA- People for the Ethical Treatment of Animals

PETA was founded in 1980, is dedicated to establishing and defending the rights of all animals. It is a non-profit organisation. PETA operates under the simple principle that animals are not ours to experiment on eat, wear, use for entertainment or abuse in any other way. PETA is a animal right organisation that opposes speciesiscm and the abuse of animals in any way, such as for food, clothing, entertainment or research. Prevention of Cruelty to Animals Act,1960, An Act to prevent the infliction of unnecessary pain or suffering on animals and that purpose to amend the law relation to the Prevention of Cruelty to Animals. Golden Rule of PETA "Do Unto Others As You Would Have Them Do Unto You" (this means animals too). PETA opposes speciesism, a human-supremacist world view and focuses its attention on the 4 areas in which the largest numbers of animals suffer the most intensely for the longest periods of time. In laboratories in the food industry, in the clothing trade and in the entertaintment business, including the cruel killing of rodents, birds and other animals who often considered "pests" as well as cruelty to domesticated animals. PETA's role in India through investigative and legislative work, public education, animal rescues, eye-catching demonstrations, celebrity involvement and outreach with PETA youth, PETA India, has drastically improved the quality of life for animals and saved the lives of countless others. PETA is at the fire front of stopping the abuse of animals used for food.

CITES- Convention on International Trade of Endangered Species of Wild Fauna and Flora-

Is an International agreement, to which States and regional economic integration organizations adhere voluntarily. States that have agreed to be bound by the Convention (joined CITES) are known as Parties. CITES signed by 184 parties. India is a CITES Party since 1976. Due to its extreme diversity, India is recognised all over the world for harbouring upto 7-8% of all the species recorded by CITES. As an active CITES Party, India prohibits the International Trade of Endangered Wild Species. Its aim is to ensure that international trade in specimens of wild animals and plants does not threaten the survival of the species. The goal of CITES is to ensure that the International Commerce in wild animal and plant specimens does not endanger the existence of the species. It provides a frame work to be respected by each party, which has to adopt its own domestic legislation to ensure that CITES is implemented at the national level. The Standing Committee noted that since the goal of CITES is the sustainable use of bio diversity, revising the Biological Diversity Act, 2002 would be the best approach to carry out this goal. The national authority responsible for implementing CITES is called the CITES Management Authority. The Additional DG (wildlife), Ministry of Environment, Forests and Climate Change, Government of India, has been designated CITES Management Authority of India. Appendices of CITES includes species that are threatened with extinction. Commercial trade of these species on a global scale is generally prohibited. Exceptions may be made in the case of scientific research or the conservation of the species. Over 40,900 species including roughly 6,610 species of animals and 34,310 species of plants are protected by CITES against over-exploitation through international trade. They are listed in the three CITES Appendices. While the more charismatic creatures, such as bears and whales, may be the better known examples of CITES species, the most numerous groups include many less popularized plants and animals, such as aloes, corals, mussels and frogs. The convention requires countries to regulate the trade of all listed specimens through permits. Its aim is to ensure that international trade in specimens of wild animals and plants does not threaten the survival of the species.

The Ministry of Environment, Forests and Climate Change notified the Living Animal Species (Reporting and Registration) Rules 2024, stating, Every person who is in possession of any animal species (in schedule IV) shall report the details and make an application for registration electronically to the Management Authority or the authorised officer within a period of six months from the date of commencement of these rules and there after within 30 days of possession. The notification also puts the onus of providing necessary import/export documents. The application shall be accompanied with copy of import licence, CITES export permit or certificate granted under the Convention in case of acquisition through import. CITES is an international agreement between Governments to prevent International trade in specimens of wild animals and plants.

MIKE Programme- Monitoring of Illegal Killing of Elephants

It was started in South Asia in 2003, after conference of parties a resolution of CITES. The main aim of MIKE was to provide the information required by the Elephant range countries for proper management and long-term protection of their elephant populations. The objectives of MIKE programme, to measure the levels and trends in the illegal poaching and ensure changes in the trends for elephant protection. To determine the factors responsible for such changes and to assess the impact of decisions by the conference of parties to CITES.

The CITES, Monitoring the Illegal Killing of Elephants (MIKE) Programme is a site-based system designed to monitor trends in levels of illegal killing of elephants and build capacity in sites spread across the range of African, Asian elephants. Information from MIKE is used by CITES parties to inform decision making on elephant conservation and management. MIKE aims to provide a reliable, robust and impartial information base to support discussions and decision making on elephant conservation and management. The objectives of the MIKE Programmes are set out in the Convention on International Trade in Endangered Species (CITES) under Resolution 10:10. The 4 main objectives are;

- Measuring trends and changes in the illegal killing of elephants.
- Assessing the impacts of decisions under CITES on elephant conservation and management.
- Information decision making on elephant management, protection and enforcement needs.

- Building capacity in managing elephants and enhancing enforcement.

Conclusion

In the post Independence India may have floated laws like Prevention of Cruelty to Animals Act, 1960, but WPA 1972, laid the real solid edifice for a legal frame work for wildlife protection in India. The WPA, 1972 celebrated completed more than 50 years, in that journey it has been some major Amendments like, 1991, 2006, 2022 etc. WPA is a landmark Act in conservation and protection of the wildlife of the country. WPA gives an elaborate definition of Hunting. Section 50 (8) in particular equips the forest officers not below the rank of Assistant Conservator of Forest to issue search warrant, enforce attendance of witness and record witness. It is noteworthy that confessions made before forest officers are admissible in courts as evidences.

The Abetment or Assistance in wildlife offence forms for the basis to un earth deep nexus of wildlife crimes as organised crimes, non-bailable and cognizable offences in case of Scheluled I , species and care of repeated offender. Also term of punishment in such cases is minimum 3 years. Forfeiture of property derived from illegal hunting and trade is too explicitly provided for under WPA. Section 57 of WPA explicitly shifts burden of Proof on the accused if they are found to be in possession of animal article.

The WPA 1991, Amendment established Central Zoo Authority (CZA) zoos are no longer a typical menagerie: collection of wild animals earlier meant for recreational purposes. Constitution of CZA under Chapter IV A of WPA clubbed with National Zoo Policy 1998, the Central Governments orders prohibiting the sale of animals by 2005 and the Recognition of Zoos Rules 2009 has greatly standardised the zoo operations in terms of animal spaces their health and their transfers.

The WPA provides for Scientific Management of wildlife under section 12(bb) that includes translocation of wild animals to alternative suitable habitat and population management of wildlife. It also permits derivation, collection or preparation of snake-venam. Due to rising human population and materialistically oriented lifestyles of today Anthropogenic pressure on forest and thus the very existence of wildlife is at cross-road. Killing an animal in Self-Defence won't be an offence upheld in Tilak Bhadur case (1979).

Implementing measures such as protected areas, sustainable practices and awareness campaigns, to mitigate the adverse impacts of de-forestation and habitat loss. The Indian Wildlife classified into six. They are;

(1) Normal Species – Population is moderate for their existence those species are known as normal species of wildlife in India. Sal, Rodents, Pine Cattle are some examples.

(2) Vulnerable Species- not yet endangered, but may become endangered. Examples- Nilgiri Langur, Nicobar Flying Fox, Bara Singha etc.

(3) Rare Species- very small population may become endangered, examples are, Desert fox, Wild Asiatic Buffalo, Hornbill, the Himalayan Brown Bear.

(4) Endangered Species- The sudden decrease in their population are known as endangered species, examples; Black Buck, Crocodile, Lion Tailed Macaque, Indian Wild Ass, Sangai, Indian Rhino etc.

(5) Endemic Species- The species of plants and animals which exist in a particular geographic region and are isolated by natural calamities, examples are, Nicobar Pigeon, Andaman Wild Pig, Andaman Tedal etc.

(6) Extinct Species- those species of plants and animals that are completely gone and can no longer be found. Examples are, Asiatic Cheetah, Pink Head Duck etc.

The Wildlife sanctuaries are established to protect the endangered species. It is an acute difficult always to relocate the animals from their natural habitat, forests and wildlife are the primary sources of the eco systems. Due to the destruction of habitats, poaching, industries, hunting or killing are main problems facing decline of population of plants and animals. The most Endangered Species in India reported in 2024, they are;

(1) Bengal Tiger

(2) Asiatic Lion

(3) Snow Leopard

(4) One-horned Rhinoceros

(5) Black Buck

(6) Lion-tailed Macaque

(7) Resplendent Tree Frog

(8) Kashmiri Red Stag

(9) Nilgiri Tahr

(10) Indian Bison (Gaur)

The New Amendments in wildlife trade rules enable issuing licences for certain schedule II species. The revised notification came into effect on January 16th 2024, the first revision since 1983. The Central Government has excluded some species from the process of issuing licences for their wildlife trade in the revised rules that have come after 4 decades. In the

Government notification dated 16th January Wildlife (Protection) Licensing (Additional Matters for Consideration) Rules, 2024, the Government offered fresh guidelines for granting licences to stakeholders involved in snake venom, captive animals, trophy animals and stuffed animals. With the new guidelines in effect, the Government has stated that, "No such licences shall be granted if it relates to any wild animals specified in the Schedule I to the Act, except with previous consultation of the Central government". The notification does not clarify the restrictions on Schedule II species have been lifted. According to the World Wildlife Report 2020 about 6,000 species of flora and fauna were seized globally from 1999-2018. In 2022, the number of cases registered under the Wildlife Protection Act in India was over 554. Over the last few years numbers of cases reduced significantly. The Wildlife Protection Act, 1972, was enacted in India to protect various wild animals, birds and plants. Animals under The Wildlife Protection Act, 1972, includes amphibians, birds, mammals and reptiles and their young ones and also includes, birds, reptiles and their eggs. Animal Welfare Act (AWA), 1966, does not cover animals used for food, fiber (including fur) or other agricultural purposes. The AWA does not cover privately owned pets, carriage horses, or hunting activities. State and local Government regulate the treatment of farm animals and pets. Poultry and fish are not included in this group. Breeding, care and slaughtering of lives stock known as animal husbandary. Livestocks are the domesticated animals raised in an agricultural selling inorder to provide labour and produce diversified products for consumption such as meat, eggs, milk, fur, leather and wool.

One of the major findings of the 2023 report with regard to Tamil Nadu is that while birds are in protected areas such as sanctuaries, national parks and conservation reserves are doing relatively well, grasslands and scrublands which are outside protected areas have drastic decline. Birds in sky island habitats such as the Nilgiris are also more protected than those in the rest of Tamil Nadu, 4 bird species-Nilgiri laughing thrush, Ashambu laughing thrush, White-bellied shola kili and Nilgiri pipit are found in Tamil Nadu and Kerala, are the highest priority comes to conservation. In Tamil Nadu coastal bird species are declining. During the vertical migration or altitudinal migration, a sizeable number of terrestrial birds from the high mountains migrate to low valleys during summer. There is another type of migration called horizontal migration. Some of the birds from the Western Indian States such as Gujarat, Rajasthan and Maharashtra will migrate to South-east Asian countries such as Malaysia, Thailand and few other countries in far-east region. A dozen rare species of birds often sighted in the Western and Eastern Ghats were spotted in a few wooded areas in Thiruvallur district. Sighting 922 birds belonging to 85 species indicates that forest areas in Thiruvallur district area an ideal habitat for these birds.

The wood areas are amid areas where urbanisation is taken place. White-rumped shama, Bonelli's eagle, White-spotted fantail, chestnut-bellied sand-grouse, White-bellied drongo and ashy Drongo also visible. The presence of a good number of birds is a sign the habitat is not disturbed. One of the objectives of the bird count is to assess quality of habitat. When degradation or any other disturbance is noticed, it can be rectified through scientific intervention. Sparrows have evolved over centuries for urban life. A 2020 survey by the state of India's Birds indicates a decline of the sparrow population in Tamil Nadu. The change in architecture, the fledging feed on worms and insects, which are absent in manicured gardens with ornamental plants and flats and other constructions. A terrestrial bird census conducted in the reserve forest lands of Ramanathapuram district recorded 6,000 birds from 121 species. The census was held on 2 & 3 March and 30 people forest officials, ornithologists and volunteers participated. The birds include the greater eagle, montagu's harrier, booted eagle, marsh harrier and kestrel. Smaller birds like the Siberian stonechat, golden oriole, Asian brown flycatchers migrating from the Himlayas, Indian paradise flycatcher, pipits, rosy starlings in huge numbers and barn swallows were recorded. This is the first time a bird census has been done in the reserve forests under the control of Ramanathapuram district forest officer. The annual bird census used to be held in the islands of the Gulf of Mannar and bird sanctuaries under the Wildlife Warden. The bird census will help us to plan further research and habitat management in these reserve forests and reserve lands.

According to Edward Wilson and others, who introduced the word Chlorophilia, is a kind of biophilia which means human beings having a natural affinity for life forms, including animals, birds, etc. Chlorophilia means the natural and irrevocable human need to be surrounded by green or chlorophyll-plant life. One trillion animals disappear from our planet each year. Human actions makes a huge price through poaching and hunting. More than 3,000 incidents of animals straying into human settlements have been reported across the state of Tamil Nadu in 2023, majority of them involving humans and elephant.

On January 3rd 2024, a 3 year old girl from Gudalur in Nilgiri District, was attacked by a leopard, one of the man-animal conflict. In 10 days, three attacks by the leopard, resulting one woman killed and eight people injured. Another incident is a leopard attacked and killed a six year old girl near famous Tirupati Temple has been captures. The presence of leopard other five places recorded, reported by the Tirupati forest officials on 14th August 2023.

In Uttarakhand, 264 human lives lost in last ten years, 61 killed by Tigers, 203 killed by leopards. Government of Uttarakhand increased from rupees four lakh to six lakh for families of those killed in wildlife attacks.

It is said in the Matangalila, the ancient Sanskrit work on the behaviour of elephants that the King of Anga ordered elephants to be captured to prevent them from raiding crops. Karnataka, Kerala and Tamil Nadu have largest populations of elephant witnesses high level of conflict. Trans- locations are a common management technique in Malaysia, Srilanka and India, with its failure. Drive operations, unplanned, unscientific drives also divert elephants from their regular routes, resulting in them encroaching human living areas. Train accidents also reason for forest elephant deaths. Use of explosives to hunt wild boars is not new in Odisha, They are either hidden in a dough or stashed inside pumpkins and pineapples to lure boards. In 2023-24, atleast 78 elephants have been killed in Odisha. 35 of them died of accidental electrocution and stepping into electrocution traps. 10 died of natural causes, 4 died due to poaching, 5 died in train/vehicle hits, 24 cases reason couldn't be ascertained, reported on 14 February 2024.

The fences are established as joint initiatives between voluntary organisations, the wildlife department, agriculture department, and the maintenance assigned to groups of local communities whose lands are protected by these structures. This requires planning as hardly faced to divert elephant movement, forcing them to go from the pathways used by people, leading to encounters. The Wildlife Protection Act 1972, makes the exception of live elephants being "gifted" or "inherited" to the people, wherein the owner has 90 days to declare this "inheritance" to the Forest Department. This clause is misused by elephant owners involved in illegal trafficking and exploitation of elephants, which allows the trade to flourish.

The Government reports says to the incidents of human-animal conflict have increased considerably due to various reasons ranging from an increase in wild animal population, habitat fragmentation and degradation, non-availability of food and water, disturbance in corridors due to development activities, change in cropping patterns, and increase in human populations. Despite the Government's effort to employ traditional methods, such as creating and maintaining water holes in protected areas, implementing soil and moisture conservation measures, establishing anti-poaching camps, solar-powered electric fences using to prevent wild animals from entering crop fields, those measures have not proven successful. The State Governments, implementing AI to reduce the intrusion of elephant into human settlement. The system operates by capturing the image of an intruding animal when it enters a settlement. It identifies the animal and generates a distinctive sound based on its frequency, which is played through speakers to move back the animal from that settlement. AI Technology will help forest officials to take immediate action.

Lack of community participation for conservation efforts cannot be successful without the participation of local people. The new Act aligns itself with CITES and included the CITES appendices but the act is unclear about the connection of protection and conservation. The schedules of the Wildlife Protection Act 1972 were rationalized in The Wild Life (Protection) Amendment Act, 2022, leading to changes in the categorization of species. Before the 2022 Amendment, Schedules were based on the level of endangerment of species. Climate Change is a significant threat to wildlife habitats, and it is likely to create threats to existing wildlife.

TABLE OF CASES

- Abdul Hakim Qureshi V State of Bihar, AIR 1961 SC 448
- Animal Wefare Board of India V A. Nagaraja & Ors, (2014) 7 SCC 547
- Animal Welfare Board of India V People for Elimination of Stray Troubles (2023)
- Animal Welfare Board V Union of India (2017), AIR ONLINE 2018 SC 1053
- Centre for Environmental Law, WWF India V Union of India, Writ Petition (Civil) No.337 of 1995
- Devaji V The State of Madhya Pradesh, MCRC-11907 -2015
- Dr. T. Patanjali Sastry, President V Chairman A.P Pollution 2001 (5) ALT 315
- In Re T. N. Godavarman Thirumulpad V Union of India (2010) 13 SCC 740
- Ivory Traders & Manufactures Association V Union of India , AIR (1997) DEL 267
- Karnail Singh & Others V State of Haryana, 2019 SCC ONLINE P&H 704,
- Maa Dasabhuja Furniture Unit V State of Orissa & Ors, AIR 2006 ORI 63, AIR 2006 ORISSA 63, (2006) 33 OCR 380
- M. C. Mehta V Union of India, AIR 1987 SC 965
- M. C. Mehta V Kamal Nath (1997) 1 SCC 388
- M. C. Mehta V Union of India, 2002 (2) SCR 963
- M. R. Ajayan V State of Kerala (2009), W.P. (C) No. 28255 of 2011
- Mohammed Hanif Qurashi & Ors V State of Bihar, AIR 1958 SC 731
- Mohd. Hazi Rafeeq V State of Uttaranchal, AIR 2006 UTTARANCHAL 18, AIR 2006 UTR 18
- Narahari Jagadish Kumar V State of Andhra Pradesh, W. P. (PIL) M.P. NO.305 of 2016 IN W.P.(PIL) No.177 of 2016
- Narmada Andolan Bachao V Union of India, Writ Petition (civil) 328 of 2002

- People for Animals V Md. Mohazzid (2015) SCC OnLine Del 9508
- Rekhchand V State of Madhya Pradesh, Criminal Revsion No. 253 of 1998, LAWS (MPH)-2008-9-11
- Satyapal Verma V State of Jharkhand, 2004 AIR (JHA) 69
- State of Maharastra V Gajanan D Jabhulkar 2002 CRILJ 349
- S. Muralidharan V Principal Chief Conservator of Forest, AIRONLINE 2019 MAD 1307
- S. P. Chockalingam v Principal Chief Conservator of Forest and Chief Wildlife Warden, W.P. Nos, 1830, 4130, 4109 of 2022
- State of Bihar V Murad Ali Khan Farukh Salauddin &... (1988) 4 SCC 655
- Scouts & Guides for Animals and Birds V Union of India & Ors., W.P. (c) No.2045/2022
- State of Gujarat V Mirzapur Moti Kureshi Kazab Jamat & Ors (2005) SCC 8 534
- State of Maharastra V Salman Khan (2016) 1 AIR Bom R (cri) 343
- State of Rajasthan V Salman Khan & Ors (2012) 07 RAJ CK 0037
- Tilak Bahadur Case, 1979 CRILJ 1404
- T. N. Godavarman Thirumulpad V Union of India, (2006) 3 SCR 1046
- T. N. Godavarman Thirumulpad V Union of India (2012) 3 SCR 460
- V.K. Venkitachalam V State of Kerala, W.P (c) No. 3049 of 2010
- V.K. Venkitachalam V State of Kerala (2015) 09 KL CK 0093, (2015) 5 KHC 417

SOURCES OF INFORMATION

- The Wild Life (Protection) Amendment Act, 2022.
- The Wild Life (Protection) Amendment Act, 2006 - K N Chaturvedi, Secretary to the Government of India.
- The Indian Wildlife (Protection) Act, 1972, Amended 1993- uploaded by Naresh Kadyan.
- Annex II (8) Gist of State Legislations on Cow Slaughter- Department of Animal Husbandary and Dairying.
- Bharatiya Nyaya Sanhitha Bill, 2023.
- Indian Penal Code - Justice Rajesh Tandon..
- The Constitutional Law of India- Dr. J N Pandey.
- Notes on Environmental Law - Anil k Nair.
- The Times of India
- Environmental Law- Usha Jaganath Law series.
- Google
- Advocate khoj
- Britannica
- Byju's
- Case mine
- Clear IAS
- Court Kutchery
- Deccan Herald
- Digi scr. Sci. gov.in
- Drishti IAS
- earth.org
- first cry
- IAS SQUAD
- I pleaders blog
- Indian Kanoon
- linked in

- India Bird watching
- Legal authority
- Lotus arise
- Prepp
- Prs India
- scribd
- Statista
- Systema naturae
- Textbook
- The Hindu
- The Indian Express
- Un academy
- Wikipedia